IMAGES
of America

BURLINGTON

I0809012

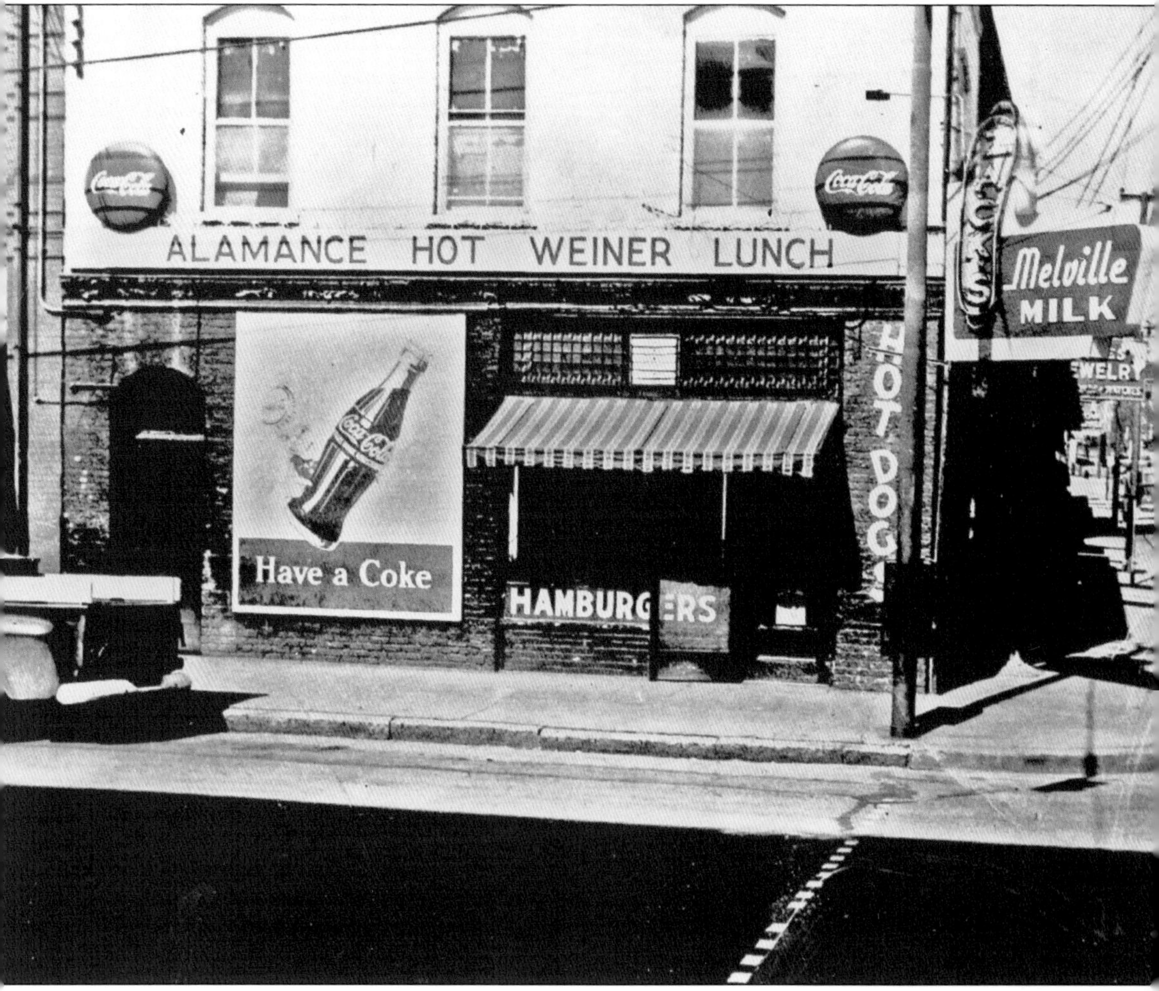

Greek immigrant Zack Touloupas started Alamance Hot Weiner Lunch in 1928 at Worth and Front Streets. Now at Davis and Worth Streets, and known as Zack's, this landmark restaurant is operated by grandson Zack Touloupas II. Some locals frequent the restaurant at least once a week, and many former residents make Zack's one of their first stops when they are in town. (Courtesy of Zack Touloupas II.)

On the Cover: This photograph, taken around 1915, shows a young pharmacist, R. Homer Andrews (right), leaning against the gleaming soda fountain in his Burlington drugstore. He became one of Burlington's best-known residents. He was involved with several drugstores and served as postmaster and as an Alamance County commissioner. An elementary school is named in his honor. Others in the photograph are not identified. (Courtesy of the author's collection.)

IMAGES
of America

BURLINGTON

Don Bolden

ARCADIA
PUBLISHING

ISBN 978-0-7385-6647-4

Published by Arcadia Publishing
Charleston, South Carolina

Printed in the United States of America

Library of Congress Control Number: 2009930170

For all general information contact Arcadia Publishing at:
Telephone 843-853-2070
Fax 843-853-0044
E-mail sales@arcadiapublishing.com
For customer service and orders:
Toll-Free 1-888-313-2665

Visit us on the Internet at www.arcadiapublishing.com

To Billie Faye and the history we have shared . . .
and to the late Dr. Hugh Lefler,
a University of North Carolina professor,
who taught me the importance of the past.

Contents

ACKNOWLEDGMENTS

My sincere thanks to all who have helped me in this endeavor. Many contributed photographs and provided information to help make this book a good view of our city and its past. I owe a special thanks to Jerri Nall and Kathy Barry of the Textile Heritage Museum at Glencoe for connecting me with Arcadia Publishing in the beginning, and also to my newspaper family at the *Times-News* who helped me in gathering photographs. I am particularly grateful to Jane Moore for sharing a spectacular collection of postcards, and to Mac Williams and the staff at the Alamance County Area Chamber of Commerce for opening their file of photographs to me. I also am grateful to Lindsay Harris at Arcadia Publishing for being so patient with me in the process of putting this book together. Most of these photographs come from my own collection, which I gathered in a 51-year history with the *Times-News*. Thanks especially to *Times-News* publisher Paul Mauney for permitting use of photographs that have appeared in the newspaper over the years. Those photographs from sources other than my files and the newspaper are credited under the photographs.

INTRODUCTION

Burlington is a community born of the railroad, bred on the loom, and built on its ability to turn adversity into opportunity. As a result, there is a rich and colorful history surrounding this North Carolina city.

In the early 1850s, the newly formed North Carolina Railroad made plans for tracks to connect Goldsboro in eastern North Carolina with Charlotte in the western part of the state. The plan included the location of facilities for the maintenance and repair of railroad engines and cars somewhere near the middle of the line.

The midpoint was in Alamance County, which had been formed in 1849, and the most desirable site was Graham, the seat of government for the new county. However officials did not want the shops nearby because they feared the activity and noise from engines might disrupt the courts. Therefore, it was decreed that the rail line could not pass within a mile of the courthouse.

Railroad officials looked elsewhere, and after a couple of other sites were rejected, attention was turned to a tract of land just west of Graham. Local citizens combined several tracts to make one large enough for the railroad, and it was accepted. Thus was born the community known as Company Shops. The railroad company constructed a number of large shop buildings for its operations, along with an office building and homes for employees. By 1856, the operation was up and running, and Company Shops was filled with activity.

The railroad company constructed a community building, which served as a community school and church. This building was known as Union School or Union Church, depending on the use at a particular moment. Later individual church groups left the Union Church and built their own denominational churches in the community. The railroad also built a large hotel next to the tracks, and over the years, both the hotel and its dining room became favorite stops for railroad travelers.

In 1886, the railroad company made an announcement that shocked the little community. The railroad shops were to be moved to a new location, and the facilities in Company Shops would be abandoned. The shops were leaving, it seemed, but the people were not. There was the seed of a new industry—textiles—already planted in Company Shops, and this industry grew into a new economic base for those living in the area. Adversity became opportunity for this community.

Textile plants had been in operation along the Haw River and Great Alamance Creek in Alamance County since the first half of the 19th century. Water from the rivers was needed to generate power for the mills, but by 1880, a new method of generating power without a water source had been developed, and as a result, textile mills began to appear in Company Shops. One of the first was the E. M. Holt Plaid Mill, named for the Alamance County man who had introduced colored textiles to the South in the 1850s, launching an industrial empire that generated mills in several locations along Alamance County's waterways.

With the departure of the railroad, local citizens decided a new name was in order, so they appointed a committee for the purpose of renaming the community. There is no factual knowledge of how the name was chosen, but the town became known as Burlington in 1887. A number of names had been proposed, including Carolinadelphia.

Burlington began its life nourished by textile mills, the Burlington Coffin Company, and a few other small businesses. On February 14, 1893, the town of Burlington was officially incorporated by the state of North Carolina. By the end of the 19th century, the Daisy Hosiery Mill had been put into operation, fueling yet another industry that fed Burlington in the years ahead.

Hosiery would indeed become a major player in Burlington's growth. The industry grew rapidly, largely by the operation of a number of small family mills. Some mills were nothing more than a couple of looms in a shed behind the house. But others were far more sophisticated, and it was not long until Burlington was heralded around the nation as the "hosiery center of the South." Many of these mills bore the names of the families who owned them, and names such as May, McEwen, Sellers, Holt, Foster, Brown, and Elder became a part of the city's hosiery history.

Because of the scope of the hosiery industry in Burlington, it is not surprising that two of the most important developments in women's hosiery were made in the town. In the mid-1950s, William Leath, then with Chadbourn Hosiery, worked with some of his associates to develop and patent the stretch yarn that revolutionized the industry. At the time, women's hosiery was made in sizes (7, 7.5, 8, 8.5, etc.), which meant retailers had to maintain a huge inventory with every size.

With stretch yarn, it was possible to have only small, medium, and large sizes, reducing the inventory needed and eliminating the need for big warehouse space. Stretch yarn also made panty hose possible, which was another revolutionary change for the industry. Several mills worked on the product, and it was Allen Gant Sr. of Glen Raven Hosiery who patented the concept.

By the early 1920s, local businessmen in the chamber of commerce saw a need for a new industry to support the local economy. They contacted a young World War I veteran in Gastonia, North Carolina, J. Spencer Love, and invited him to join in developing a new textile company. Love was part of a textile family, and he knew the operations well. In 1923, he joined the local group in forming Burlington Mills. The operation was chartered in November 1923 and began production in the summer of 1924.

What had formerly been a cornfield became home to a plant producing textile products and employing local workers. Along with the plant, the company built houses to rent to prospective employees, giving rise to a community known to this day as "the mill hill." An employee could rent a five-room house for $1 per week.

Textile companies produced cotton goods at the time, but the market for those products went into steep decline, and Love's first year was horrendous. He faced a difficult time, but he made it an opportunity. The first of the man-made fibers—rayon—had just been introduced to the marketplace. However, rayon was untested and not well known. Love decided to stake the future of his new company on rayon.

His gamble was a huge success. In just a few years, Burlington Mills was growing rapidly. The one mill soon became five, all in Burlington. And, in the years to come, the company, later known as Burlington Industries, would become the largest producer of textiles in the world, with plants in 25 countries and more than 20,000 employees. Burlington Mills was the company that made Burlington, North Carolina, a name recognized around the globe.

The Great Depression was difficult for the county, but unemployment was not as big a problem as in most places. Burlington Mills workers received comfortable pay increases in those years, and hosiery mills continued to operate. However, there was a large textile plant that opened in 1929 on the east side of town that closed within three years due to the Great Depression. The plant also produced rayon goods but was not able to match the successes of Burlington Mills. The vacated plant became known as the Rayon Plant and played a major role in the town's industrial history in years to come.

A difficulty for the textile plants during the Great Depression was the effort by labor groups to unionize workers. There were some strikes with violence, but the union efforts failed. This period in Burlington's history was chronicled in a novel entitled *The Bridge* by the late Doug Marlette.

Burlington's mill communities were tightly knit and proud. One expression of that pride was displayed through athletic teams. A number of mills in the area fielded semiprofessional baseball teams in the 1920s and 1930s, and the rivalries were fearsome. Mills hired the best players, and in order to keep them, gave them the best jobs in the mills. Mills raided other mill teams to obtain better players, offering them a better job, and stars often moved across town to the rival team.

When World War II came, Burlington residents quickly adapted to rationing, shortages of many goods, and the absence of many young men and women who left for the military. Just two months after the war broke out, the federal government obtained the vacant Rayon Plant and announced that Fairchild Aircraft would occupy the site in order to build a training airplane for the military. Hundreds of workers from across the nation were brought to Burlington, and a new community was built near the plant to house them. The government also took over an airfield across the road from the plant. The operation known as Huffman Field was moved near the village of Alamance to provide space for Fairchild Airport, where airplanes produced in the factory would be tested. Many women moved into the workforce, particularly at Fairchild Aircraft, to fill jobs left open because men were called into the military.

Fairchild Aircraft operated until 1944, when the government demand for twin-engined training airplanes ended. Four-engined bombers were in use by that time, and the Fairchild AT-21 Gunner was obsolete. Firestone moved into the plant and produced artillery pieces for the military until the war's end in August 1945.

The Western Electric Company then moved into the plant and began producing telephone equipment. It was not long, however, until the plant's major production again went to the government. One of the major projects was the production of equipment for the military's antimissile systems. Guidance systems for the Nike family of antimissiles were produced in Burlington, and at peak production, more than 3,000 people were employed in the Western Electric plant, which had become known to the government as the Tarheel Army Missile Plant.

In the early 1970s, new adversity struck. The United States entered into a treaty with the Soviet Union that effectively eliminated the use of antimissile systems such as those produced in Burlington. The treaty came at a particularly bad time for the county. The textile industry was still the leading employer in Burlington, but a severe recession hit the industry in the 1970s. At one time, unemployment was at 20 percent.

At that point, local leaders began an intensive effort toward industrial diversification to end reliance on one industry. Other companies were successfully brought into the area in the diversity effort. Again, adversity became opportunity for the county. In the latter years of the 20th century, textiles began to fade quickly as companies moved overseas. Even Burlington Industries, the textile giant of the world, fell in the era of corporate takeovers and now continues as part of a new company—the International Textile Group—that combined the remnants of Burlington Industries and the Cone Mills Corporation.

As one economic support in the community faded, another appeared—the medical laboratory testing industry. Dr. Jim Powell, a member of the family that created the Carolina Biological Supply Company nearby many years ago, joined his brothers in forming a small medical testing laboratory in Burlington. It was not long before their company merged with Hoffman–La Roche, and then, some years later, a company known as the Laboratory Corporation of America was born. It is the second-largest testing lab in the country, and, known widely as LabCorp, the company is headquartered in Burlington. In 2009, it was the largest single employer in the area.

Although the company has operations in many areas of Alamance County, LabCorp has always been centered in downtown Burlington. Because of that, many of the historical buildings have been preserved as LabCorp facilities, including the tallest, a nine-story building constructed as a bank in 1929. In 2009, LabCorp solidified its downtown presence with the opening of an ultramodern national headquarters building.

In the 1960s, racial unrest occurred in Burlington. There was rioting on one occasion, rising out of problems with integration of the local schools. The U.S. Army National Guard was brought in to restore calm. With the help of biracial organizations, however, school integration was accomplished far more orderly than in neighboring areas.

The water supply was also a major problem for many years in Burlington. A climax occurred in 1954 when the city's supply almost completely dried up during an extended drought. Industry was in peril, water use was restricted, and the future was uncertain. Hurricane Hazel hit Burlington in October 1954 and ended the shortage, but the city, under the expert guidance of city manager J. D. Mackintosh, went to work with the city council to prevent future shortages.

A new reservoir opened in 1957, and a second was opened in the 1970s. The result was that Burlington has one of the best water supplies in North Carolina and is the envy of other communities across the state. The water supply was a problem, and the city worked to overcome it. Adversity came, and the community saw it as an opportunity.

Such has been the history of this North Carolina city.

One

The Early Years

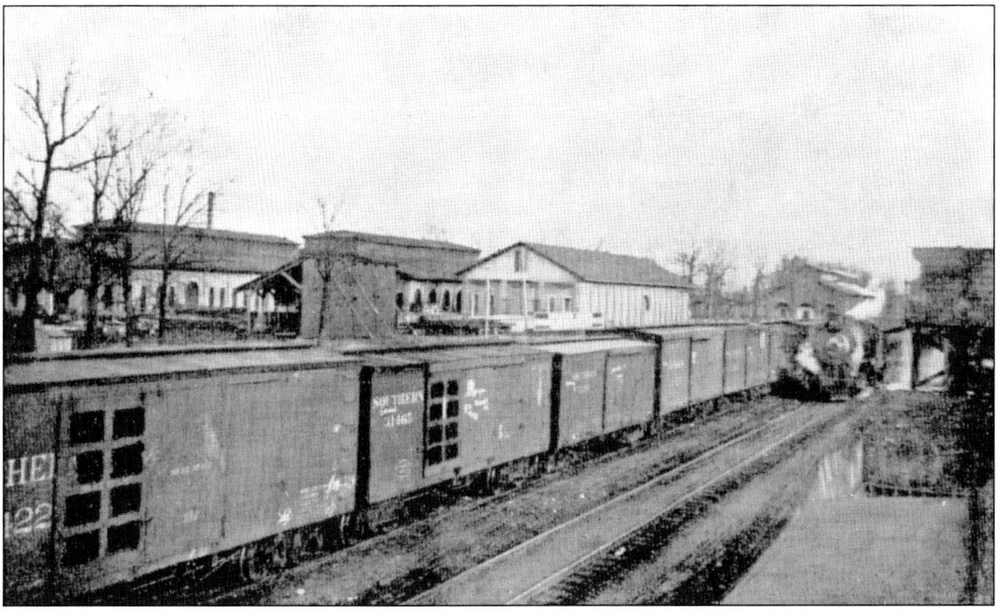

Burlington was a railroad town from the mid-1850s to 1886. The North Carolina Railroad operated its maintenance shops in Burlington during those years. This scene from the early 1900s shows a freight train stopped beside the depot (at right) with the old shop buildings in the background. At the time of this photograph, the Virginia Bridge Company occupied the shop buildings. (Courtesy of Jane Moore.)

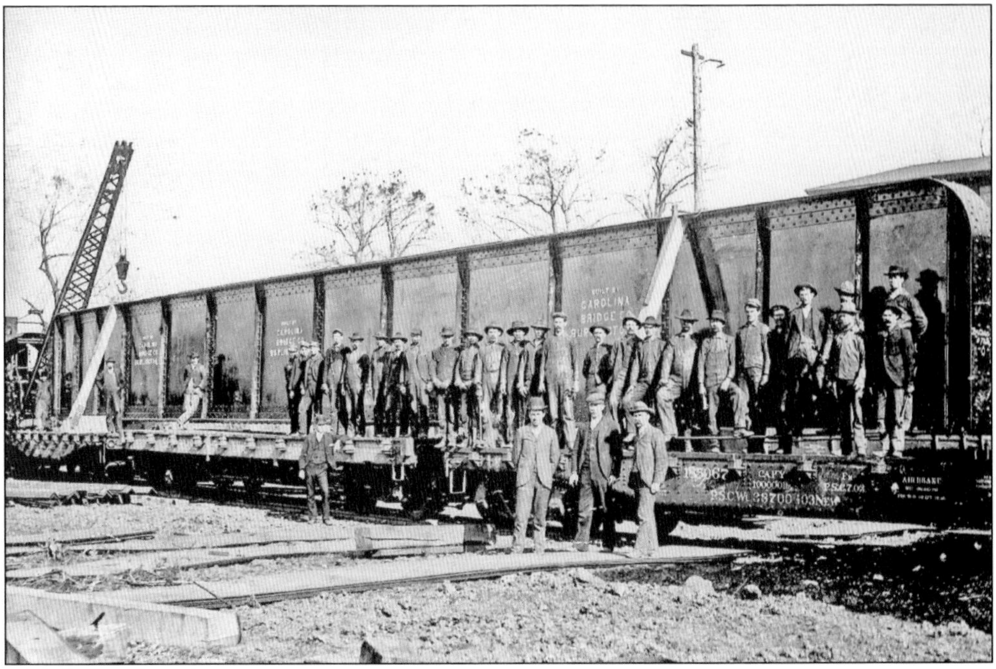

A large, steel bridge beam is loaded on a freight car for shipment at Burlington's rail yard in the early 1900s. After the Company Shops ended operations in 1886, the buildings were occupied by the Virginia Bridge Company and later the Carolina Bridge Company. Bridge components were shipped from Burlington across the nation.

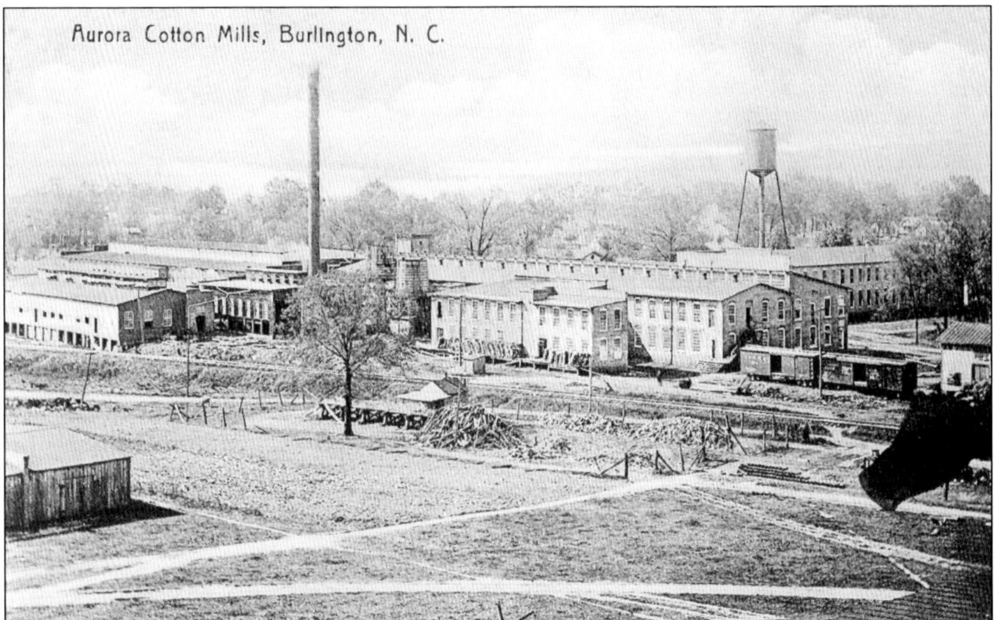

Aurora Cotton Mills was one industry that provided jobs locally after Company Shops closed in 1886. Aurora Cotton Mills was located on East Webb Avenue and was built in the early 1880s. It was the first cotton mill in the county that was not built beside a river. Water had been an essential power source until the 1880s, when other sources were developed.

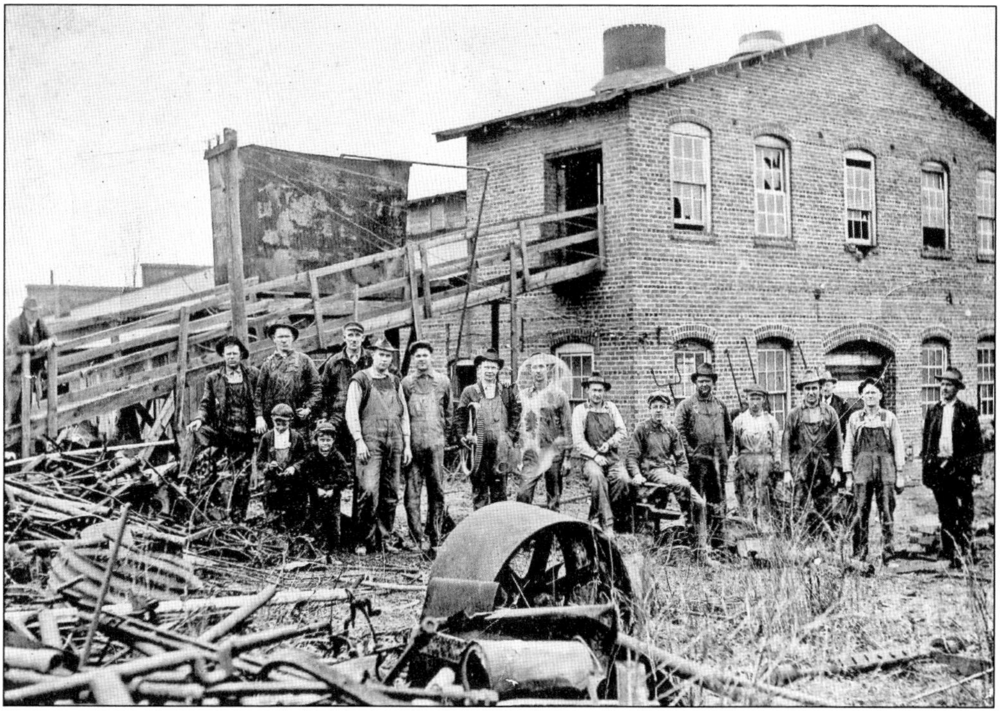

Sykes Foundry was one of Burlington's early businesses, and it became one of Burlington's major industrial operations in the town's early years. Employees are seen here in front of the foundry in 1923. The company has been located in east Burlington throughout its history, and it is now known as Sykes Supply Company.

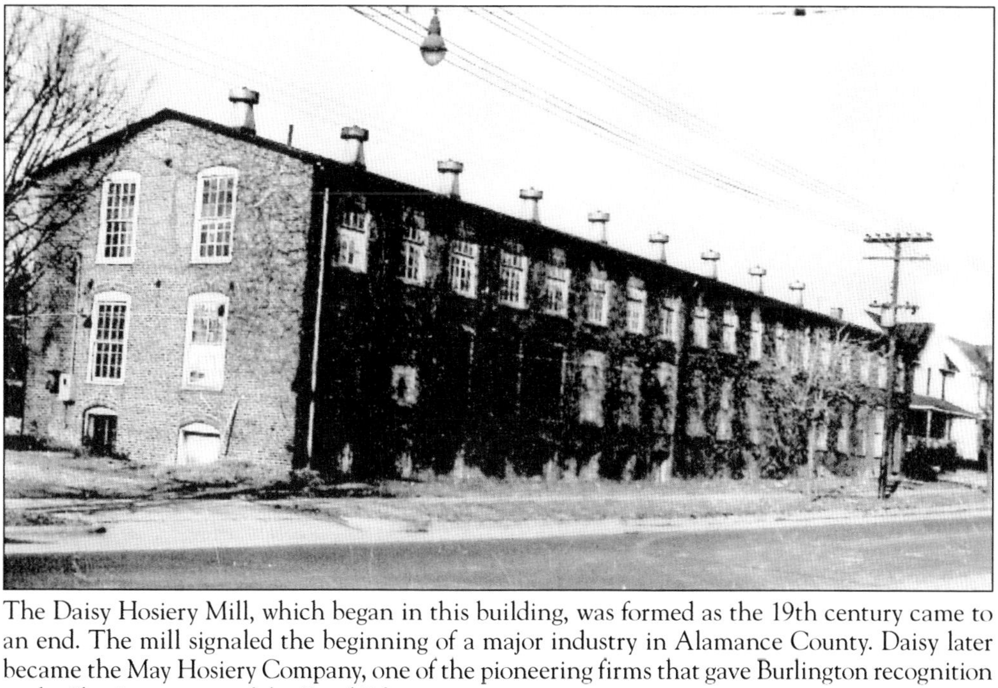

The Daisy Hosiery Mill, which began in this building, was formed as the 19th century came to an end. The mill signaled the beginning of a major industry in Alamance County. Daisy later became the May Hosiery Company, one of the pioneering firms that gave Burlington recognition as the "hosiery center of the South" for many years.

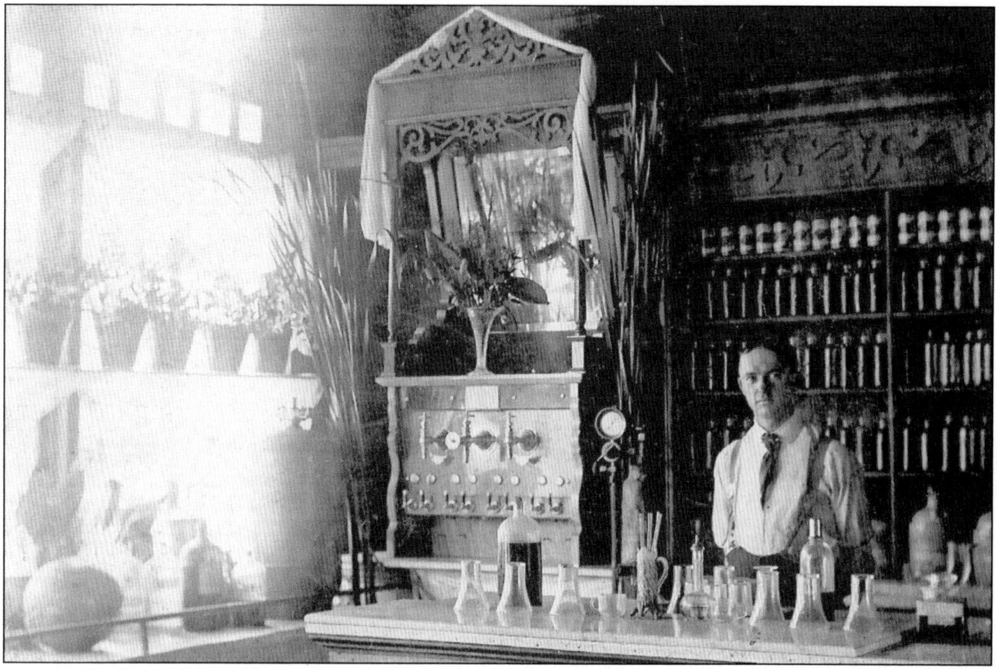

Corney Dallas Whitesell was one of the early merchants in Burlington. He is shown here in 1900 working in his drugstore. Early druggists did not have the endless array of pills of a modern pharmacy, so they actually mixed compounds, using beakers like those on the counter, and dispensed from bottles like those on the shelves in the background. (Courtesy of Linda Angel.)

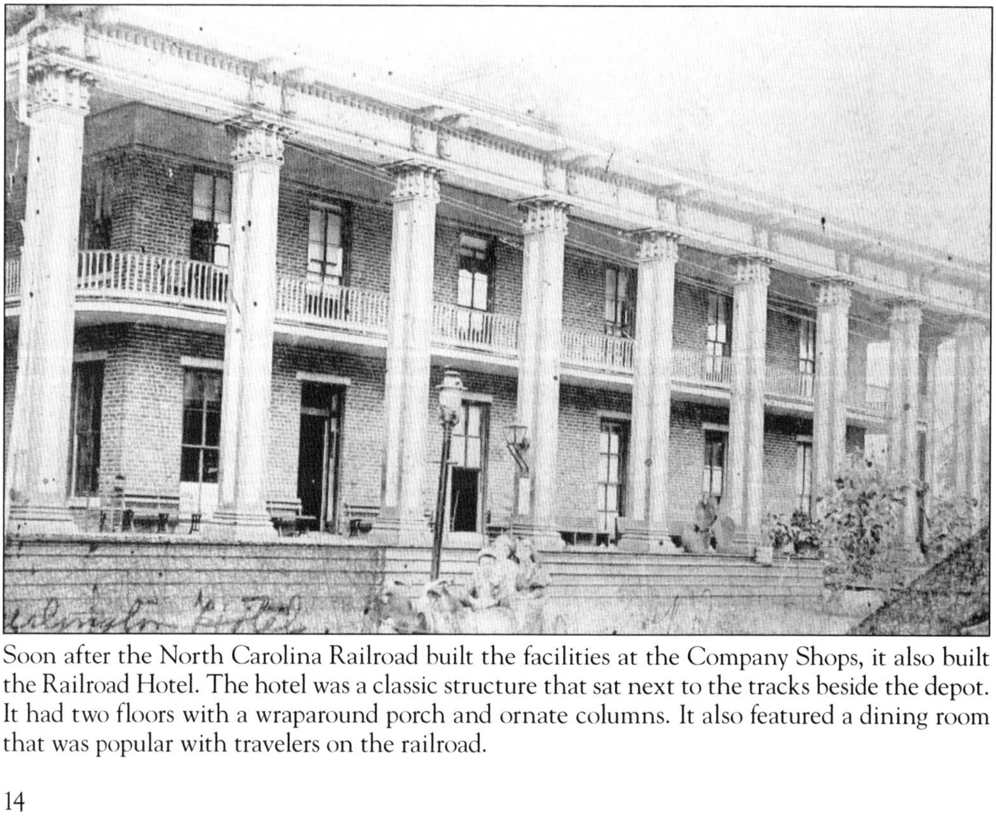

Soon after the North Carolina Railroad built the facilities at the Company Shops, it also built the Railroad Hotel. The hotel was a classic structure that sat next to the tracks beside the depot. It had two floors with a wraparound porch and ornate columns. It also featured a dining room that was popular with travelers on the railroad.

The Railroad Hotel remained in operation after the Company Shops closed, but early in the morning of May 24, 1904, a fire broke out in the hotel and quickly consumed the entire structure. This is one of a series of spectacular photographs of the fire as it burned in the predawn hours.

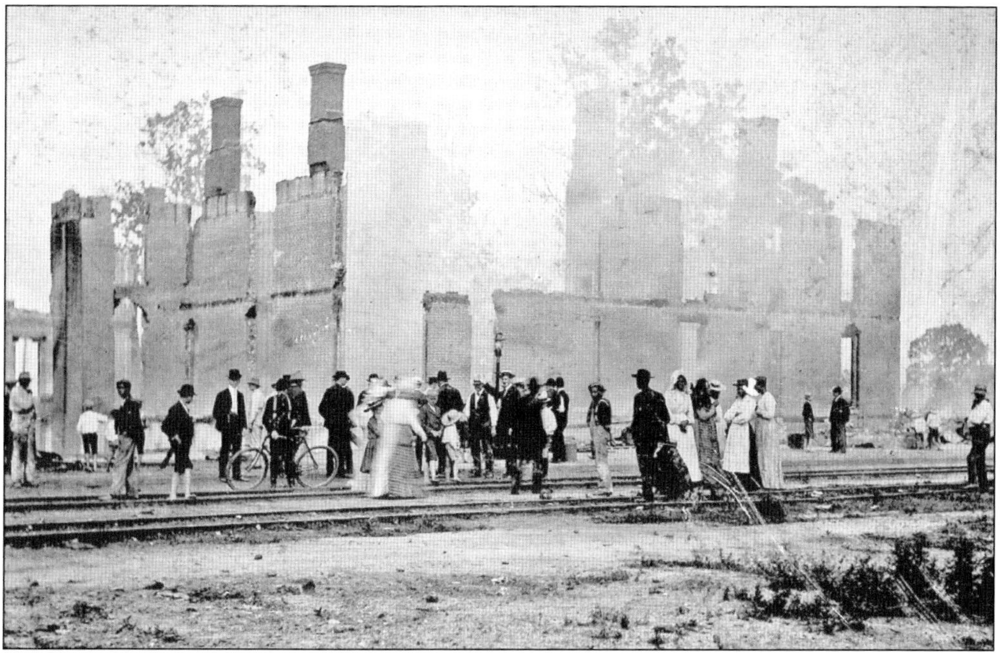

Smoke rose from the ruins of the Railroad Hotel in 1904. Burlington residents gathered the morning after the fire to see the damage. Only brick walls and some chimneys remained standing in the wake of the fire. Reportedly, a disgruntled employee who had been fired from the hotel returned after dark and set the hotel ablaze. The facility was never rebuilt.

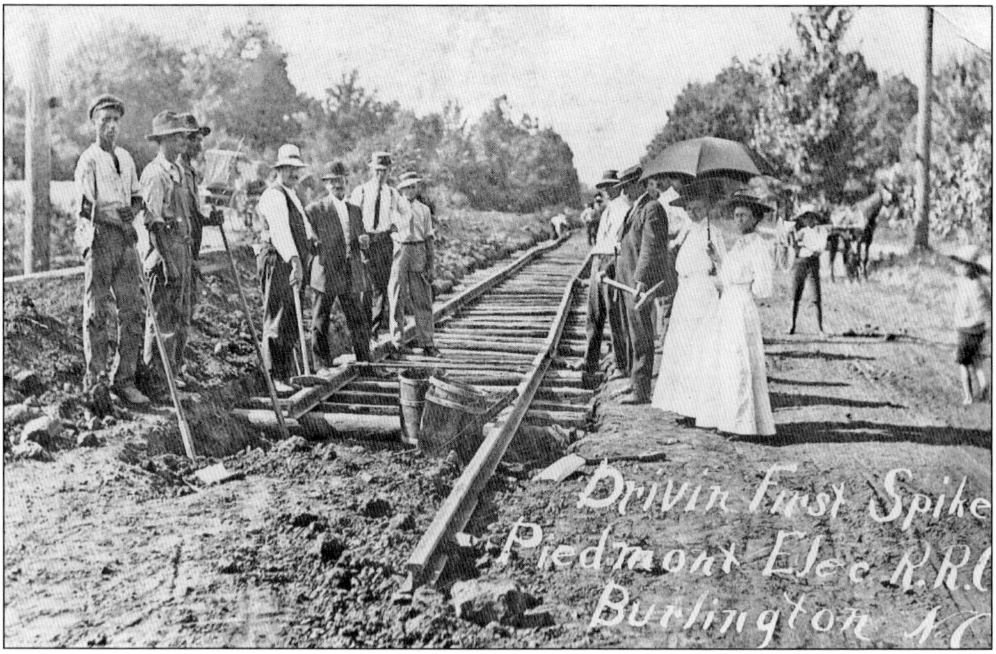

A special ceremony was held in 1911 when the tracks of the Piedmont Electric Railway Company were connected to complete construction of the line linking Burlington, Graham, and Haw River with streetcar service. This service allowed people for the first time to live in one of those communities and work in another. Streetcars were popular with workers, schoolchildren, and families looking for Sunday afternoon entertainment.

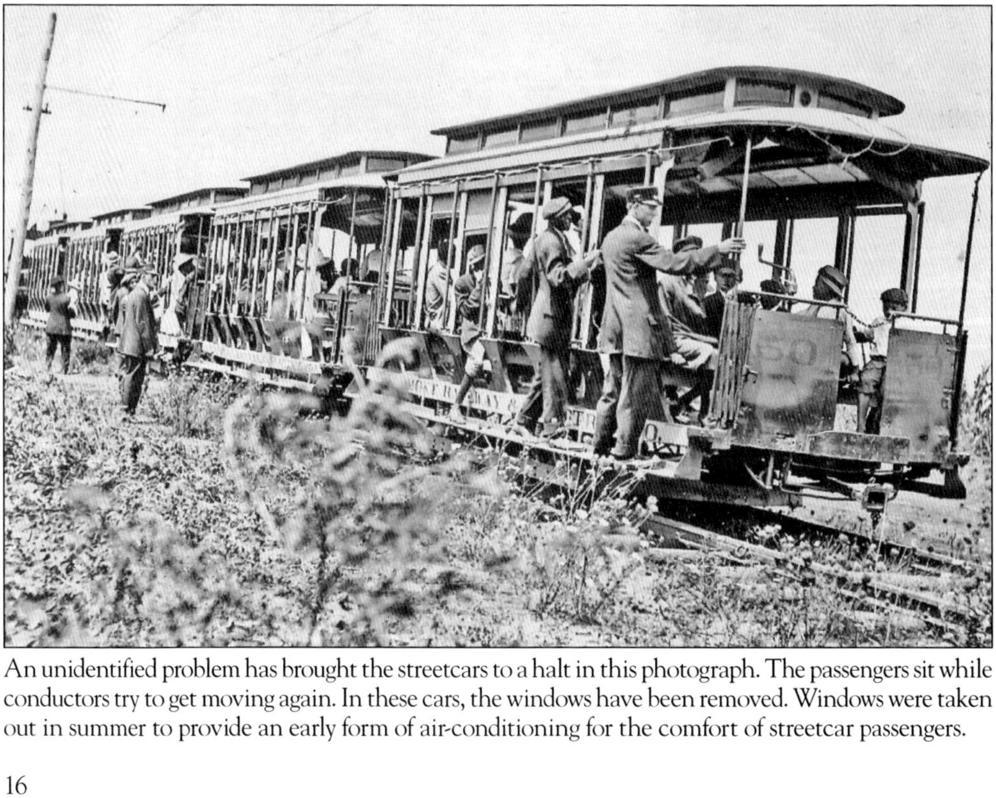

An unidentified problem has brought the streetcars to a halt in this photograph. The passengers sit while conductors try to get moving again. In these cars, the windows have been removed. Windows were taken out in summer to provide an early form of air-conditioning for the comfort of streetcar passengers.

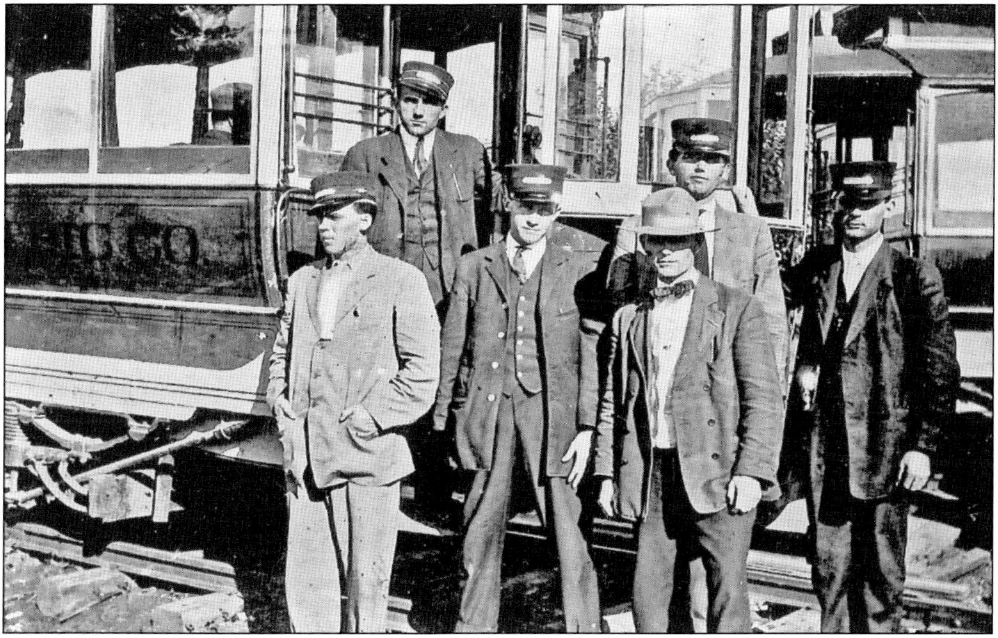

These six men were among the crewmen who operated the streetcar line out of Burlington from 1911 into the early 1920s. Cars ran from 6:00 a.m. until almost midnight. Some of these crewmen had arrangements with local eating establishments, and it was not uncommon for streetcars to stop while a conductor bagged a rabbit running along the tracks. The animal was then sold to the restaurant.

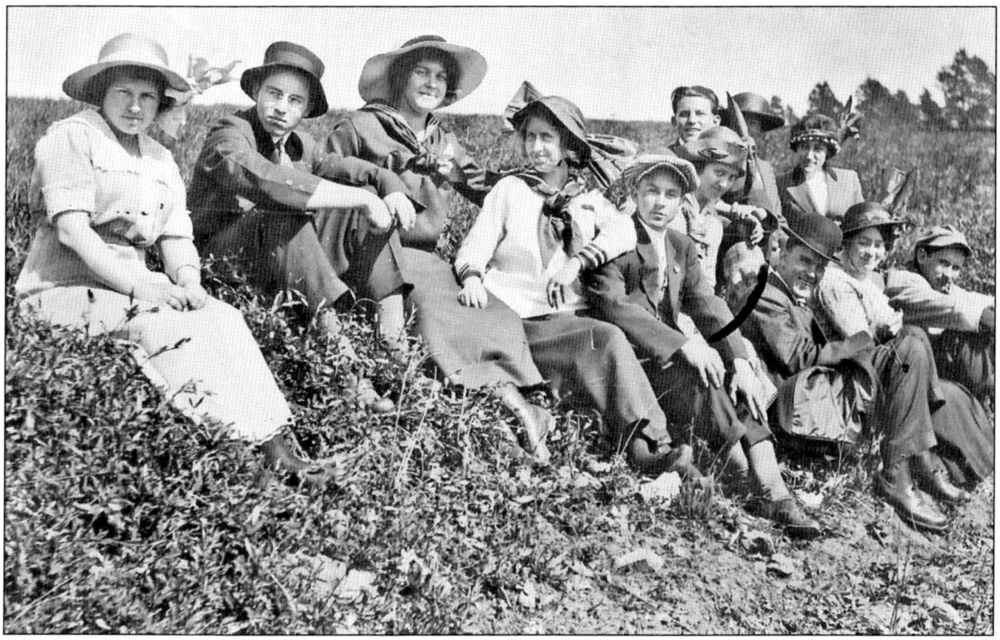

Streetcars were an opportunity for family outings. Some rode on Sundays for entertainment, while others chose to sit on the banks beside the tracks and watch the cars go by, like the group pictured here. Also on Sunday outings, the best dresses, suits, and hats were required. Most of the tracks were removed in World War II, but some still remain buried under the asphalt.

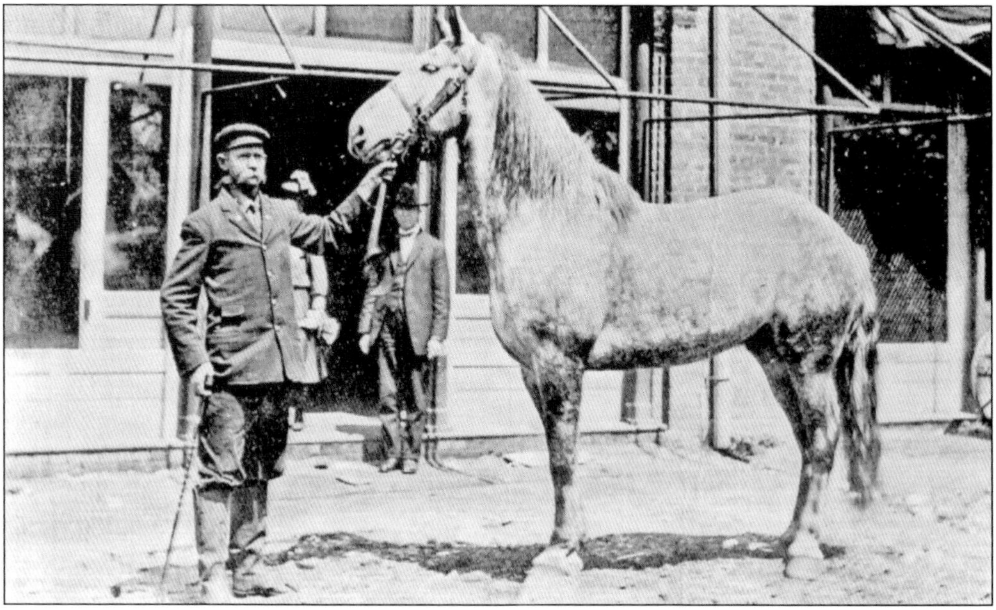

This was the Burlington Fire Company No. 1 in 1906. The horse was kept in a stable in town, and when a fire occurred, volunteers hooked the horse to the hose wagon and headed to the blaze. Horses continued in the fire service until the town purchased its first fire truck around 1918. (Courtesy of Jane Moore.)

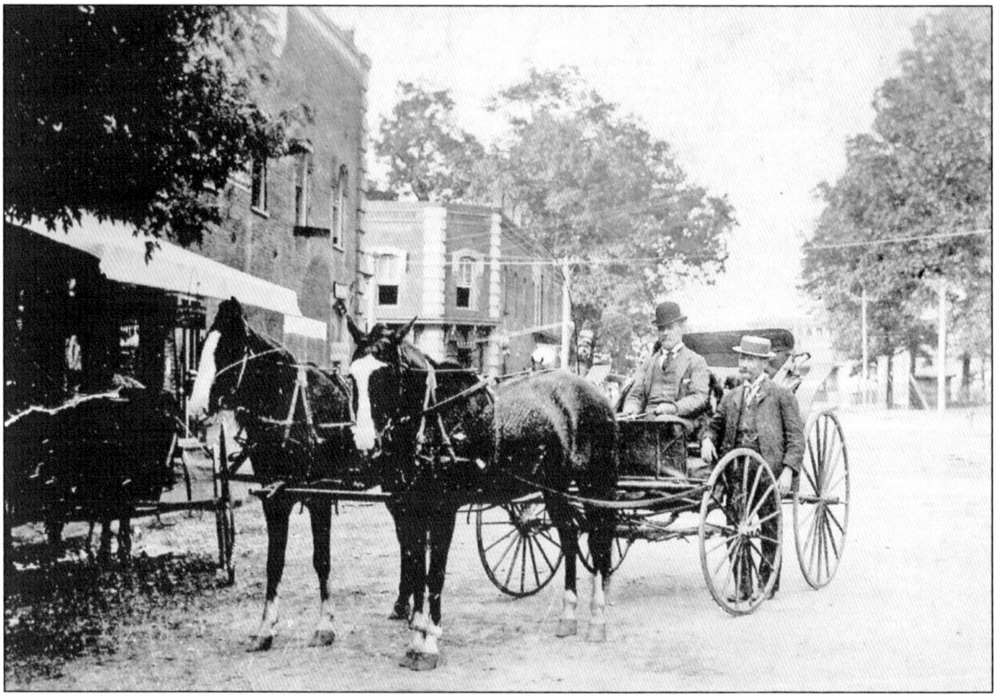

The horse and buggy formed the primary mode of transportation in early Burlington. W. G. Stafford and T. H. Stroud are seen here on Burlington's Main Street around 1909. The horses were named Nip and Tuck, and were well known to early Burlington residents. In those days, hitching posts were as common along Main Street as parking meters were decades later.

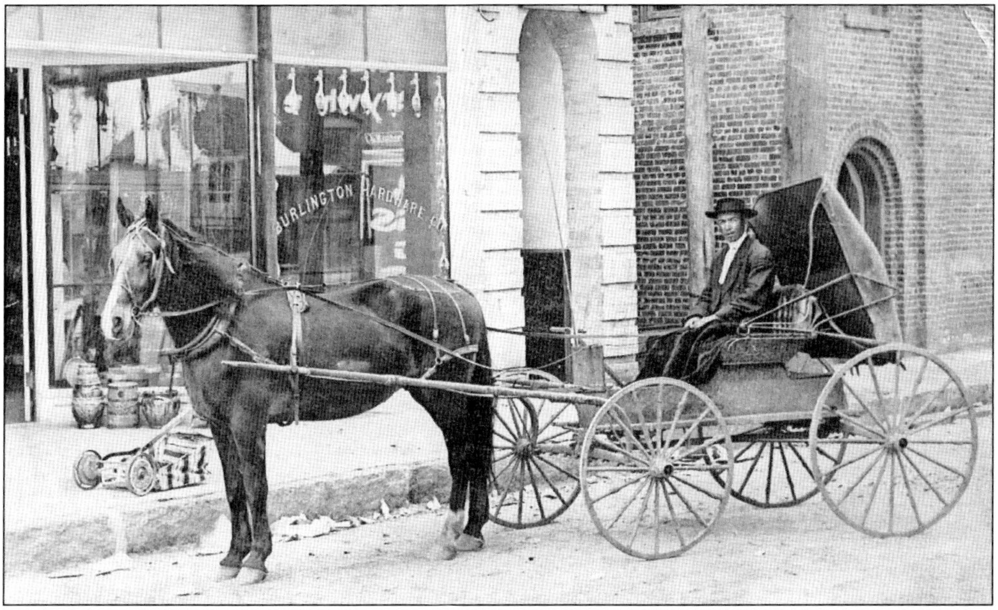

George May poses in his buggy on Burlington's Main Street in the early 1900s. May is parked in front of the Burlington Hardware Store, one of the most popular businesses in the city in those years. When this photograph was made, Main Street had not been paved, and there is a very high curb along the street. (Courtesy of Virginia May Corbett.)

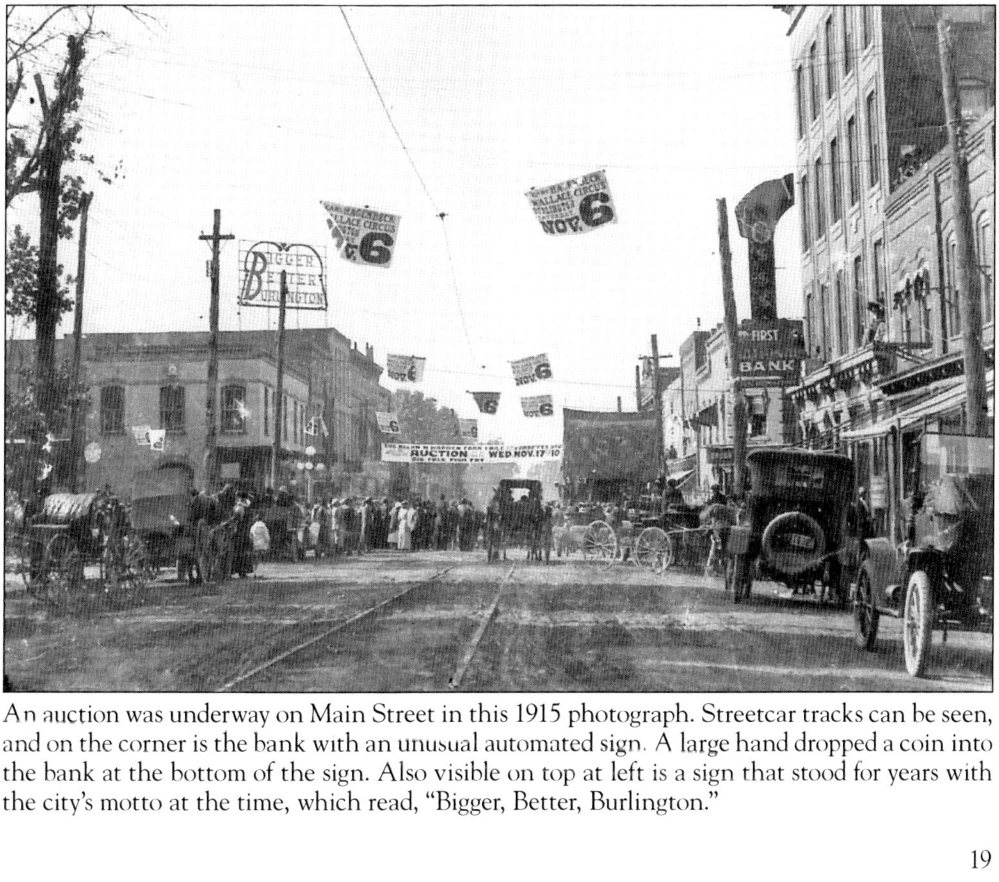

An auction was underway on Main Street in this 1915 photograph. Streetcar tracks can be seen, and on the corner is the bank with an unusual automated sign. A large hand dropped a coin into the bank at the bottom of the sign. Also visible on top at left is a sign that stood for years with the city's motto at the time, which read, "Bigger, Better, Burlington."

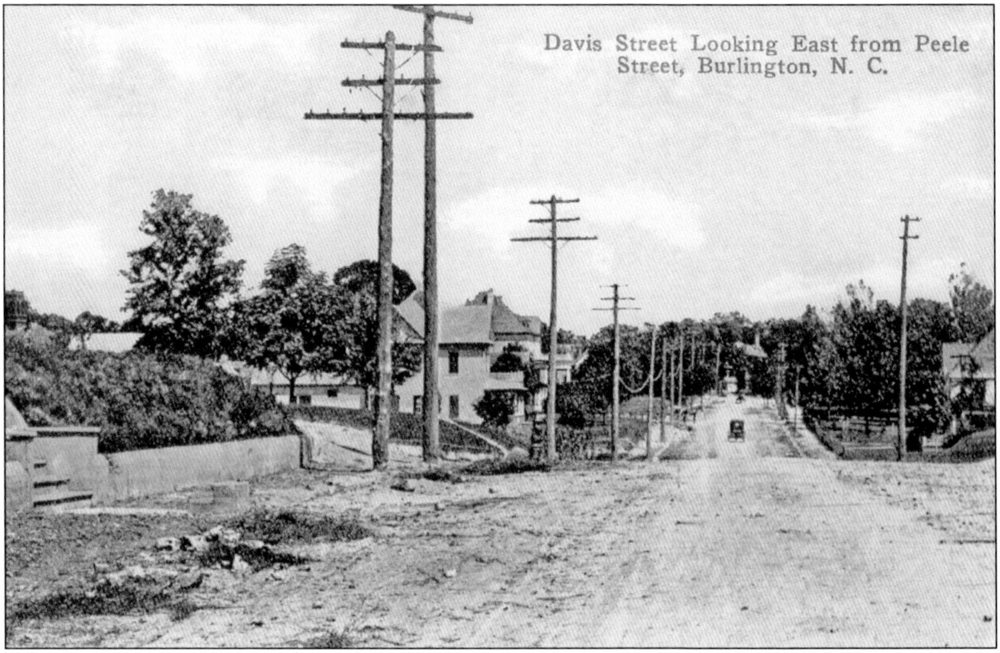

West Davis Street is one of the city's major residential streets, but in 1913, it was a dirt street that had yet to be fully developed. This photograph was made at Peele Street looking east to the downtown area. Later some of the city's finest homes were constructed on this street. (Courtesy of Jane Moore.)

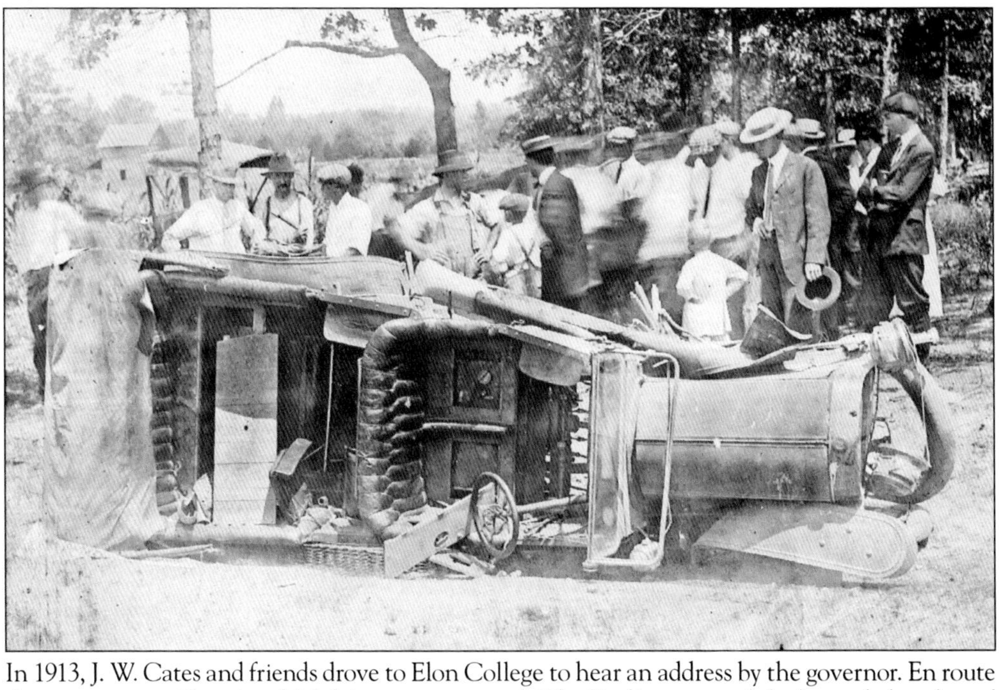

In 1913, J. W. Cates and friends drove to Elon College to hear an address by the governor. En route there was an accident in which his car overturned. The Burlington coal dealer and church and civic leader was injured and never fully recovered from the accident before his death several years later.

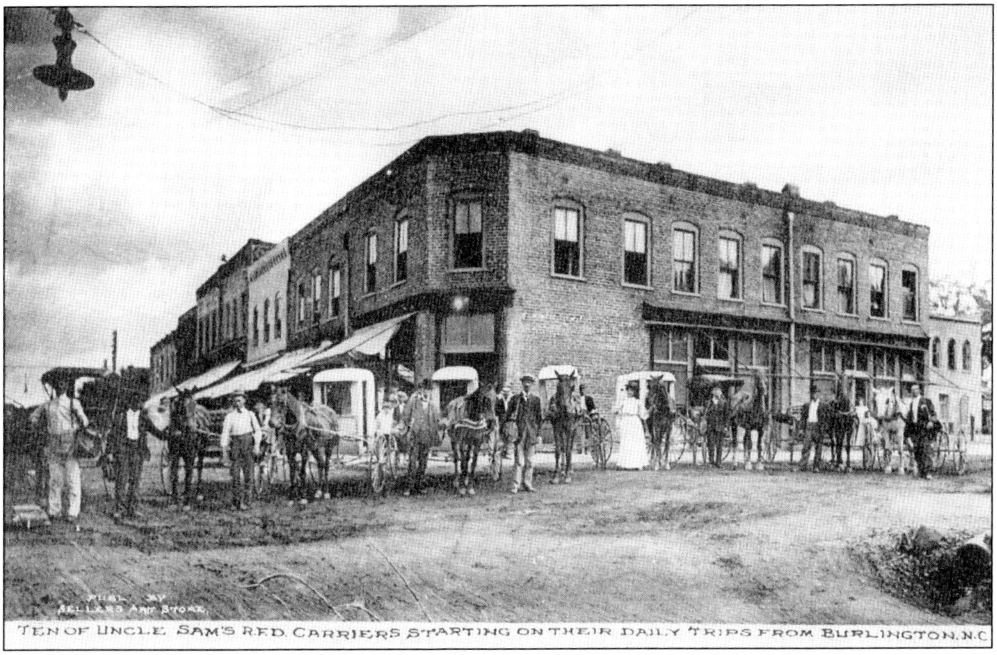

Burlington's postal carriers posed for a group photograph in 1909 in front of the post office near the intersection of Spring and Davis Streets. In the middle of the group is Alice Fowler. The female postal carrier had a rural route for many years and made her rounds each day through all types of weather by horse and buggy in the early years of her career.

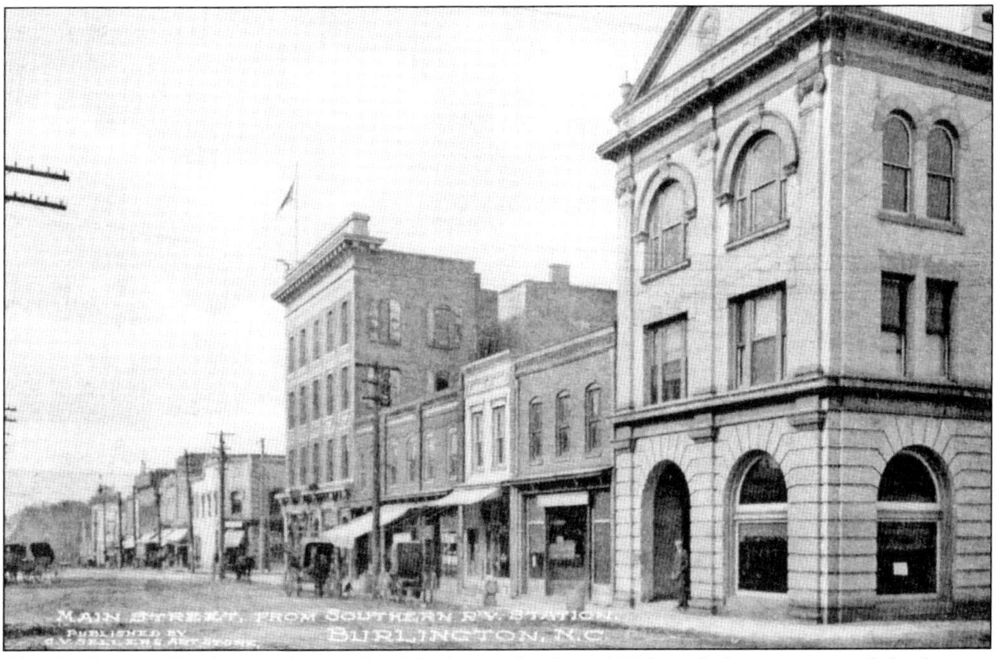

The Piedmont Hotel, at right on this block, was built in 1906, and this was one of the busiest business blocks in the years that followed. The Piedmont Trust Company occupied much of the ground floor, and the upper floors were hotel rooms. This entire block disappeared in the area's redevelopment during the 1970s. (Courtesy of Jane Moore.)

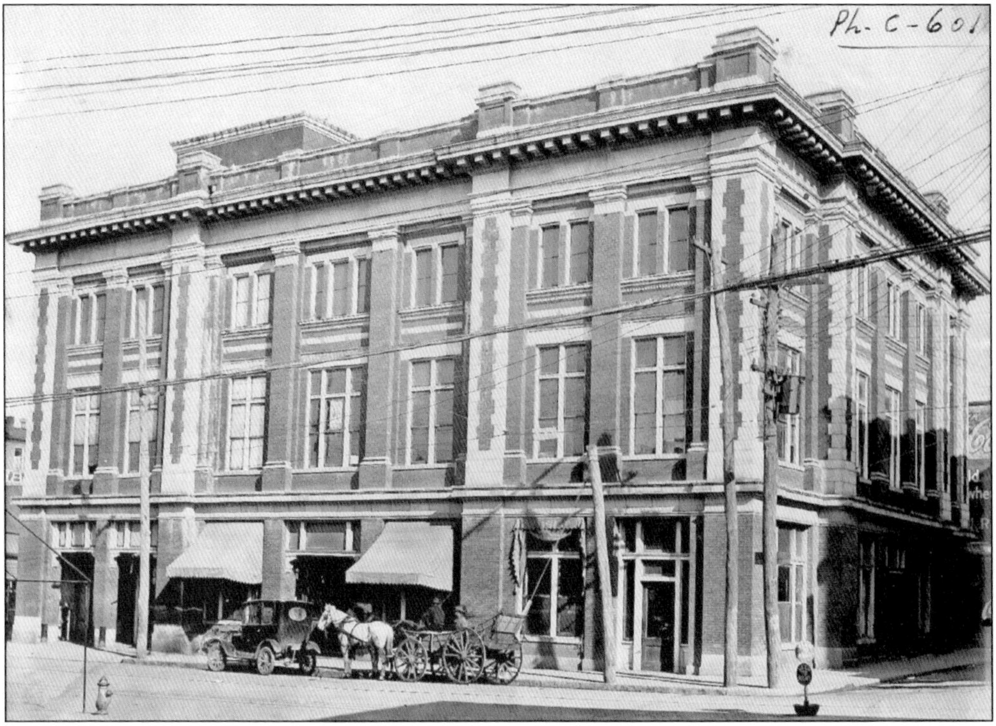

Burlington's city hall was built in 1916. It stood at the corner of Front and Worth Streets, and for many years, the building housed all offices of city government, including police and fire departments, tax offices, and the mayor's office. There was an auditorium on the second floor that served as a courtroom and also as the site of professional boxing matches and community programs. The building was replaced in the 1960s.

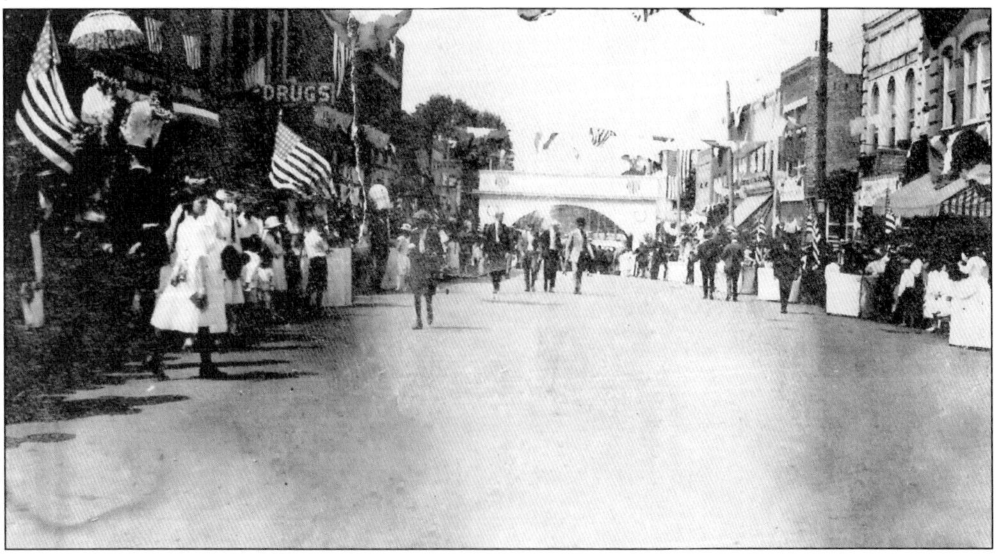

On May 30, 1919, Burlington hosted a huge Memorial Day program to welcome troops home from World War I. A large white arch was built across Main Street at Davis Street, and a parade of troops and patriotic floats passed under it. The arch was built to remind the troops of the Arc de Triomphe in Paris, where many of them had recently served in the war.

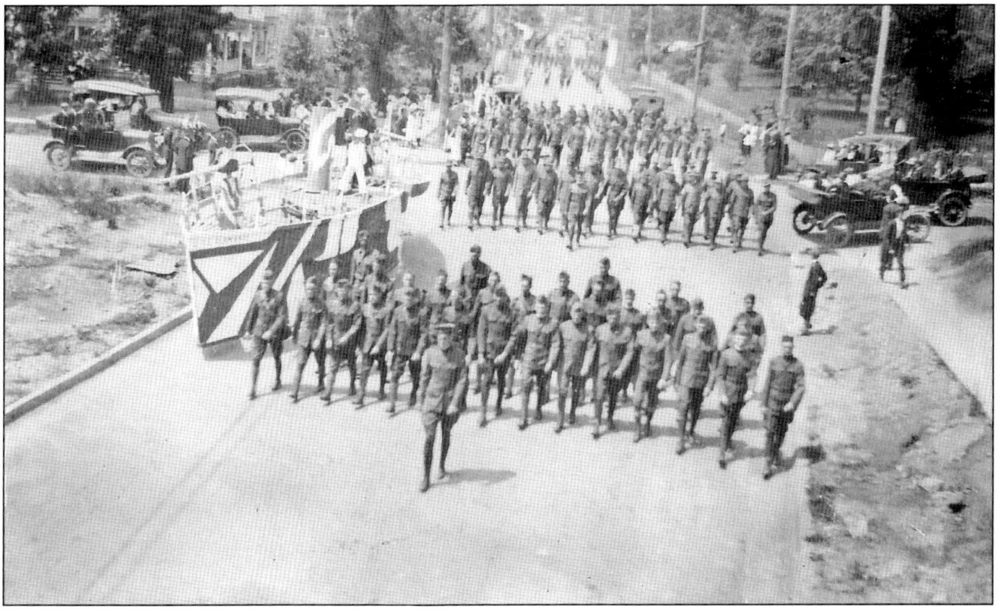

The World War I parade passed from the business district into residential areas, and these troops were part of the group that paraded on to the Burlington High School grounds on Broad Street. A full day of patriotic activities was held there to celebrate the end of the war. Many local troops served in a U.S. Army National Guard unit that was composed of Alamance County men.

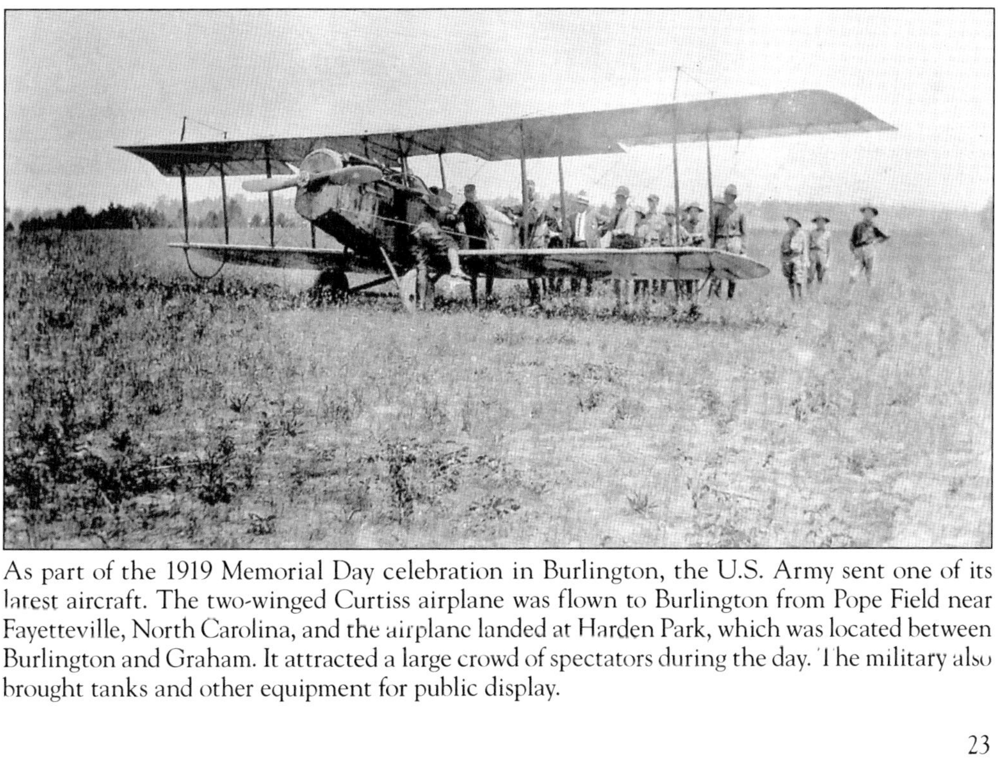

As part of the 1919 Memorial Day celebration in Burlington, the U.S. Army sent one of its latest aircraft. The two-winged Curtiss airplane was flown to Burlington from Pope Field near Fayetteville, North Carolina, and the airplane landed at Harden Park, which was located between Burlington and Graham. It attracted a large crowd of spectators during the day. The military also brought tanks and other equipment for public display.

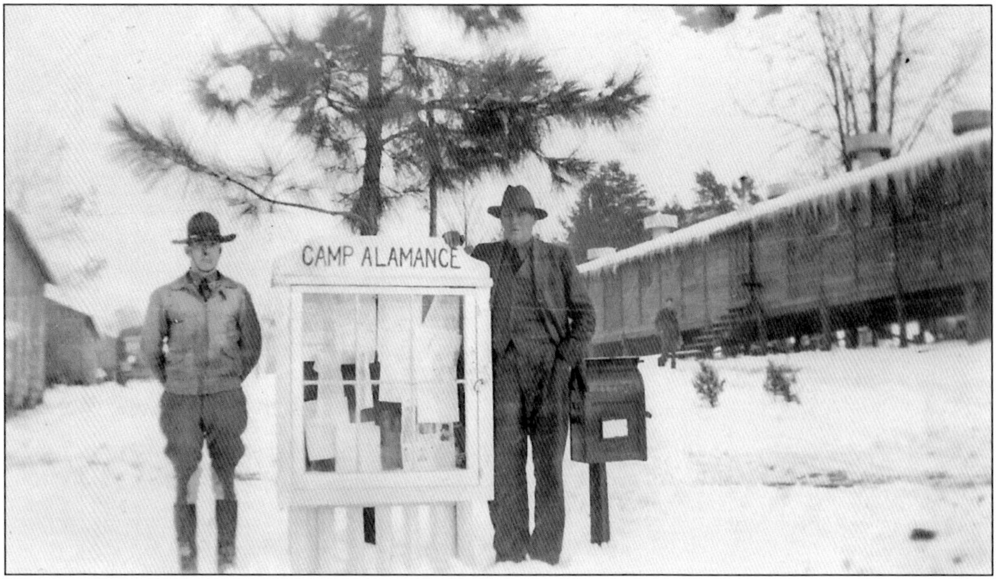

Burlington was the site of a Civilian Conservation Corps (CCC) camp during the Great Depression. Camp Alamance was located on the east side of Burlington in the area north of where the Western Electric plant was later located. The CCC program was a public works relief program for unemployed men. This program operated in every state as well as in territories. (Courtesy of Victor Seamon.)

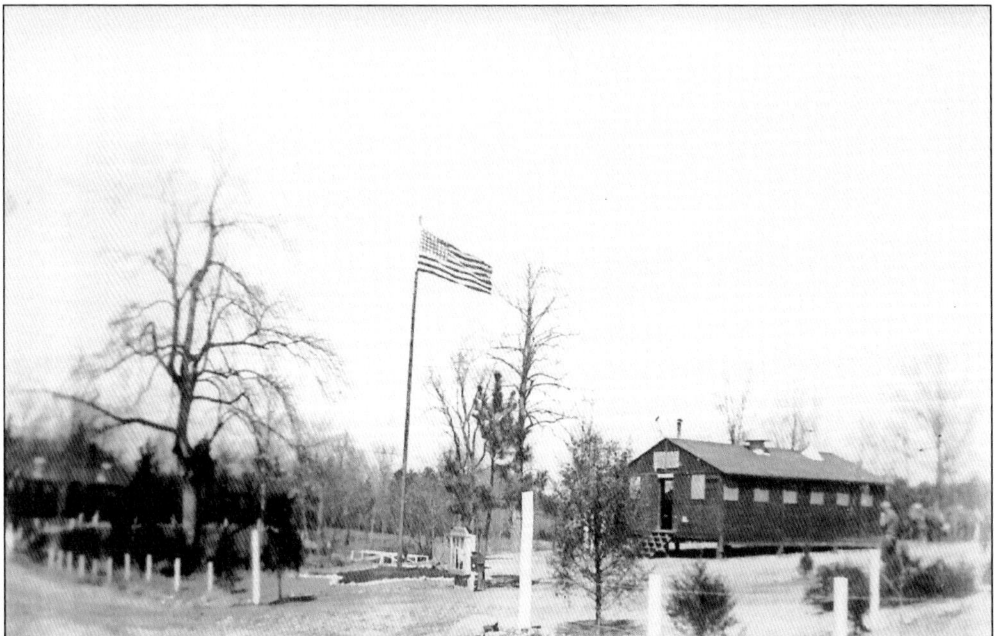

The CCC camp was a quasi-military operation with the men living in barracks, wearing uniforms, and following a military-like chain of command. Men in the camps needed the jobs desperately, and in order to maintain order, they were under the threat of "dishonorable discharge" for bad behavior. They worked in natural resource conservation and in various public works projects such as road construction. (Courtesy of Victor Seamon.)

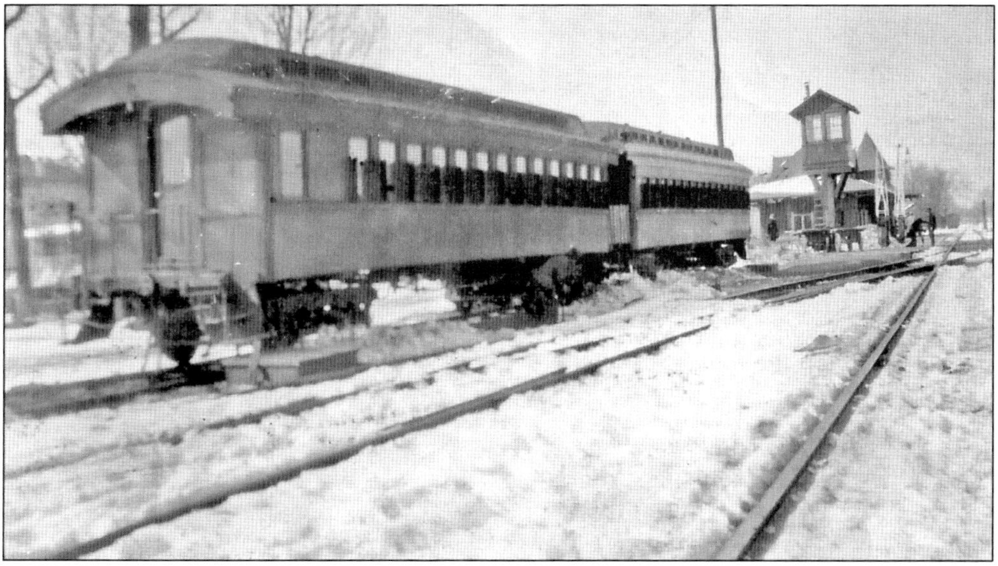

Passenger cars sat idle on a sidetrack at the Main Street railroad crossing in the 1930s. In the background are the signal house and depot. A railroad employee manned the signal house, and it was his duty to lower the crossing gates when a train approached to stop motor vehicles from crossing the tracks. In later years, automated gates replaced the gatehouse.

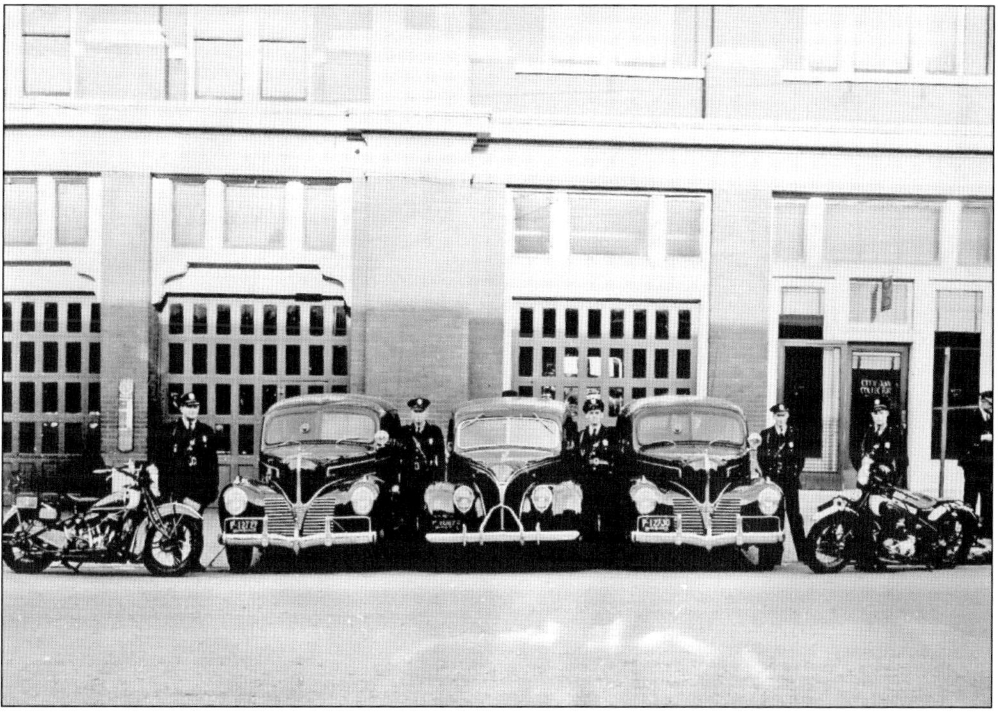

Burlington's police officers posed for this photograph in 1940 in front of the old city hall's fire station doors. They are displaying the city's patrol vehicles. Officers seen in the photograph are, from left to right, D. D. Matthews, Dean Poe, Charles Pyles, Jack Hall and Jesse Winningham. These men were familiar to Burlington residents in the 1940s, 1950s, and 1960s. Matthews later served as the police chief in Burlington, and Hall became a police lieutenant.

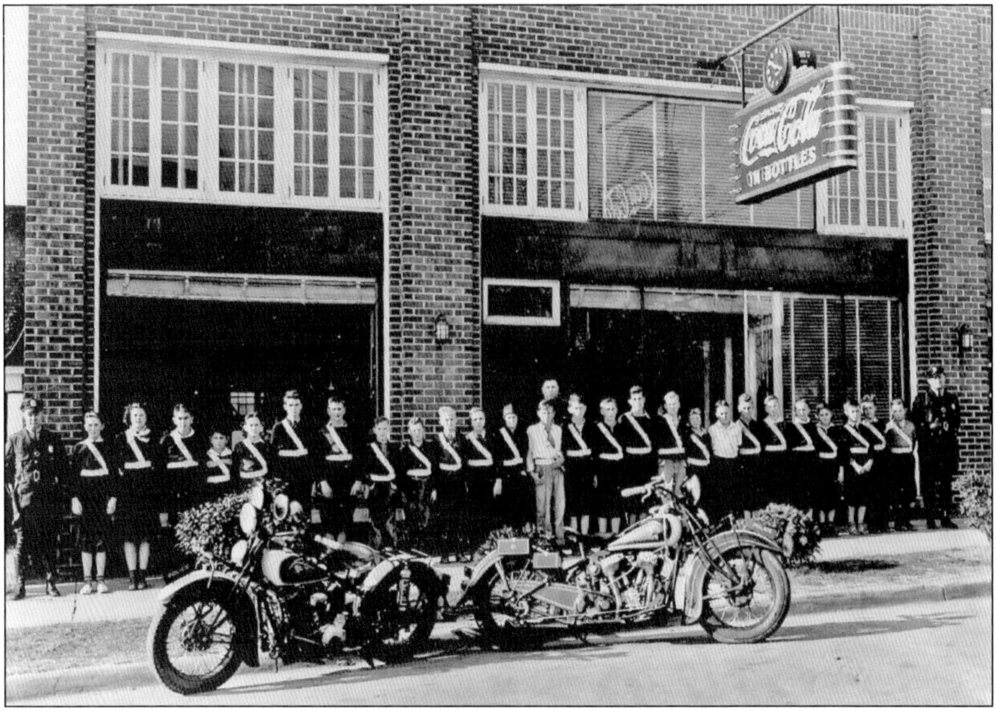

For many years, the Burlington Police Department and the local Coca-Cola Company operation sponsored the Schoolboy Patrol. Young students enlisted to help other students cross busy intersections near the schools. This group served in the mid-1930s. They are seen in front of the Coca-Cola Company plant on South Main Street. At left is officer Jesse Winningham, and at right is officer D. D. Matthews. (Courtesy of Wayne Beam.)

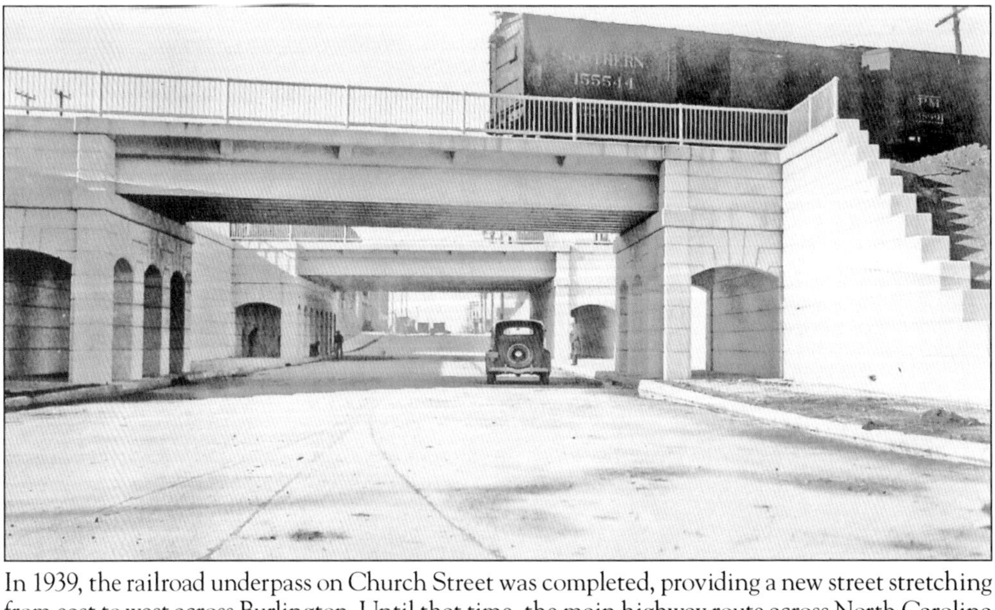

In 1939, the railroad underpass on Church Street was completed, providing a new street stretching from east to west across Burlington. Until that time, the main highway route across North Carolina went down Burlington's Main Street. When the underpass opened, Church Street became the route of the cross-state traffic. (Courtesy of Richard Campbell.)

Two

THE WORLD WAR II YEARS

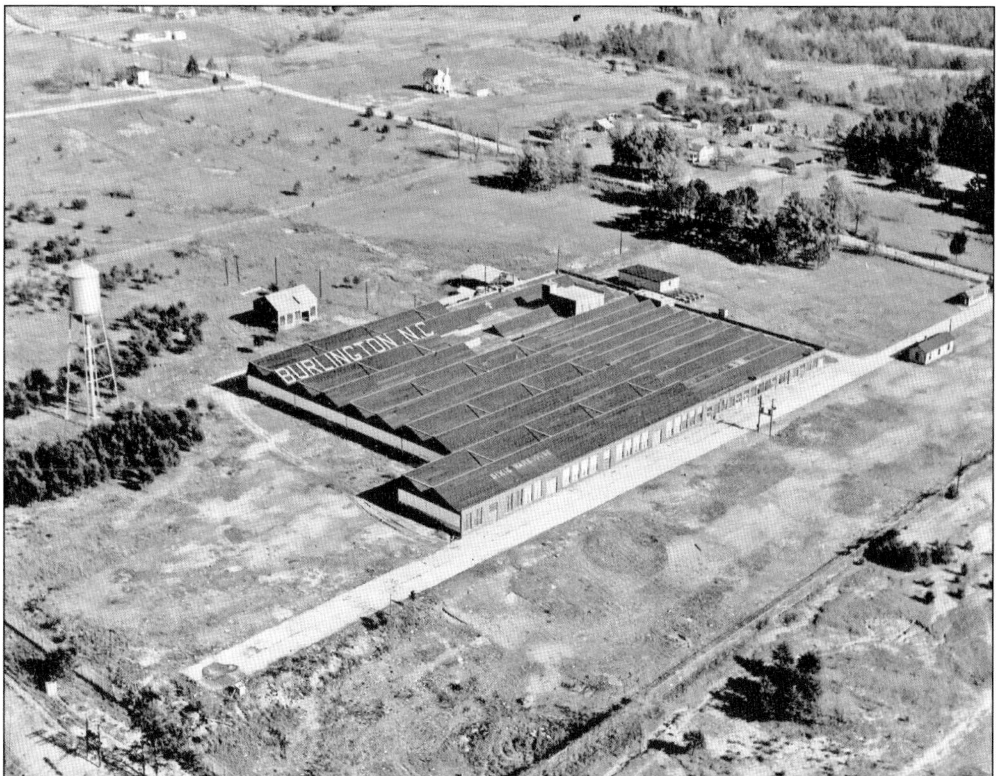

After World War II began, the government made the rayon plant on the east side of Burlington available to Fairchild Aircraft to build training airplanes for the U.S. Army Air Corps. This plant had been built in 1929 as a textile factory but closed three years later during the Great Depression. After the war, the building housed the Western Electric Company, which produced components for the Nike antimissile system.

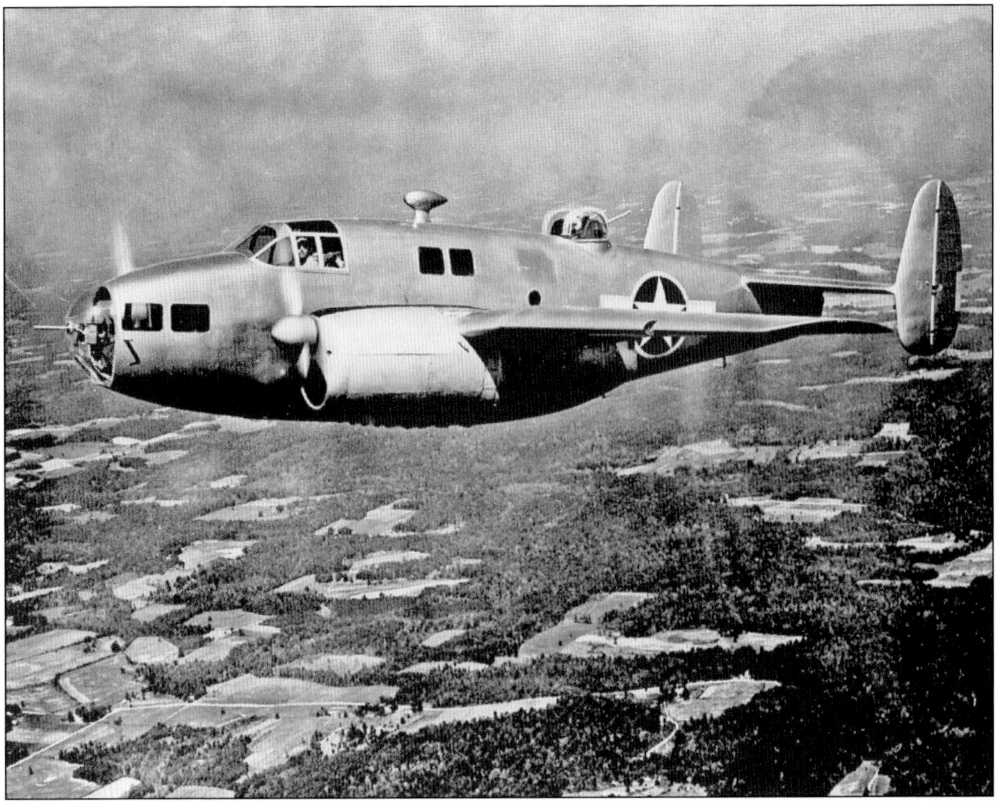

Fairchild Aircraft produced the AT-21 training airplane. This training airplane was different in that it was built mostly of plywood. The AT-21 was designed to train crews for twin-engined bombers, but production was halted in 1944 as the air corps put more emphasis on four-engined bombers. The Firestone Company later moved into the plant to produce artillery pieces for the military until the end of the war.

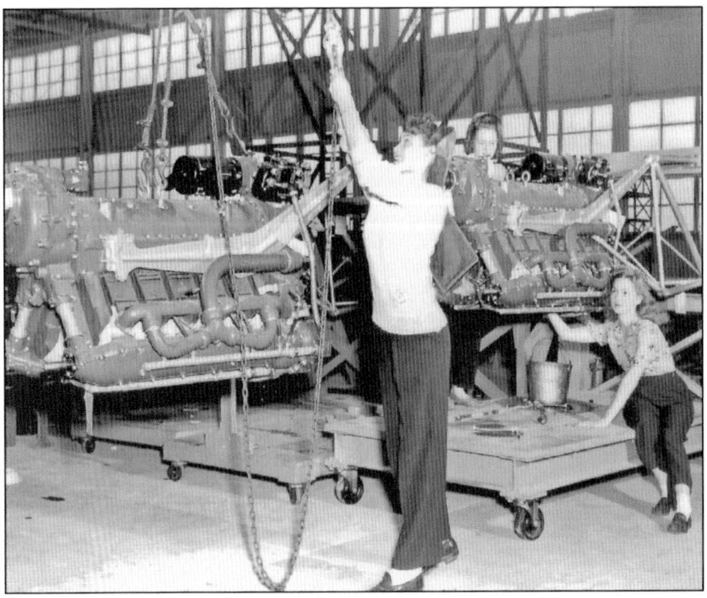

Many of the employees in the Fairchild plant were women. Here, three women move engines for the airplanes to the assembly line. When the war started, many women moved into the workforce for the first time in Burlington. Large numbers of men went into the military, leaving jobs vacant. Women had to fill many of those spots. Workers were imported from other Fairchild locations as well.

On May 19, 1943, Fairchild held a special ceremony to mark the flight of its first airplane produced in the Burlington plant. Hundreds of people turned out to see the flight and to hear North Carolina governor J. Melville Broughton speak. The Fairchild Airport was located across the road from the plant. Today a Wal-Mart store occupies much of the old airstrip.

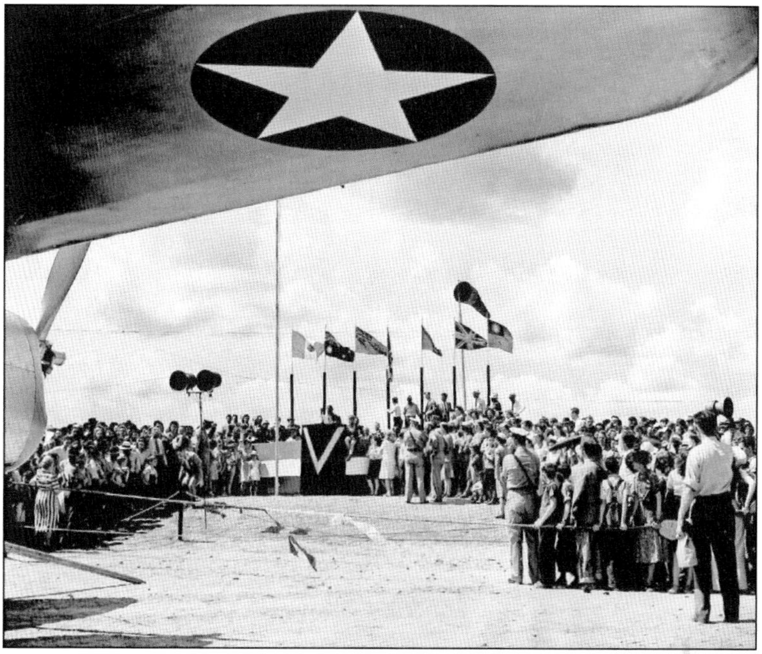

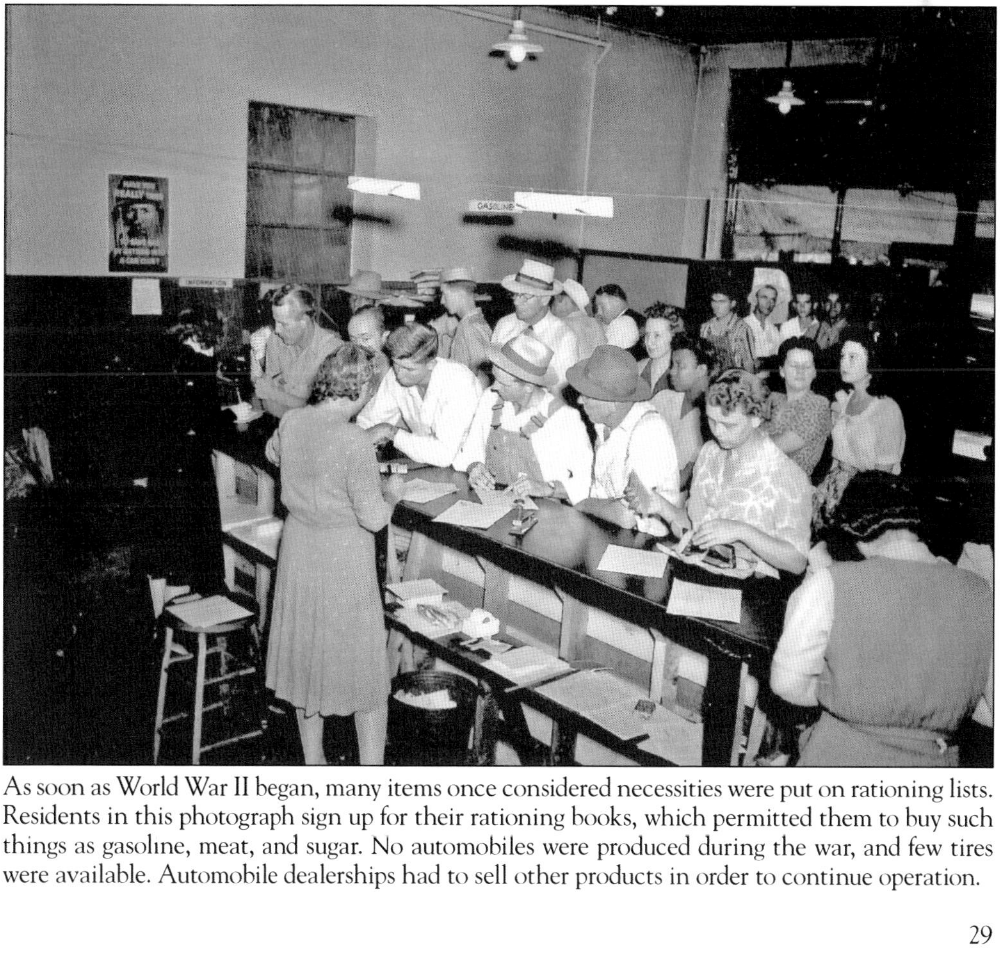

As soon as World War II began, many items once considered necessities were put on rationing lists. Residents in this photograph sign up for their rationing books, which permitted them to buy such things as gasoline, meat, and sugar. No automobiles were produced during the war, and few tires were available. Automobile dealerships had to sell other products in order to continue operation.

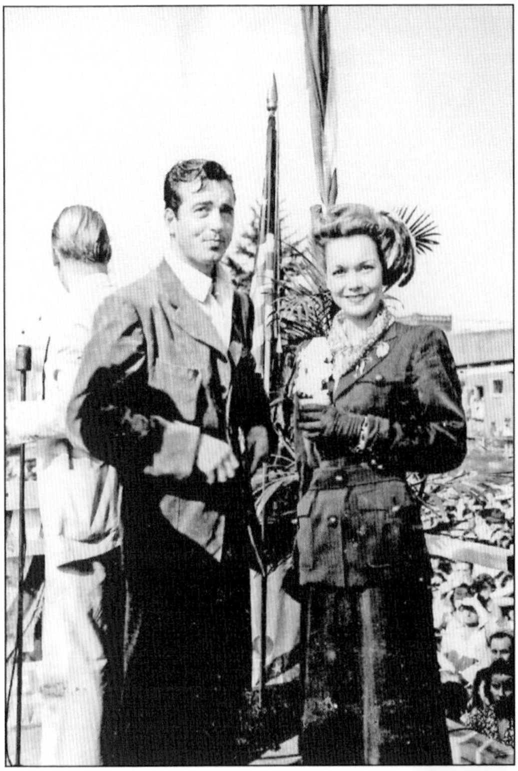

Movie stars John Payne and Jane Wyman came to Burlington in 1942 to promote war bonds. They appeared on East Front Street, and a huge crowd of residents turned out to buy thousands of dollars in bonds. Bond sales were heavily promoted throughout the war. School children helped by filling books with saving stamps. The books were then traded for bonds for the war effort.

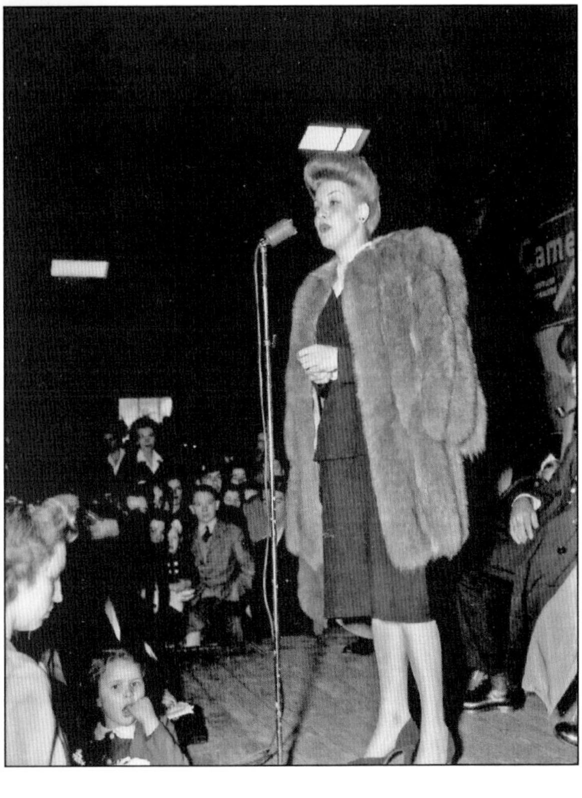

Another movie star, Ann Savage came later in the war to promote bond sales. With her was actor Lon Chaney, and they appeared in an event at one of the tobacco warehouses. They sold thousands in bonds, and they even sold personal items such as cuff links and earrings to raise money for the war effort. Several other stars, including Lucille Ball, came to Burlington for war bond appearances as well.

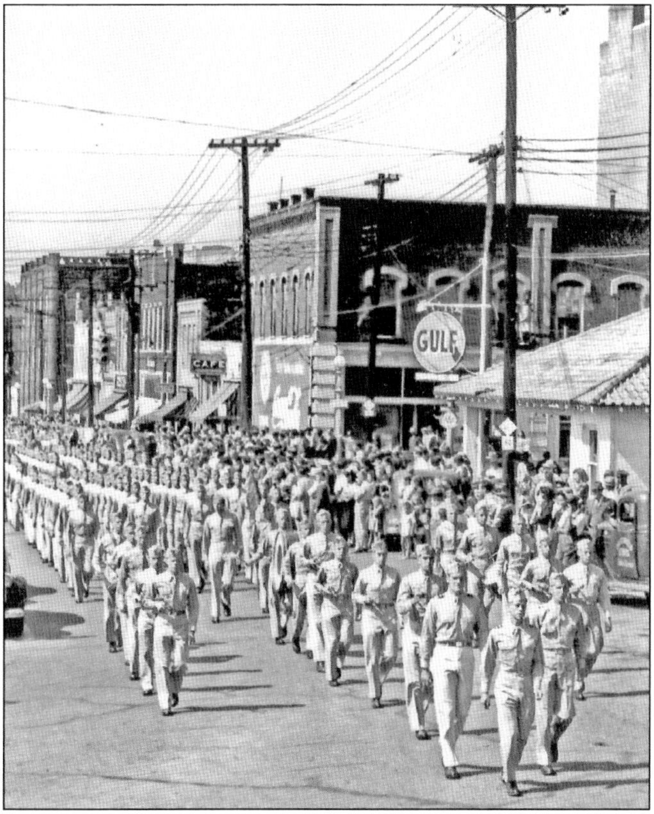

Patriotic parades were held on a regular basis in Burlington throughout the war years. This group of military personnel marches up Spring Street past the Front Street intersection. Often these parades were used to promote war bond sales, and some were staged to boost the morale of those on the home front during the war.

Below, members of the American Legion lead a parade up South Main Street during World War II. The Gate City Motor Company building in the background was later home to the *Times-News*, the local newspaper. Walter B. Ellis Post No. 63 of the American Legion was named for the first serviceman from Alamance County to be killed in World War I.

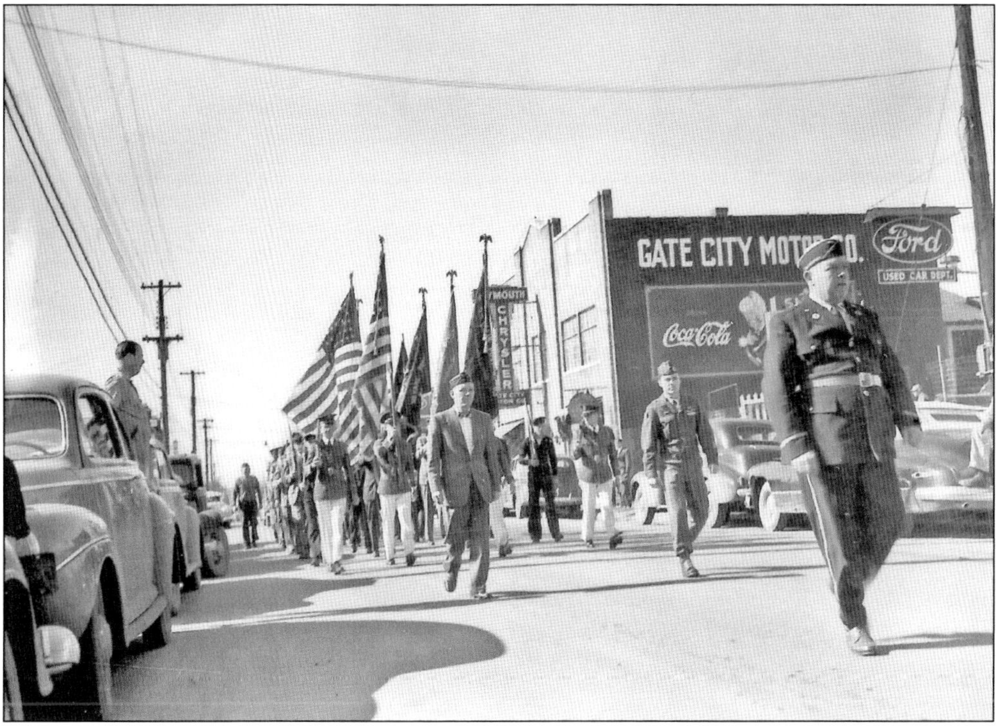

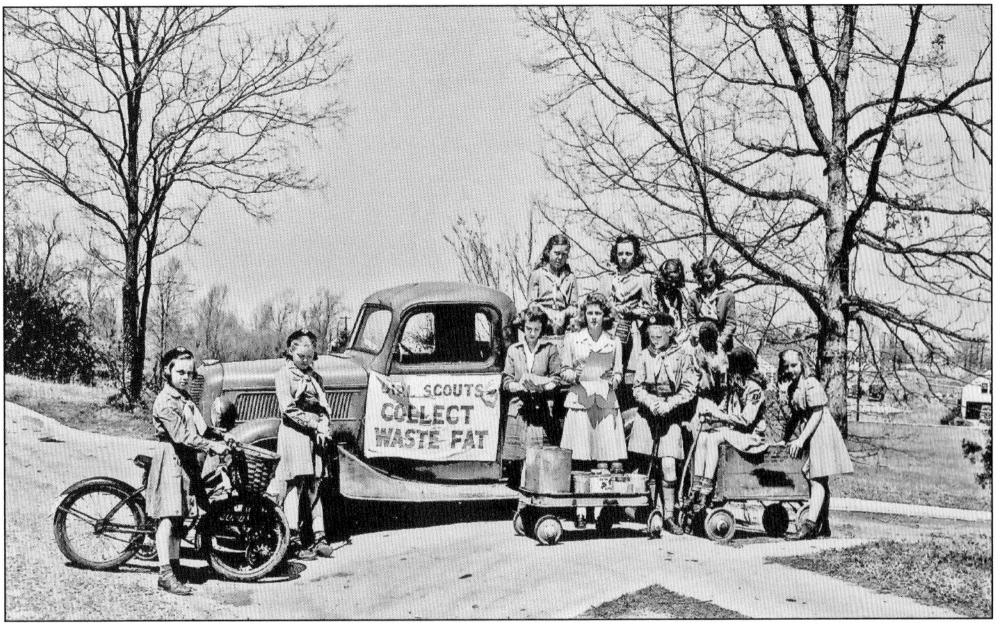

Girl Scouts and other youth organizations helped in the war effort by collecting materials needed by the government and the military. These girls made regular collections of cooking fat from local homes and restaurants, which was used in the production of munitions. Other children scoured their neighborhoods for scrap metal, which they sold to local metal dealers. The metal was melted down and used for military purposes.

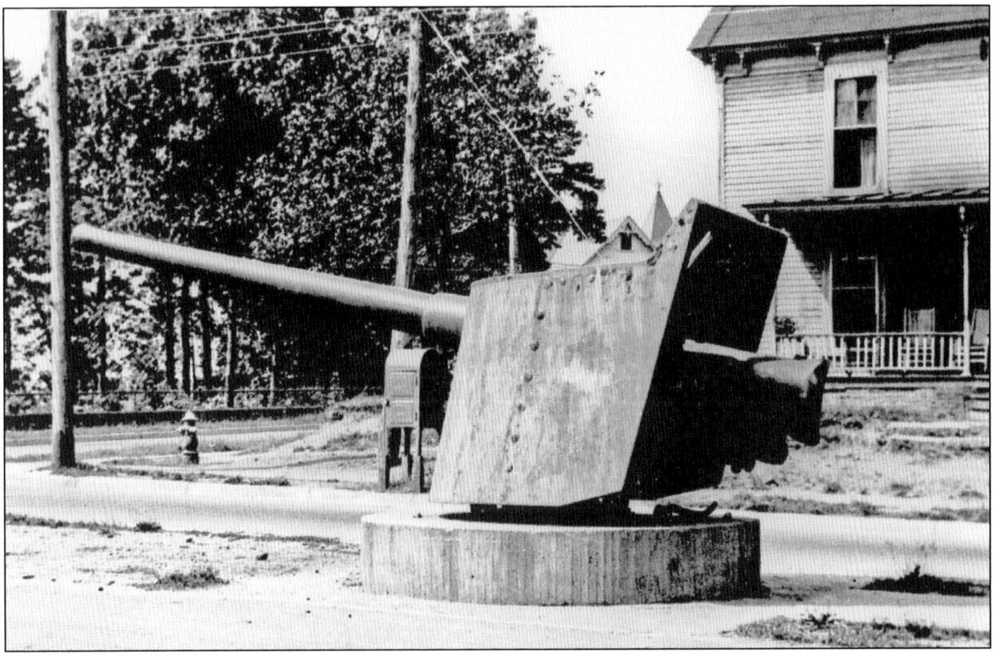

The Big Gun sat for many years on East Webb Avenue at Anthony Street. The World War I navy gun sat there as a reminder of the war. It was a major landmark, still remembered by many. In 1942, the gun was recycled for use in weapons during World War II. Many of the old streetcar rails in city streets were taken up at that time for the same purpose.

From left to right, Casey Jones, Max Marion, and Buddy Baker sat on the steps of a housing unit at Fairchild Heights, a community built during World War II for Fairchild Aircraft workers. Workers lived in concrete buildings that resembled barracks. There was a post office, a chapel, and a store in the village, which was later the site of the Eastlawn School and the Alamance-Burlington School System offices. (Courtesy of Buddy Baker.)

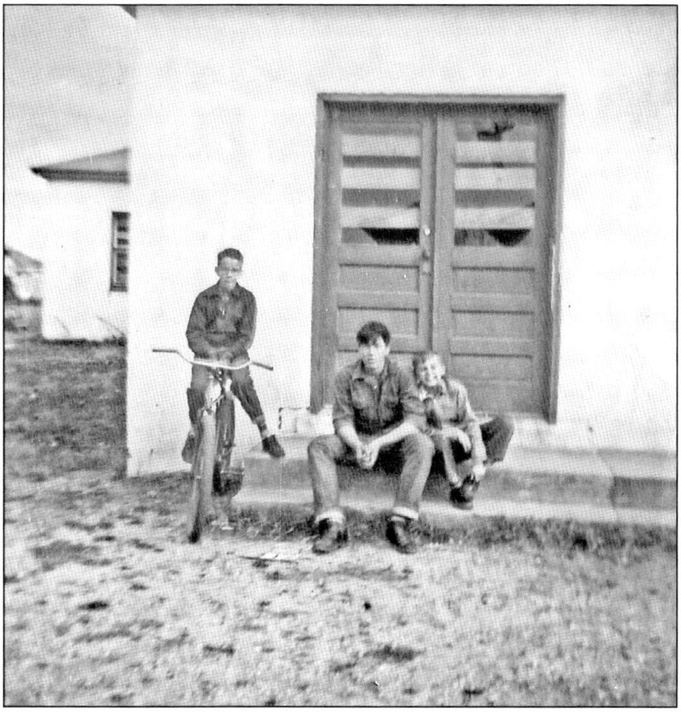

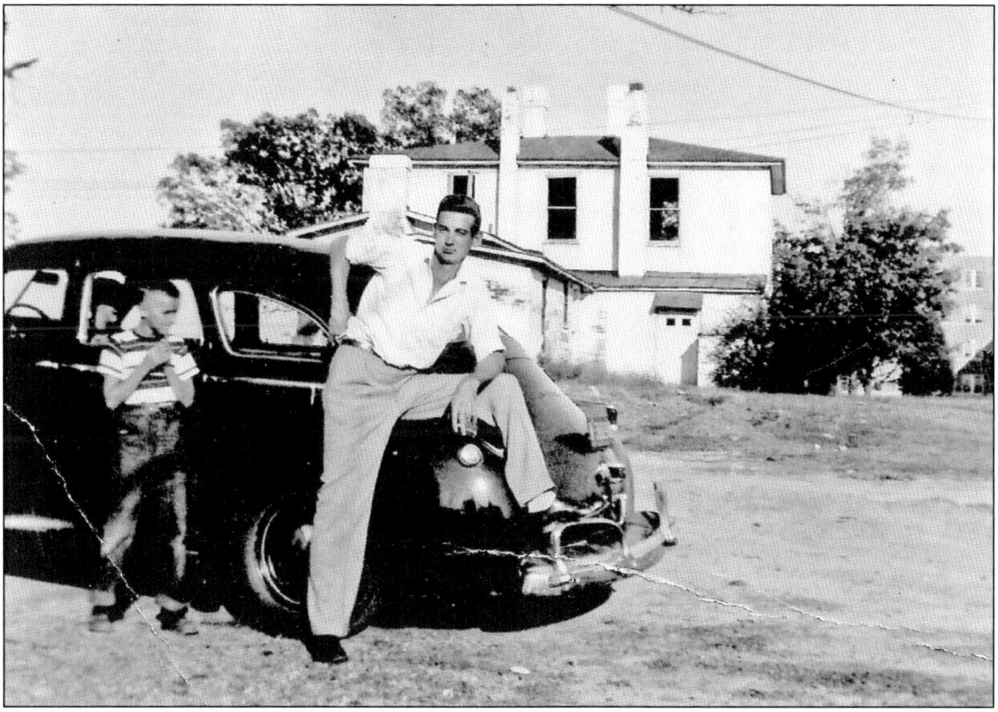

David Baker and his son Buddy relax by the family car after the war years. They lived on the east side of Burlington, which was, at the time, near the Alamance General Hospital, partly visible at far right. Buddy Baker became city manager of the City of Burlington near the end of the 20th century. (Courtesy of Buddy Baker.)

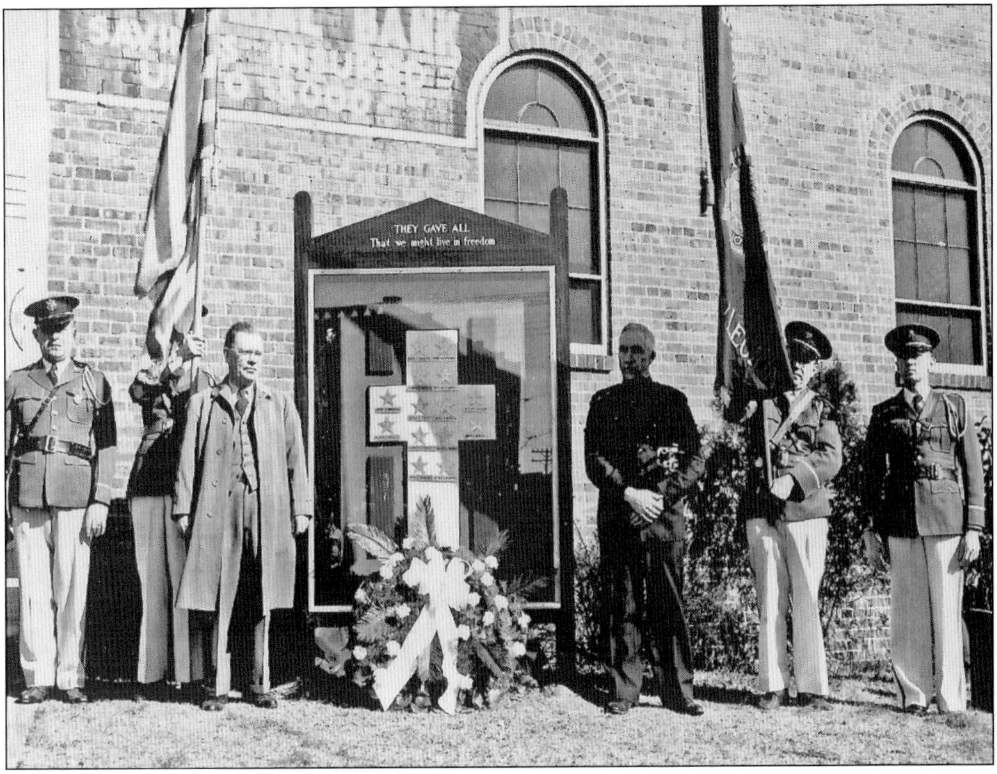

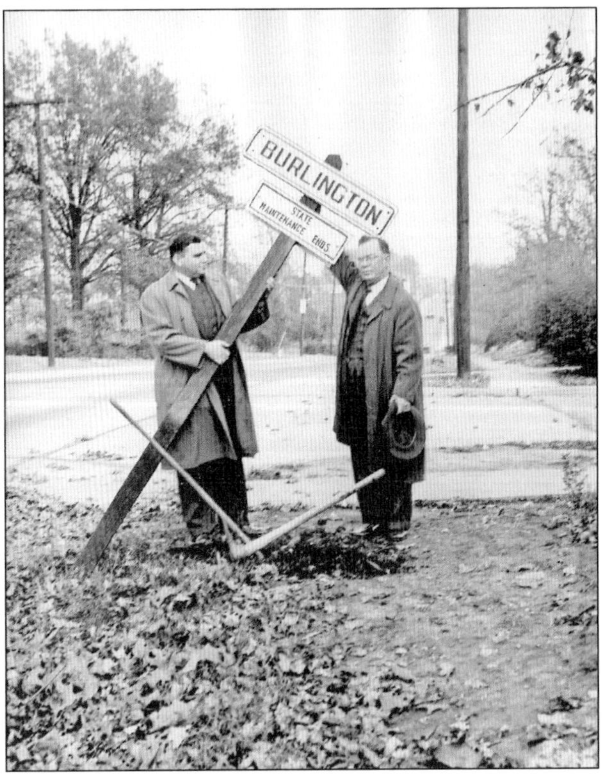

A memorial was erected on the lawn of the May Memorial Library early in World War II to honor Alamance County's war casualties. There were 14 gold stars on it when Mayor Earl Horner unveiled the memorial. Before World War II ended, more than 200 men and women from Alamance County were killed in action.

On November 17, 1943, Burlington expanded its city limits for the first time. Burlington Chamber of Commerce president Ralph Scott (left) and Mayor Earl Horner placed the new sign at the corner of South Church Street and Glenwood Avenue. The city grew from about 10,000 people to about 23,000 with this expansion.

Nylon was taken by the military during World War II, so there was none available for ladies hosiery. When the war ended, the May-McEwen-Kaiser Hosiery Company on South Main Street staged a celebration in the middle of the street to welcome nylon back to the public. Several models appeared on the street, and Rosalyn Troxler was chosen as the "Nylon Queen" and sat atop hosiery cases to don a pair.

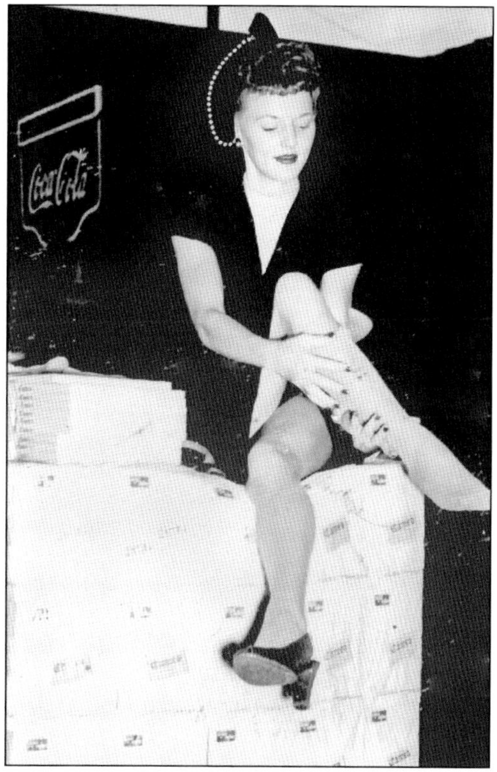

One of the major problems in Burlington during World War II was the polio epidemic. A number of cases were reported in the area, and young people were placed under quarantine. Children could not attend movies, go to playgrounds, or congregate in any public area. Iron lungs were used for the most serious cases. The Burlington Kiwanis Club donated this unit for use by area patients.

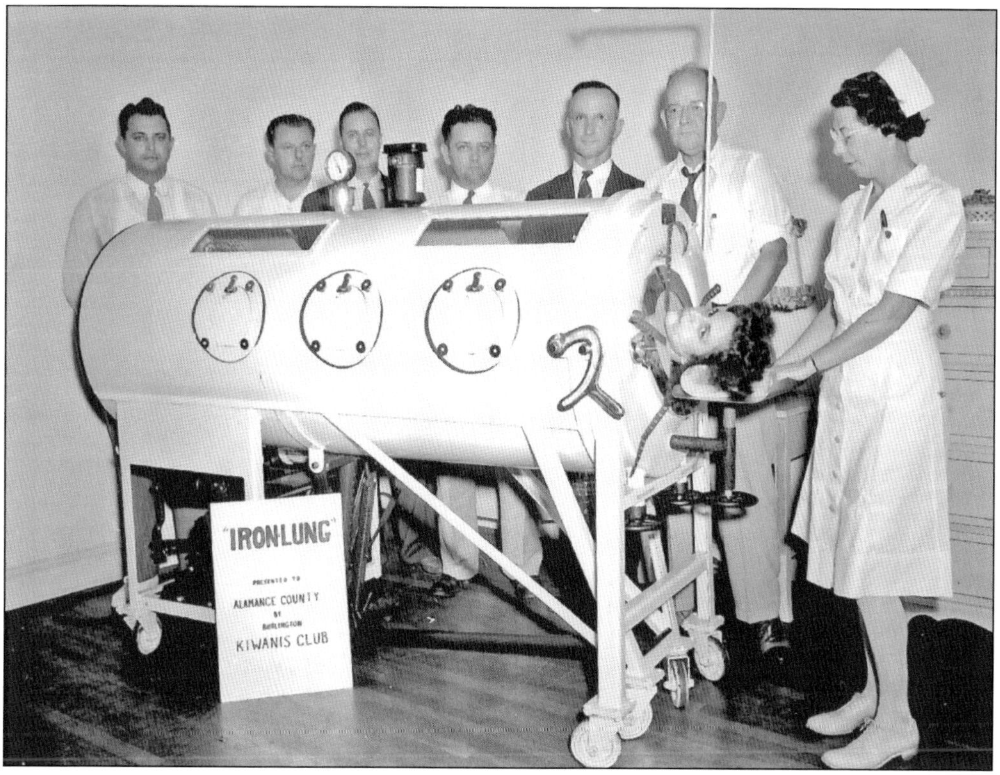

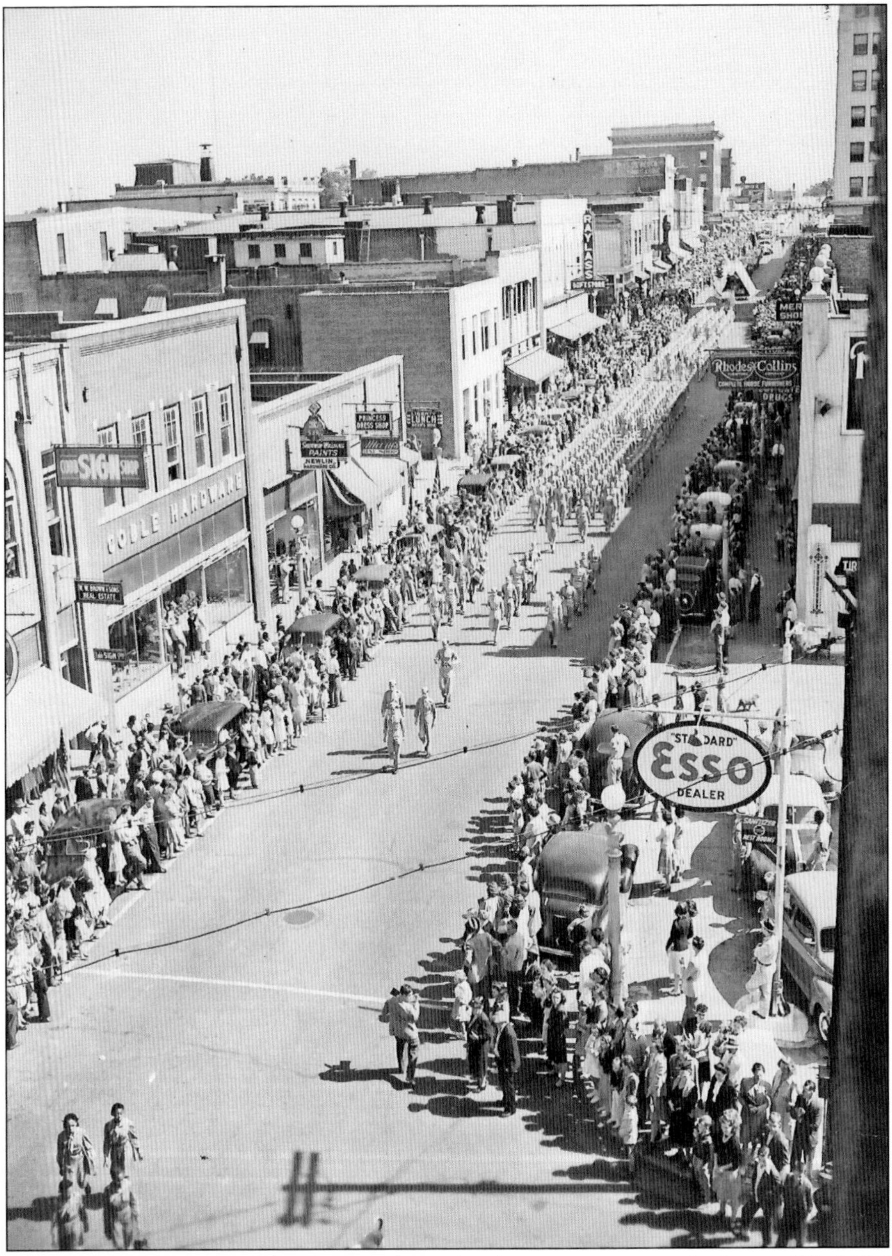

Thousands of Burlington residents turned out for this patriotic parade during World War II. Military personnel, both men and women, marched down Burlington's Main Street to inspire those on the home front to support the war effort. People in Burlington felt the war's impact in many ways—through rationing, the draft of fathers and sons into the military, shortages of necessities, and through the loss of loved ones in faraway places. This photograph was taken from a window of the Alamance Hotel at Main Street and Maple Avenue. The Esso station, at right, was replaced by J. C. Penney and later still, by a LabCorp operation. The entire block at left, which includes Coble Hardware, was leveled and replaced by a bank and its parking lot. As businesses moved out to shopping centers, the entire landscape downtown was changed, and the appearance of the street in this photograph is only a memory now.

Three

Burlington's Schools

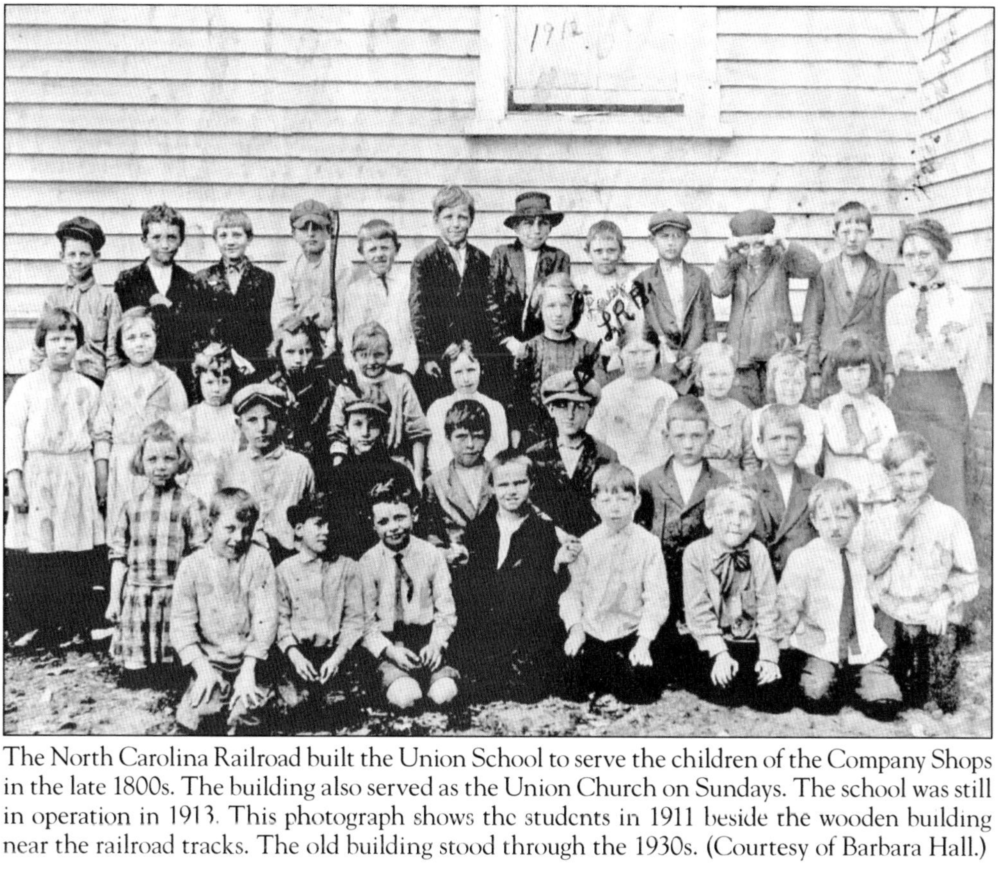

The North Carolina Railroad built the Union School to serve the children of the Company Shops in the late 1800s. The building also served as the Union Church on Sundays. The school was still in operation in 1913. This photograph shows the students in 1911 beside the wooden building near the railroad tracks. The old building stood through the 1930s. (Courtesy of Barbara Hall.)

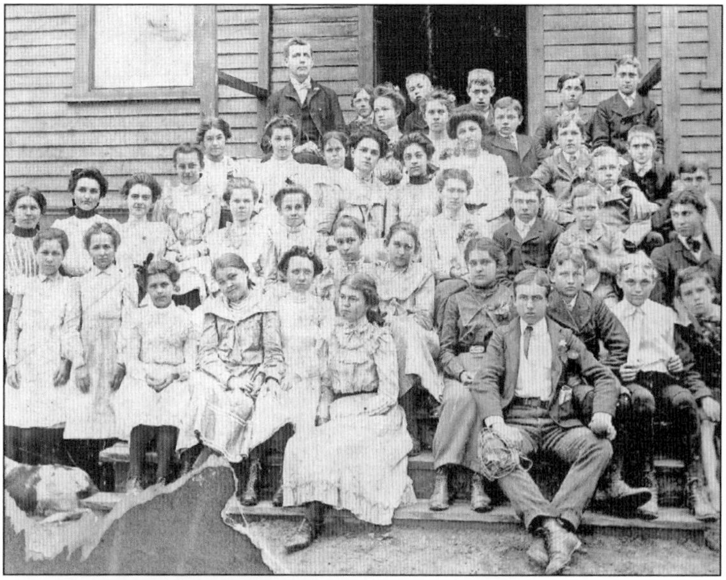

In 1913, these Burlington students posed on the steps of the school with their superintendent, Frank Curtis, who is on the top row at the far left. In 1916, Burlington High School was built on Broad Street, and the building was used until 1951, when Williams High School was opened on the west side of downtown Burlington.

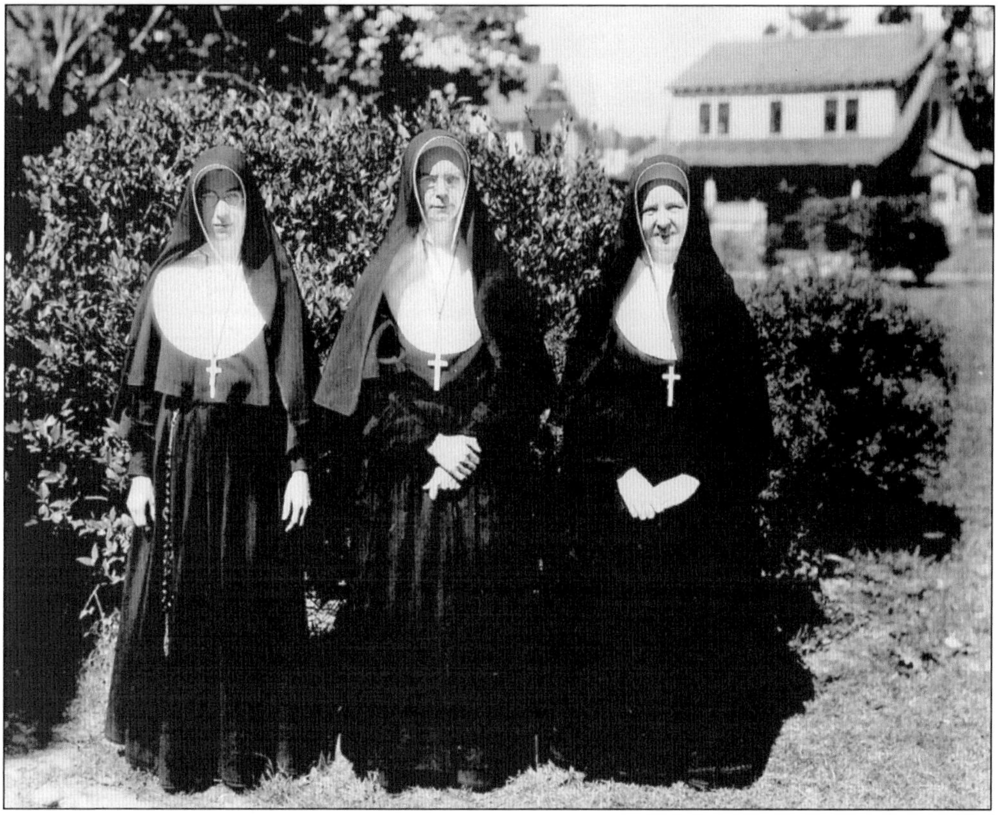

The Blessed Sacrament Catholic Church opened a school in 1935 with 35 students. Among the early nuns to serve the local church and school were, from left to right, Sister Miriam Vincent, Sister Mary Edmunds, and Sister Gaudentia. A new classroom unit was built in 1951 adjacent to the church. In 1995, the school moved to the Hillcrest School building, which had been vacated by the Burlington City Schools. (Courtesy of Blessed Sacrament Catholic Church.)

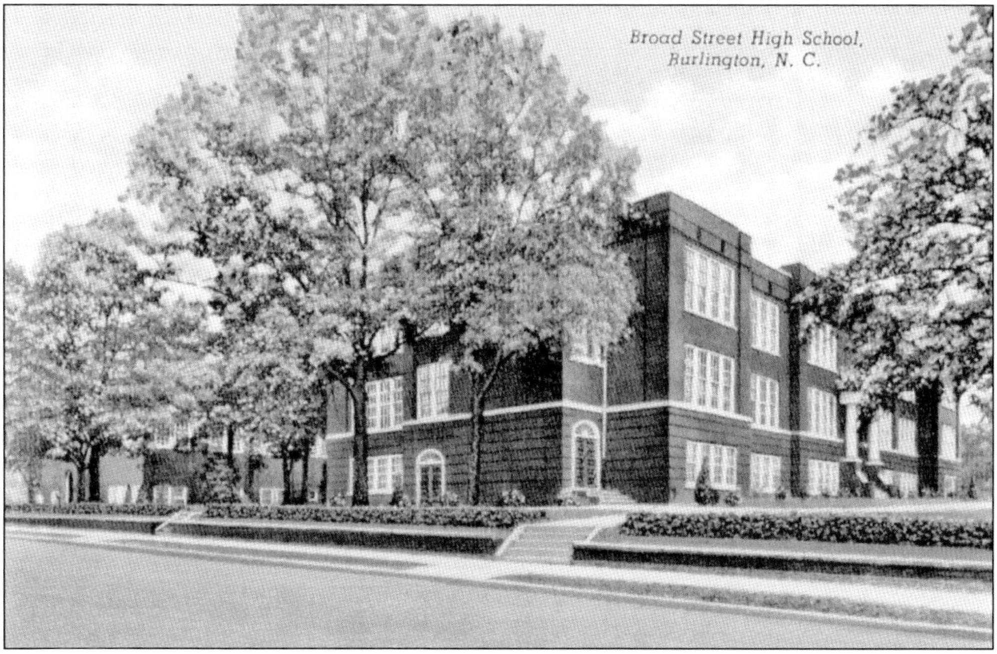

Burlington High School was constructed on Broad Street in 1916. A classroom building with an auditorium was built first, followed by a multipurpose gymnasium-auditorium-cafeteria, and finally by an eighth-grade classroom building. The school operated through the 1950–1951 academic year, when the new Williams High School opened. This location then served as a middle school for several years. The city recreation department now uses the gym.

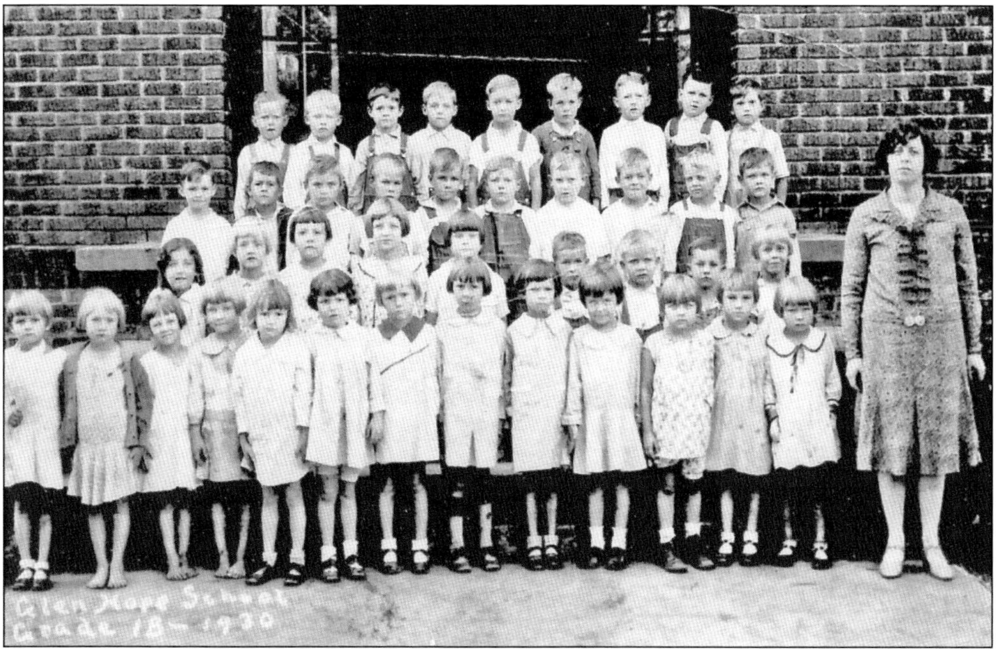

A Mrs. Walker's first grade class posed for this photograph on the steps of Glenhope Elementary School in 1930. Glenhope was on the east side of Burlington and held grades one through seven. Even though the building was outside the city limits for many years, it was a part of the Burlington City Schools.

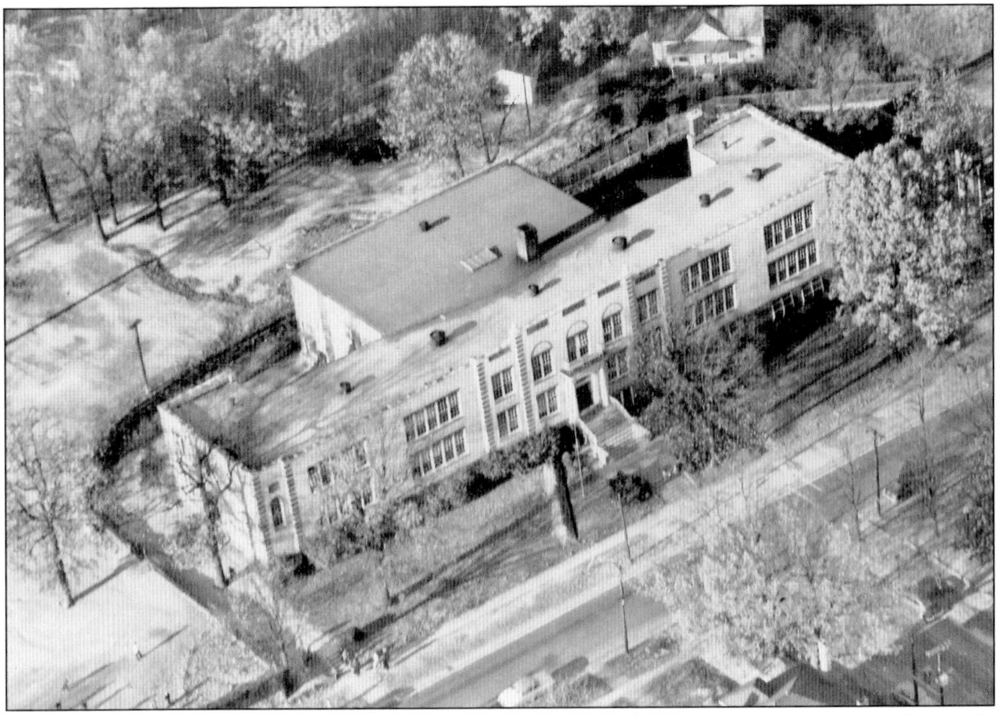

The Fisher Street School was another Burlington elementary school. It served students on the north side of Burlington and was identical to the Maple Avenue School on the south side. Both schools had seven grades, and students moved on to eighth grade at Burlington High School. Students went through 11 grades until 1945, when 12th grade was added. (Courtesy of Terry Woodings).

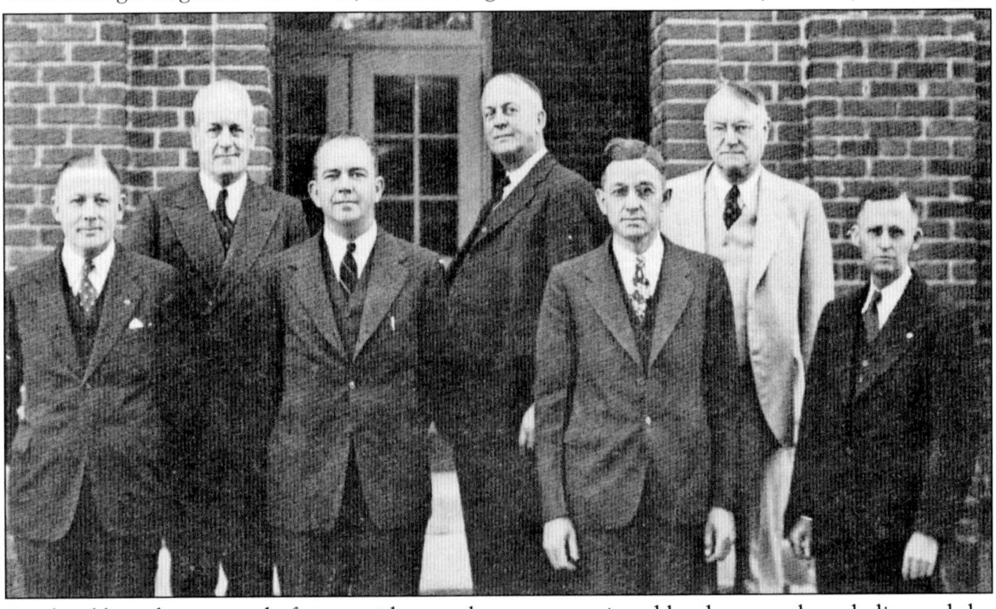

A school board composed of city residents, who were appointed by the town board, directed the Burlington City Schools system's operations. This group served the system in 1938. From left to right are Jerry Strader, Harold Eaton, Ed Curlee, J. A. Lowe, Walter M. Williams, Joe Gant, and Dr. H. V. Murray. (Courtesy of the Burlington City Schools Report to the People, 1963.)

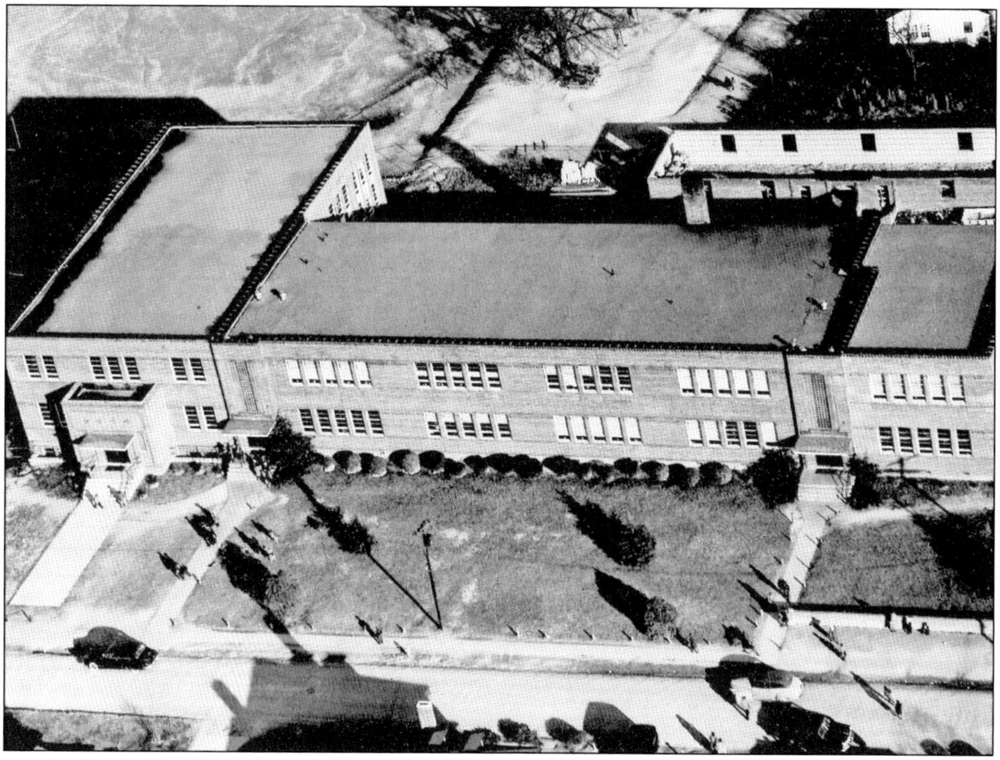

The Jordan Sellars High School (shown here) and the J. F. Gunn Elementary School served African American students during the years of racial segregation. In the upper right of the photograph is a roofless building that had been a cannery during World War II, serving residents near the school who grew their own vegetables. (Courtesy of Terry Woodings.)

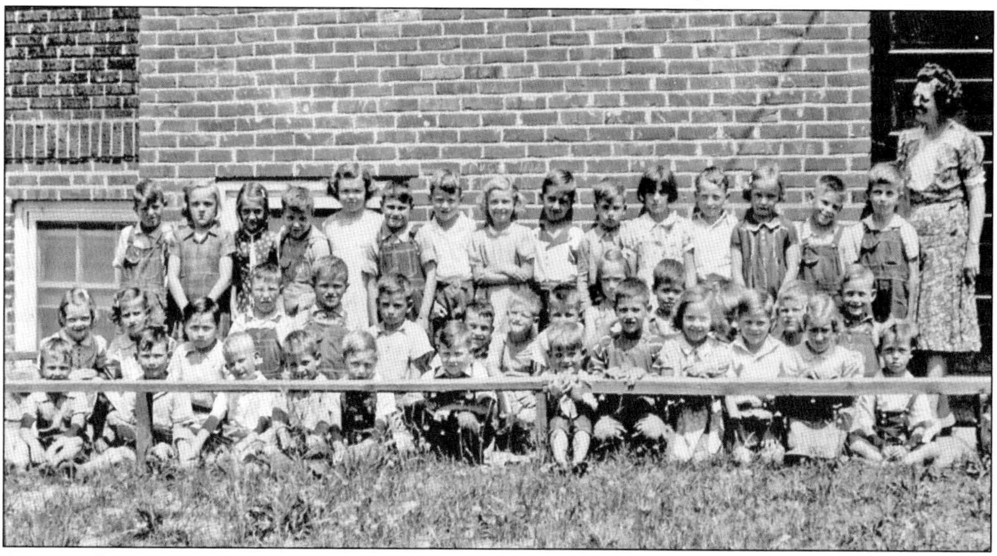

Ann Bridges was the first-grade teacher at the Glenhope School in 1941. She posed with her class beside their classroom. The parents of many students in this school worked at Burlington Mills and lived in the community known as the Mill Hill, adjacent to the textile mill that made the name Burlington known the world over.

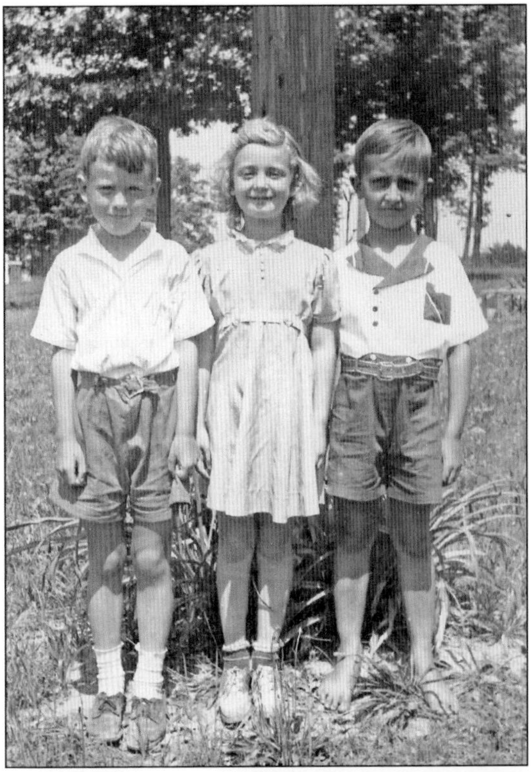

From left to right, Walter Seamon, Arlene Stafford, and Don Bolden were members of the Glenhope School's first grade in 1941, and they were the only three in the class to achieve perfect attendance for the year. Seamon moved to Virginia to work after college, but Stafford became a local high school teacher, and Bolden became editor of the city's newspaper, the *Times-News*.

Below, this class of kindergarten students graduated from the Blessed Sacrament Catholic School in 1945. For many years, this was the only private school in the community, and many parents who were not Catholics sent their children to the school from kindergarten through the elementary years. The school has continued in operation since 1935. (Courtesy of Blessed Sacrament Catholic Church.)

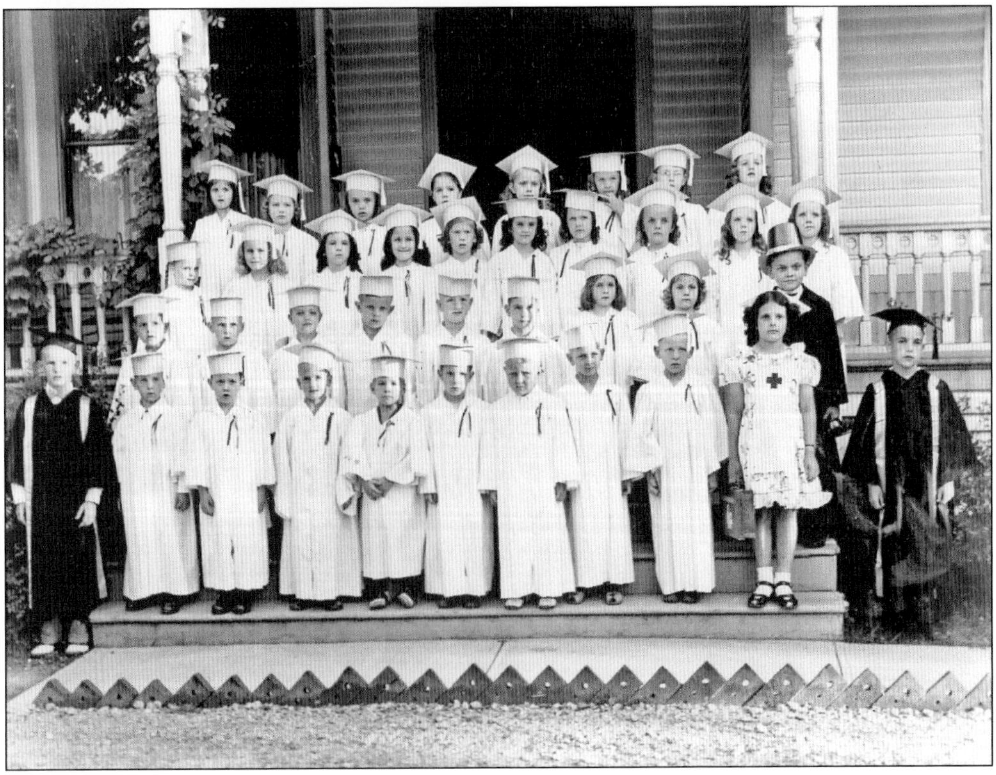

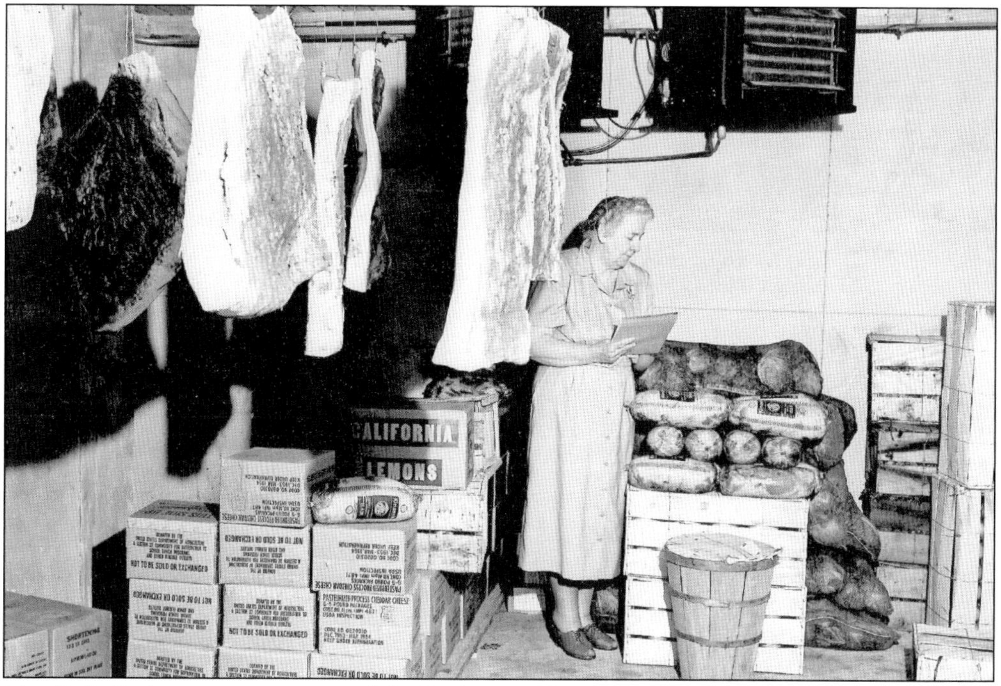

Mrs. R. L. Barham was supervisor of the Burlington City Schools cafeteria program in the 1950s and 1960s. She is shown here in one of the food storage areas used by the cafeteria operation to provide meals on a daily basis to all students in the various city school facilities. (Courtesy of Terry Woodings.)

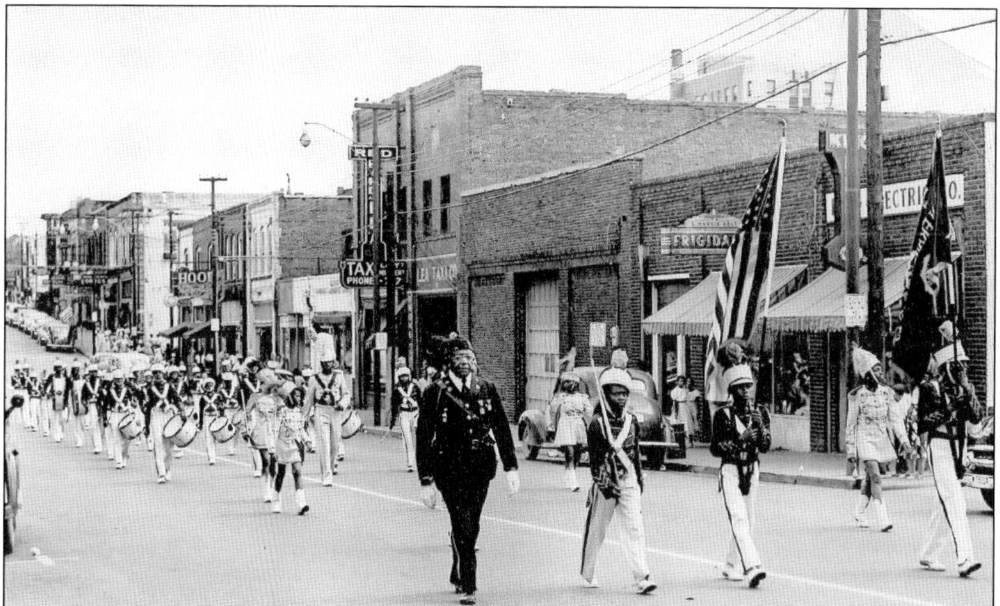

The band from J. F. Gunn Elementary School led a parade along Front Street in the 1950s. Many students from the elementary school band moved on to play in the Jordan Sellars High School band. The high school band was one of the most popular in the Piedmont North Carolina region for many years and was constantly in demand for parades and special events.

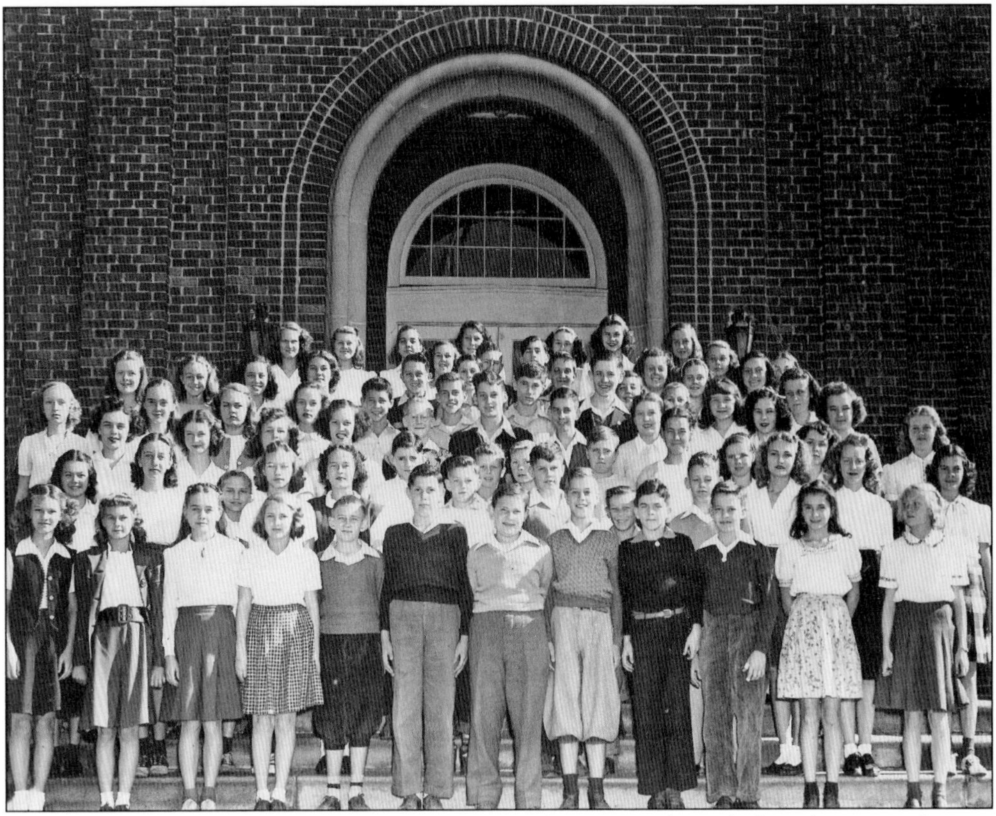

The Hillcrest Elementary School served west Burlington students before they moved on to Burlington High School. This group of students formed the Hillcrest Elementary School glee club during the 1946–1947 school year. Hilda Somers directed the musical group. The school, located on Hillcrest Avenue, was later relocated to West Davis Street, and the Blessed Sacrament Catholic School then moved into the Hillcrest Avenue location. (Courtesy of Terry Woodings.)

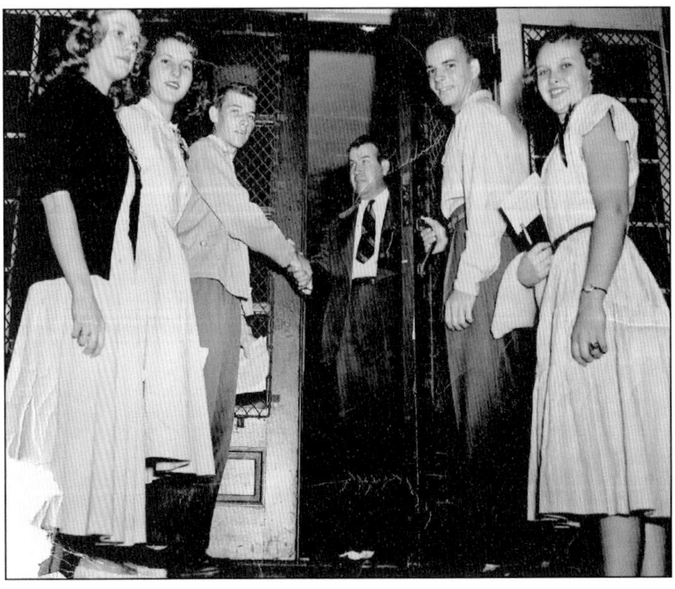

Principal C. C. Linnemann (center) opened the door to greet the new student body officers at Burlington High School at the beginning of the 1948 school year. Those serving in student government roles that year were, from left to right, Sue Steele, Sally Goldman, Pete Barnwell, Richard Pitts, and Ruth Ann Sullivan.

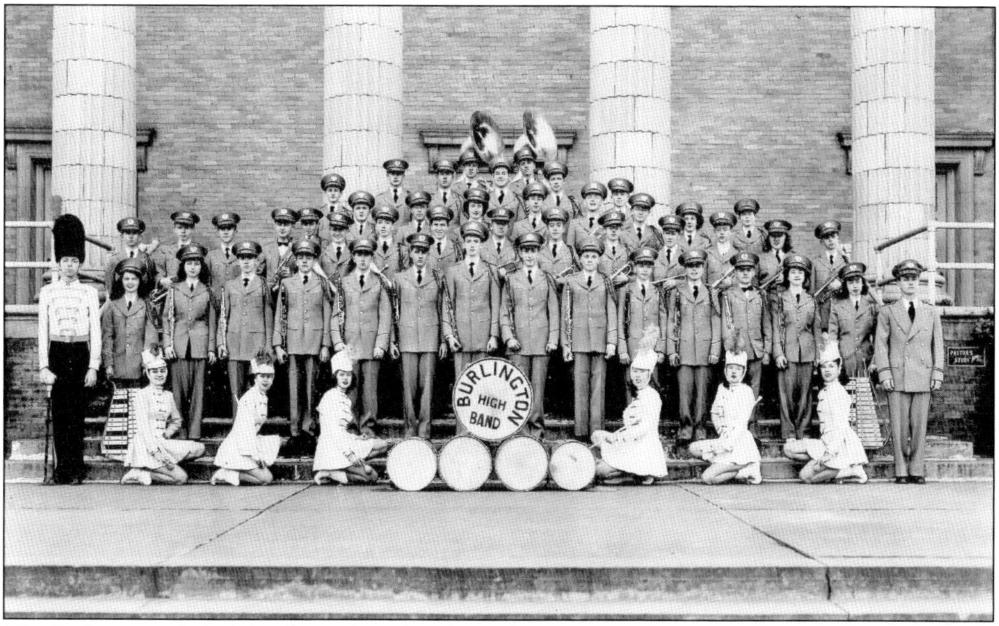

The Burlington High School marching band posed in 1949 on the steps of the First Baptist Church of Burlington just a few blocks from the school on Broad Street. The band was directed by James Cole (at far right) and was always featured in community parades in Burlington. In 1949, the band was part of several centennial parades in the area to mark Alamance County's 100th birthday.

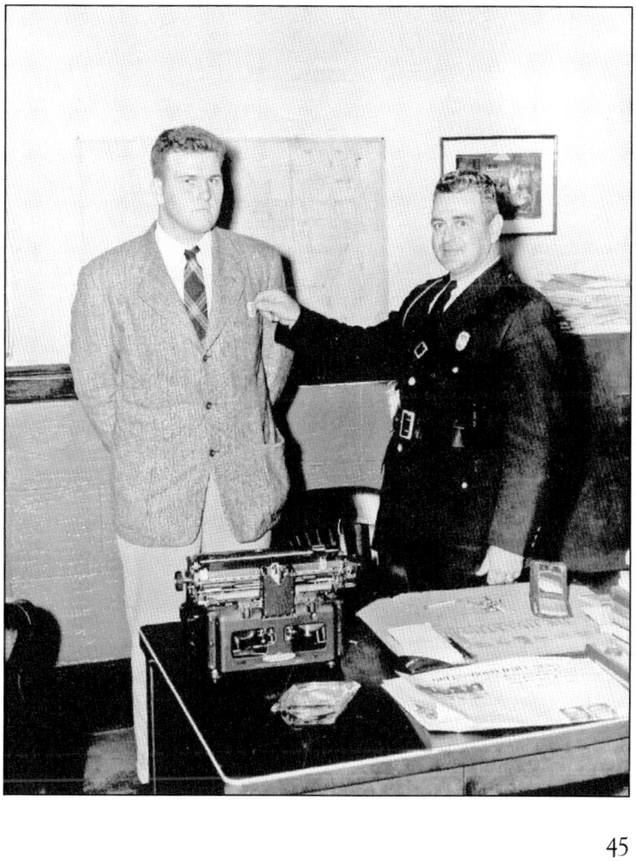

Robert Marshall, a popular Burlington High School football player, became chief of police in Burlington when students took over city offices for a day in the late 1940s. This was part of a special program in which high school students assumed the duties of city officials for one day each year. At right is Burlington police chief D. D. Matthews.

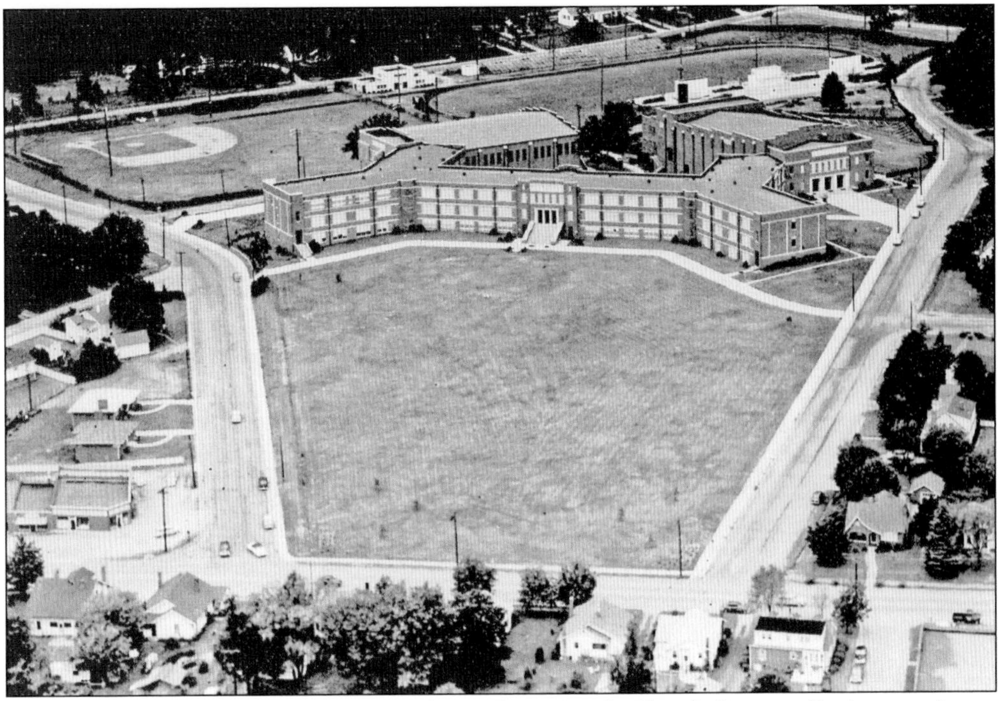

Williams High School opened in September 1951 on South Church Street in Burlington. It was located on the site of the old Piedmont Country Club golf course. The school replaced Burlington High School and was named for Walter M. and Flonie Williams. Walter Williams was a textile executive and former school board member. (Courtesy of Alamance County Area Chamber of Commerce.)

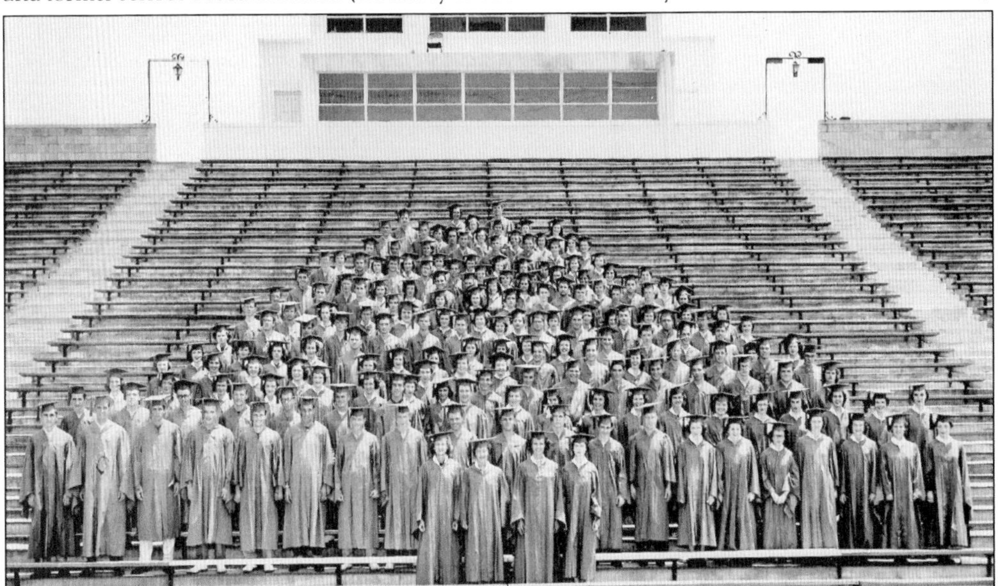

The class of 1952 was the first graduating class at Williams High School. The class photograph was taken in the stadium behind the school. The stadium was built prior to the school. For many years, the stadium was the home field for Elon College before Rhodes Stadium was opened in 2001. This stadium has been the site of many community programs in addition to athletic events.

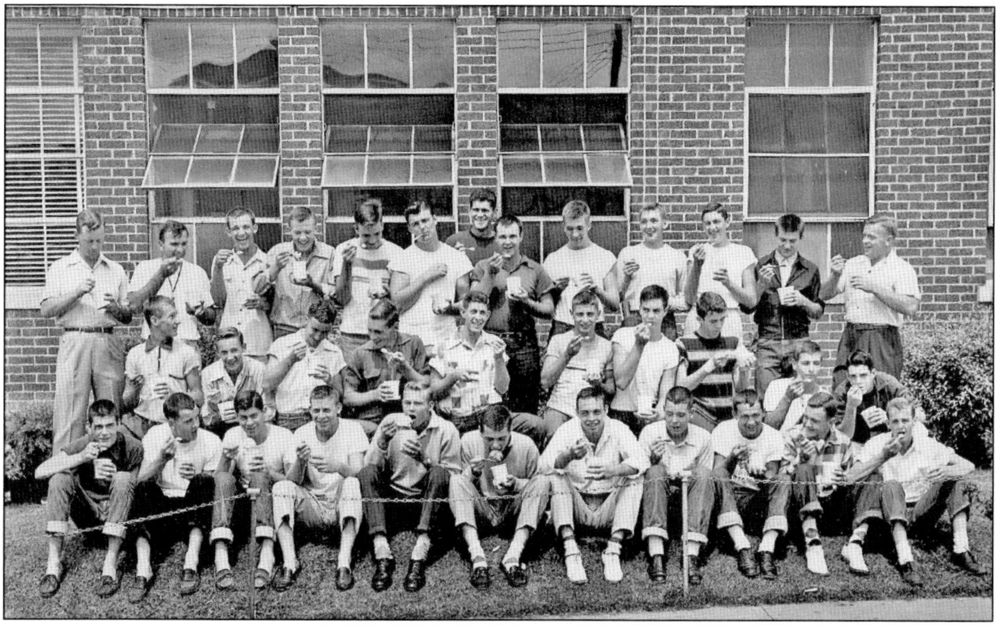

Melville Dairy, located on Worth Street in the downtown area, was one of Burlington's best-known businesses for many years, and in 1952, the company celebrated its 25th anniversary. Many events were held to mark the event, and one of the memorable moments was this picture of the 1952 Williams High School football team eating ice cream in front of the dairy.

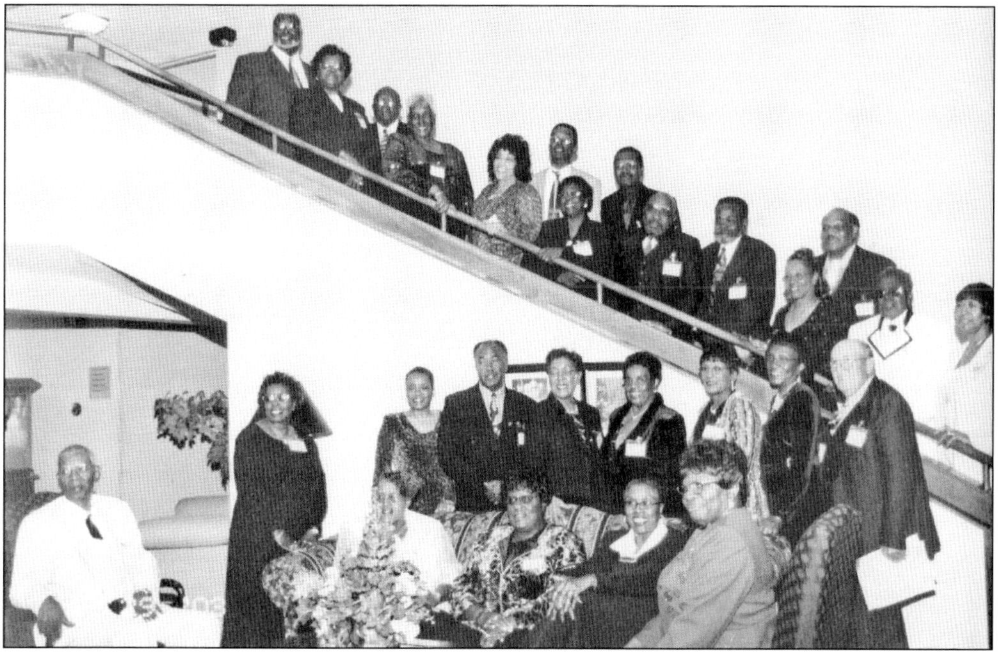

Jordan Sellars High School closed during the integration process in the 1960s, but the school's students keep its memory alive in class reunions. The class of 1958 is shown here as the students gathered for a reunion. Jordan Sellars High School was the only high school for African American students in Burlington during the years of segregation. The students moved to Williams High School when integration was completed. (Courtesy of Leroy Richardson.)

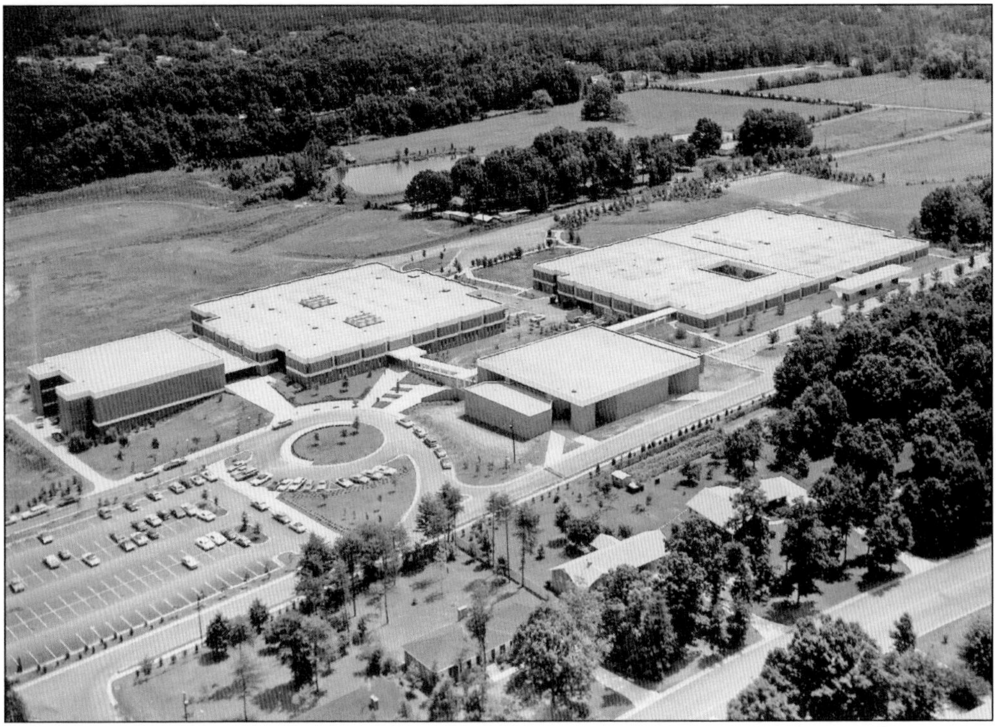

In 1970, a second high school opened in Burlington. Cummings High School opened in eastern Burlington and was named for Hugh M. Cummings, a local businessman whose contributions helped make the school possible. J. A. Freeman was the school's first principal, and he served for 20 years before moving to the city school office. Broadview Middle School and Cummings High School share adjoining campuses off North Church Street. (Courtesy of Terry Woodings.)

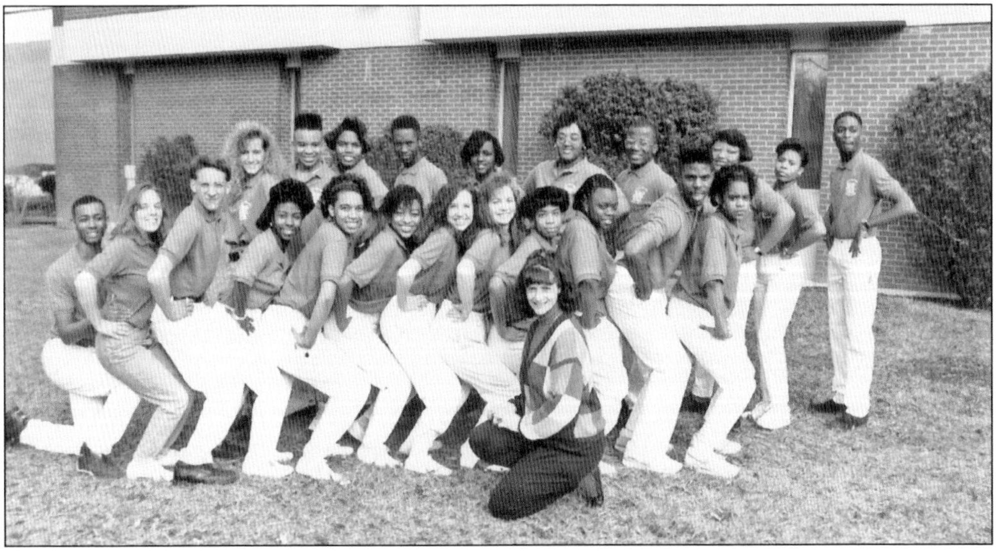

In 1989, the Cummings High School show choir traveled to the Soviet Union to participate in an international music festival near the Black Sea in the city of Sochi. The students visited several locations in communist countries before the collapse of the Berlin Wall. One month after the choir's visit there, the wall was torn down. (Courtesy of Cummings High School.)

Four

Sports and Recreation

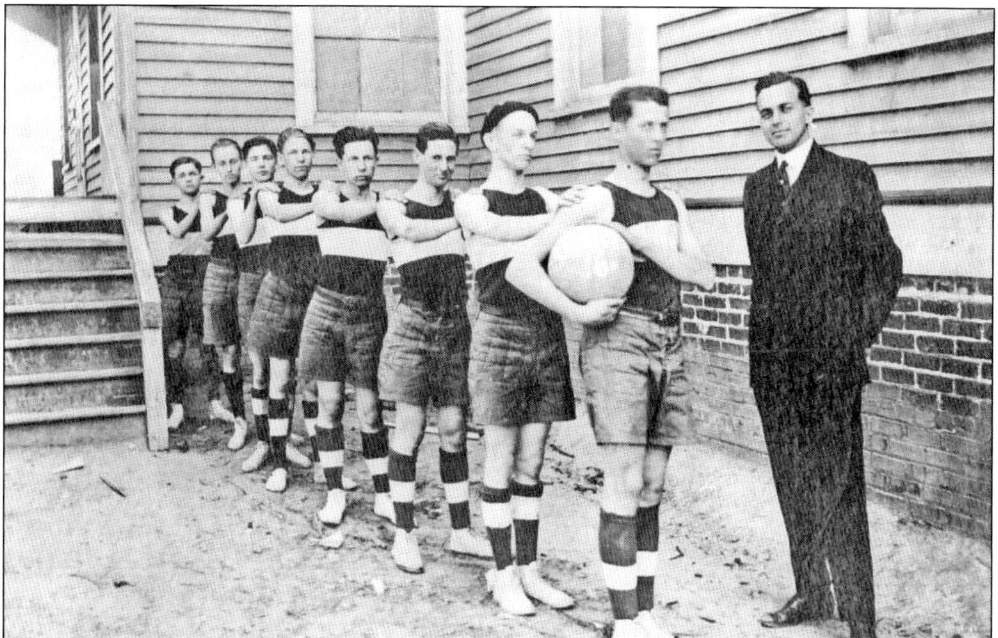

This basketball team represented Burlington High School in 1916. J. H. McEwen (at right) was the team's coach and the school principal. Team members were Bob Hay, Dunlop White, Keener Isley, Clarence Tickle, Layton Hodge, Marvin Holt, Harlan McPherson, and Henry Atwater. They posed in front of the old school building. A new school was being constructed at the time this photograph was made.

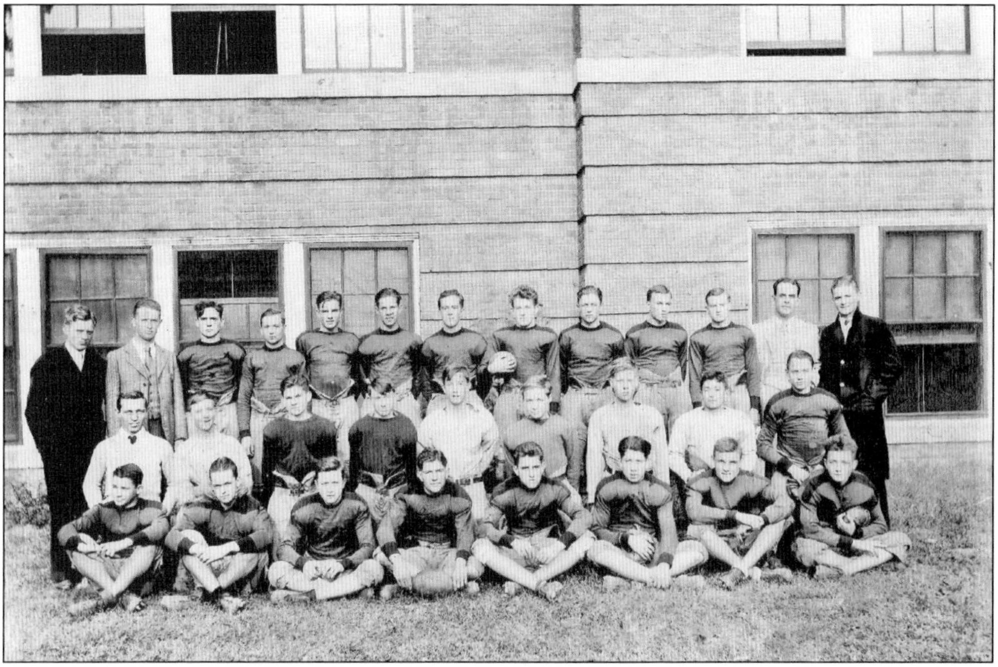

One of Burlington High School's football teams in the 1930s posed beside the school for this photograph. In the third row at far right is Robert Atwater, a team manager, who later operated auto dealerships in Burlington for many years. Next to him is Brodie Hood, one of the coaches. Hood later operated the Hood's Sporting Goods store on Front Street in Burlington.

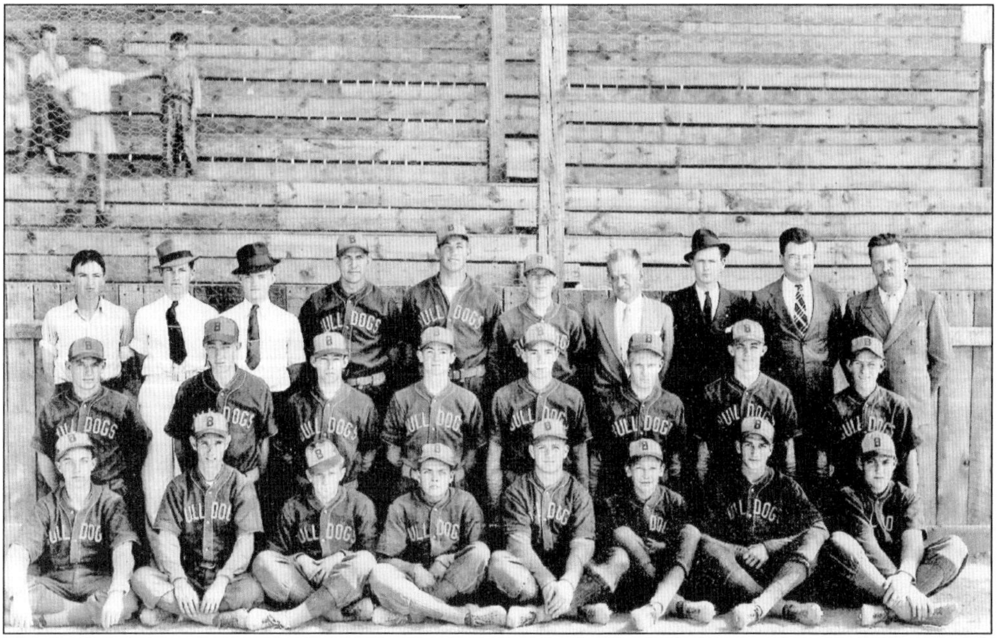

The 1936 Burlington High School baseball team won the state high school championship. The team played games at the old Hillcrest Park behind Hillcrest Elementary School. The grandstand is shown in the background. The high school also played football there, and many area semiprofessional teams played games at Hillcrest Park. (Courtesy of George Hardie.)

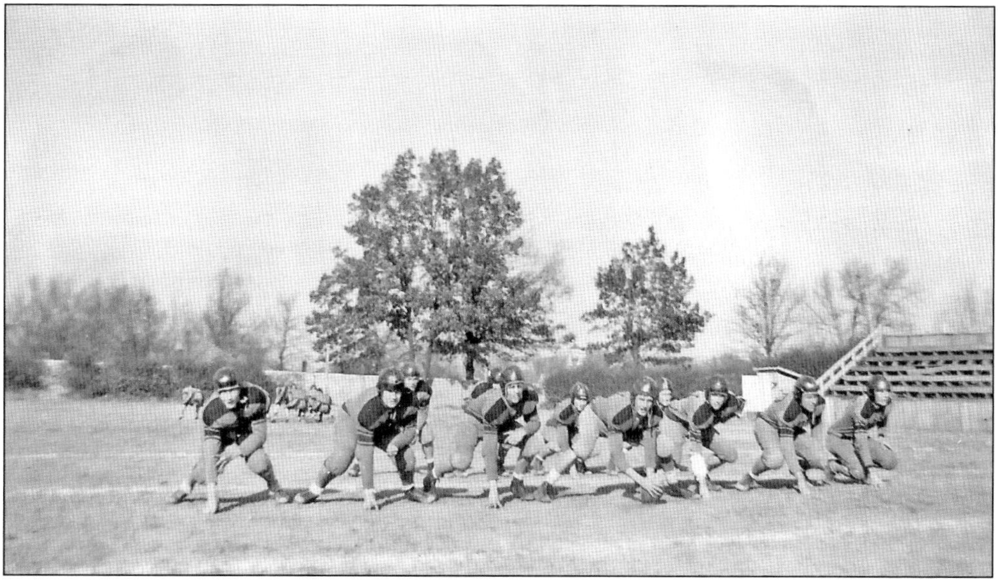

The Burlington High School's football team is shown at practice in 1944 at the Hillcrest Elementary School field. At that time, Burlington High School played against high schools in the Piedmont region, including Greensboro, High Point, and Winston-Salem. By 1944, the team played some home games at the old Elon College baseball park on Williamson Avenue.

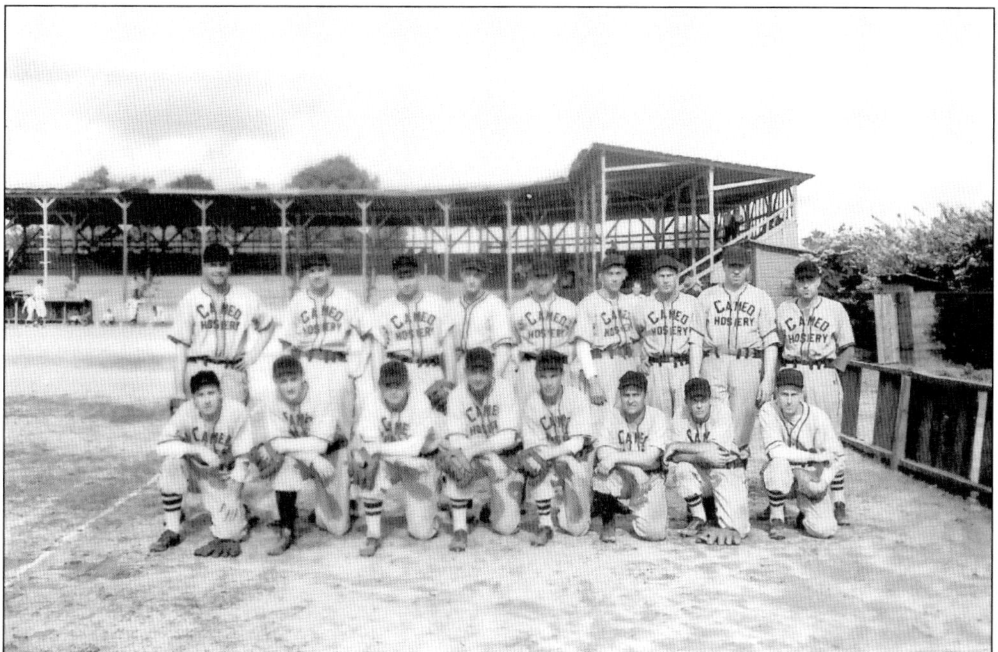

The Cameo Hosiery baseball team played home games in the 1930s and 1940s at the old Hillcrest Park. The grandstand is in the background. In 1943, the Cameo team hosted the navy preflight team from the University of North Carolina at Chapel Hill for two games. The navy team featured Boston Red Sox star Ted Williams, who was then in training at Chapel Hill.

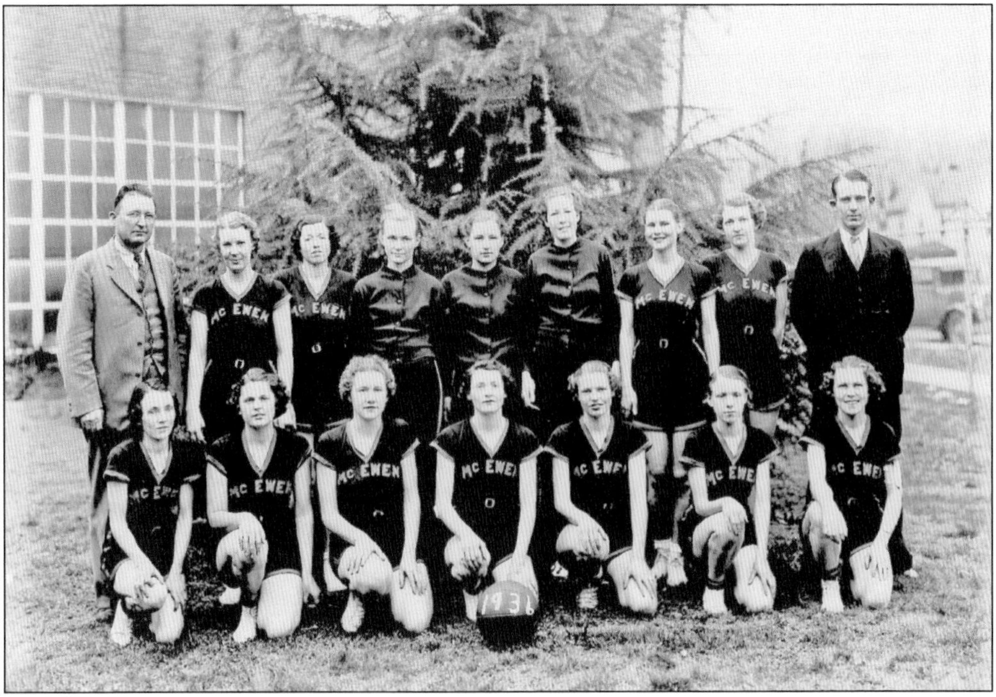

The hosiery mills were proud of their baseball teams, but the ladies had their sport as well. This women's basketball team represented the McEwen Hosiery Mill in 1936. At the time, women's teams had six players; three on offense and three on defense, but no one crossed the center court line. Players were on offense or defense but never both.

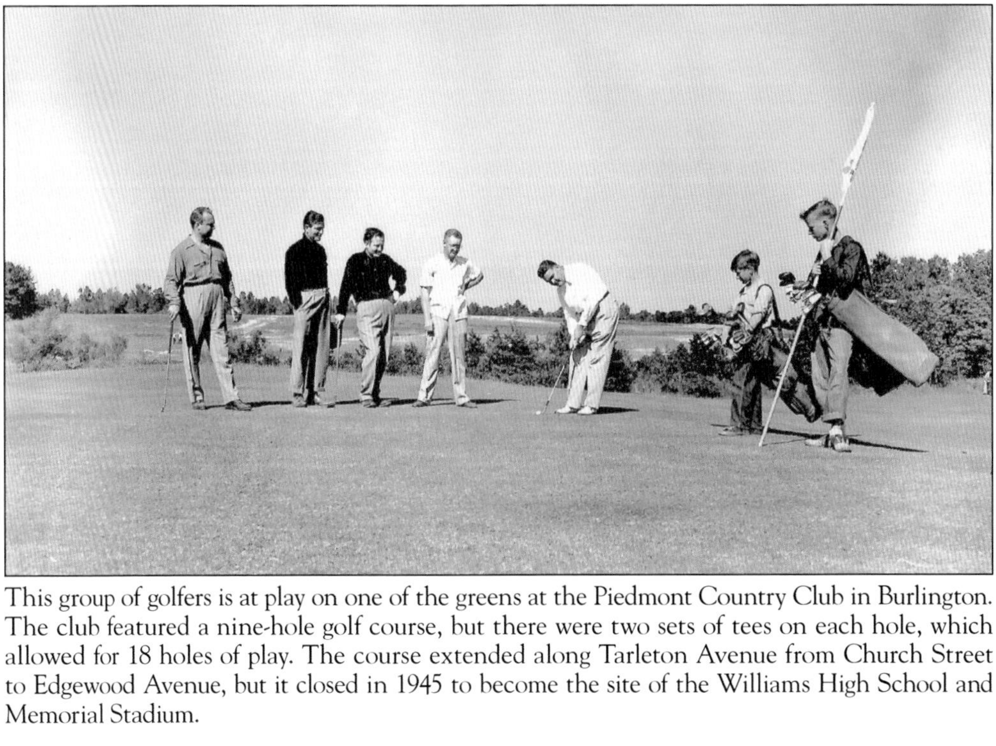

This group of golfers is at play on one of the greens at the Piedmont Country Club in Burlington. The club featured a nine-hole golf course, but there were two sets of tees on each hole, which allowed for 18 holes of play. The course extended along Tarleton Avenue from Church Street to Edgewood Avenue, but it closed in 1945 to become the site of the Williams High School and Memorial Stadium.

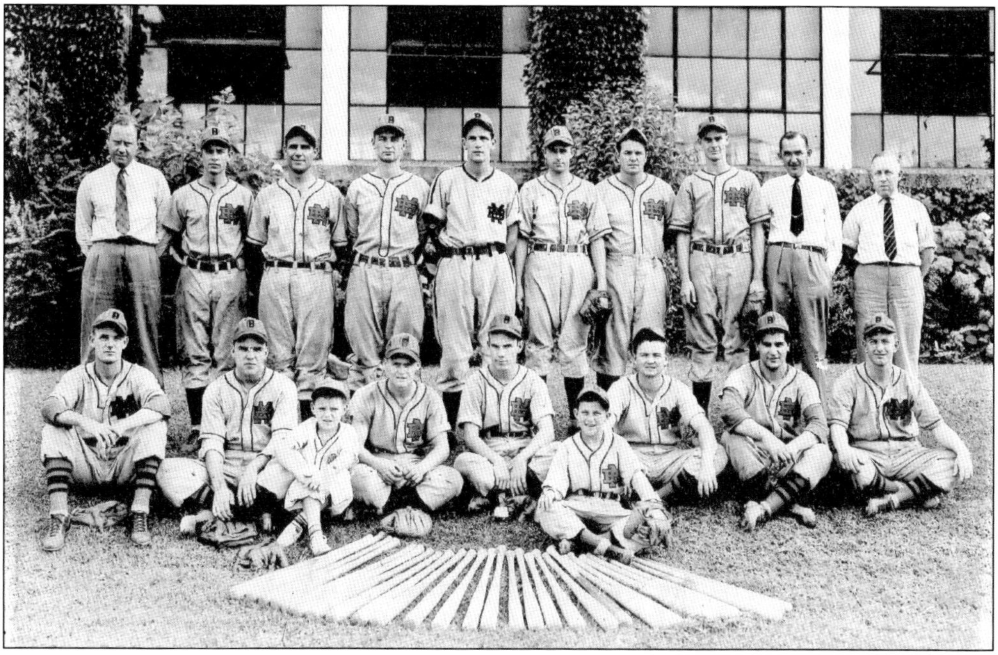

The Burlington Mills baseball team won the 1941 state semiprofessional championship. This team represented the Piedmont Heights plant on Graham Street. That was the site of the original Burlington Mills plant, which opened in 1924 on what had previously been a cornfield. At least two players on this team, Max Wilson and Tal Abernathy (first row, second from left), later played major league baseball.

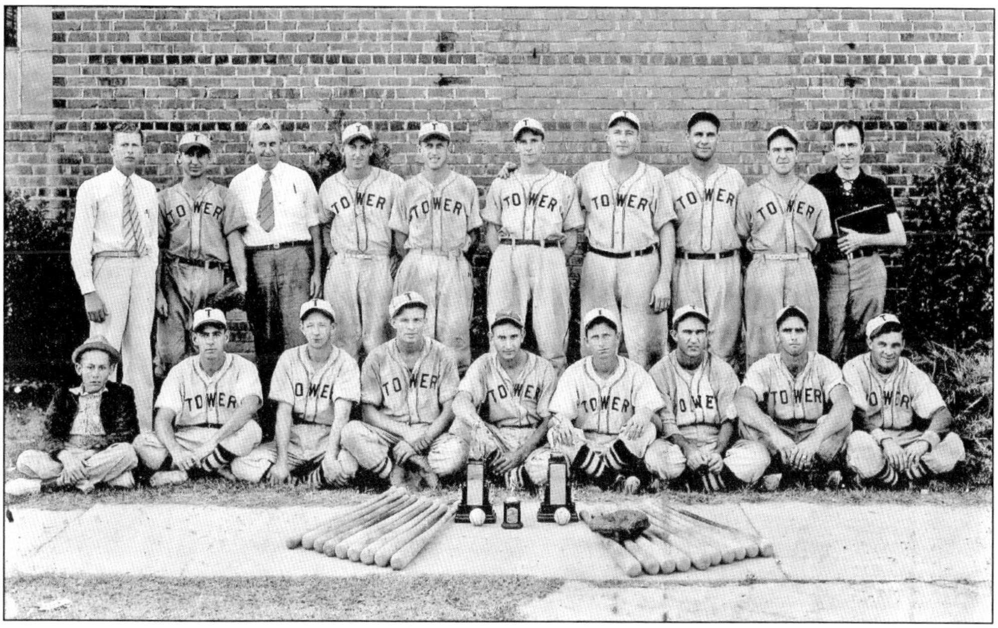

The Tower Hosiery Mill fielded a league championship team in the 1937 baseball season. This team also featured a player who would go to the major leagues, Ray Scarborough (standing, fourth from left). In the second row, mill executive E. E. Chapman is on the far left, and mill owner Reid A. Maynard is third from left. (Courtesy of William Cross.)

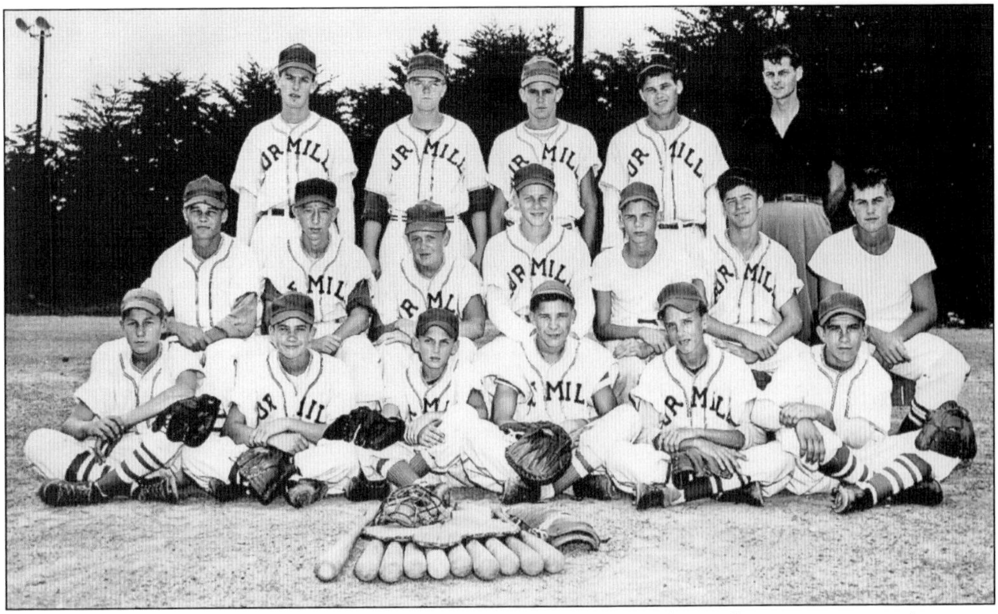

In the 1940s and 1950s, mills in Burlington often sponsored youth teams in city leagues. Burlington Mills sponsored this team, and the children lived in the area known as the Mill Hill, the community around the Piedmont Heights plant. Earl Bolick (third row, far right) was the coach of this team.

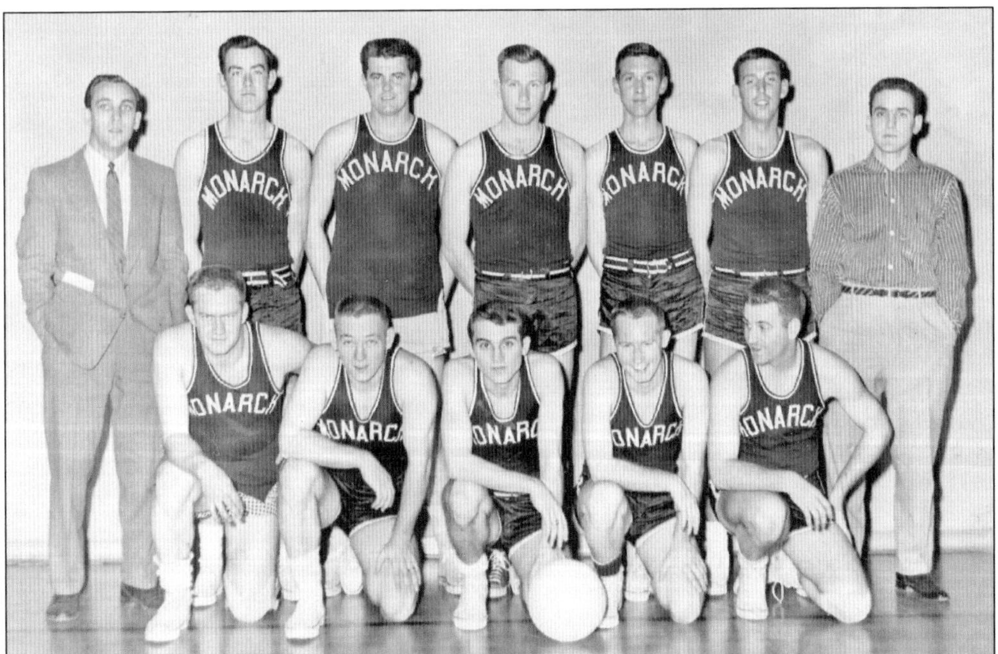

The Monarch Hosiery Mill sponsored this youth team in the YMCA league in the 1950s. In this photograph are, from left to right, (first row) Pete Sykes, Dick Keziah, Bobby Harrison, Harvey Sharp, and Ronnie McIntyre; (second row) coach Fred Lail, Jimmy Lee, Bud Mullins, Glenn Walker, Mull Miles, Jack Sutton, and assistant coach Paige Stout. Several of these players later starred for area high schools. (Courtesy of Mull Miles.)

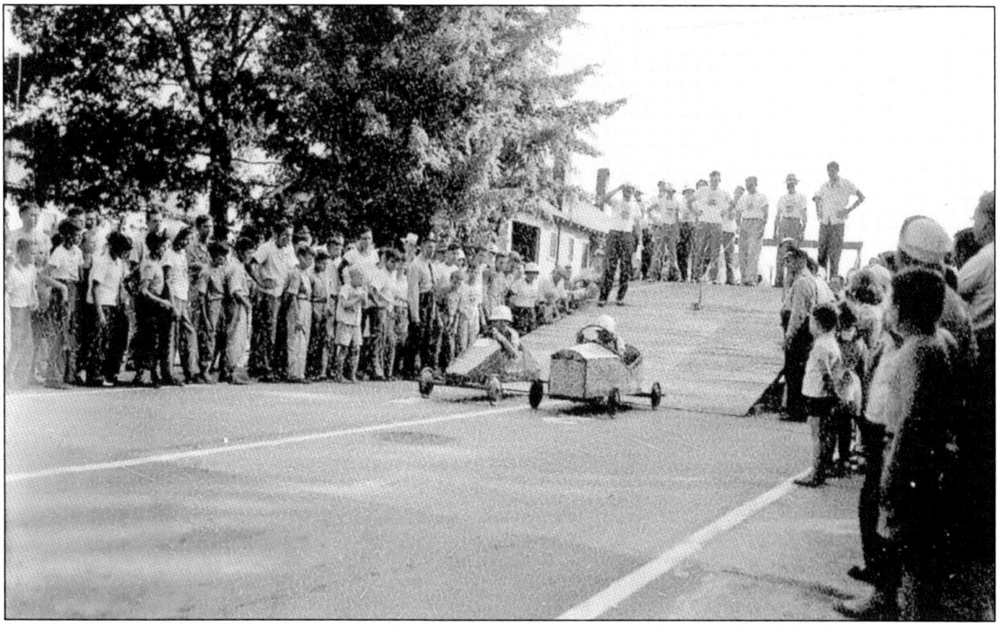

Two soapbox derby racers are down the ramp and on the way to the finish line. The track was set up on South Church Street. The ramp was at the Glenwood Avenue intersection at the Rich and Thompson Funeral Home. Each year, the winner of this race went on to Akron, Ohio, to represent Burlington in the national finals. Local businesses sponsored the young racers, who built their own cars.

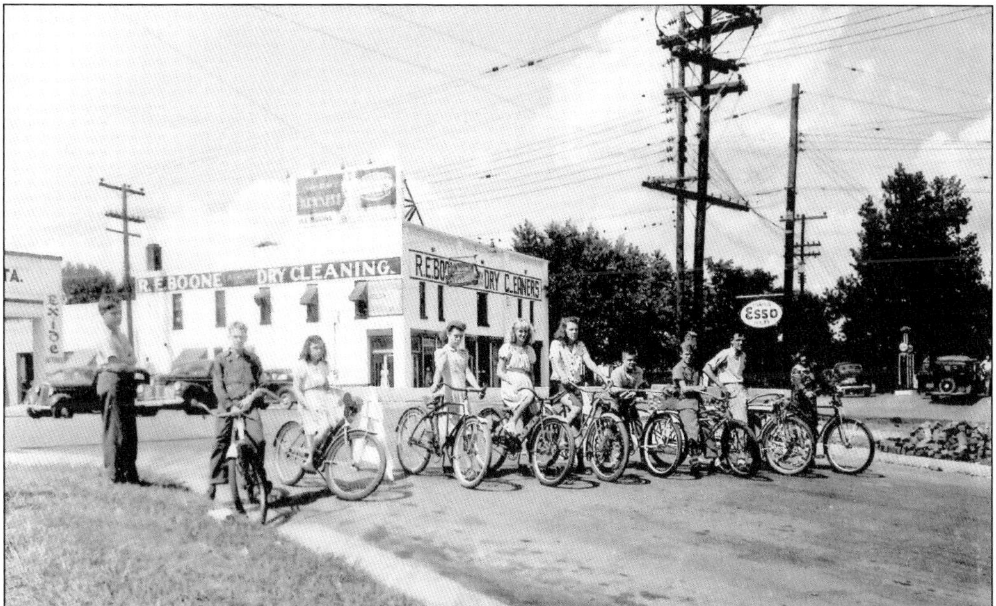

A group of young bikers gathered at the corner of Main and Trade Streets before racing off to the Eva Barker Playground, a favorite summer spot in the 1950s for children on the east side of Burlington. R. E. Boone Laundry and Cleaners, a North Main Street business for many years, is in the background.

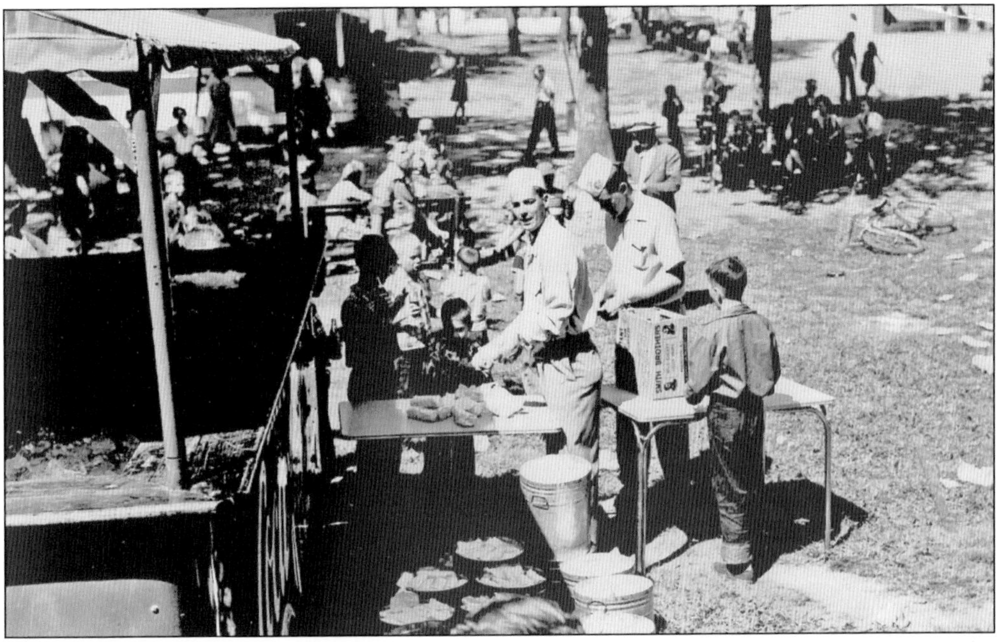

The Fourth of July has always been a big event at Burlington's City Park. Three-legged races, the greased pole, and many other events were once a part of the celebrations. Hot dogs were on the menu as well, and Burlington High School basketball coach Warren Burns (standing, facing the camera) serves some at one of the events during the 1950s.

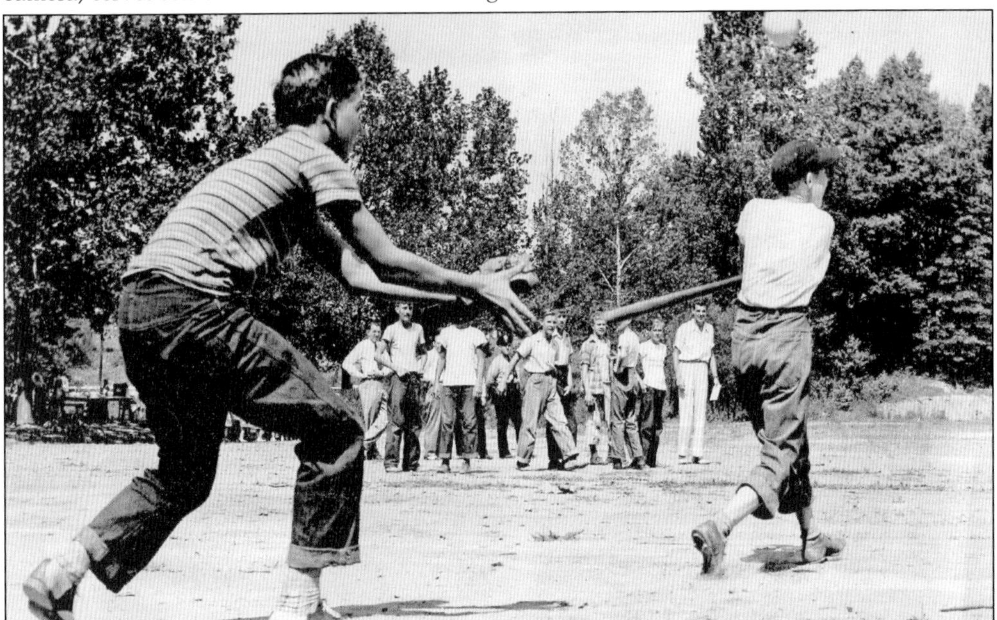

Burlington's City Park has always been the place for softball in the community, whether in organized leagues, state and national tournaments, or a pickup game among kids in town. The park grew from small beginnings to become one of the premier recreational centers in the state, complete with a carousel, a miniature train, tennis courts, and various rides.

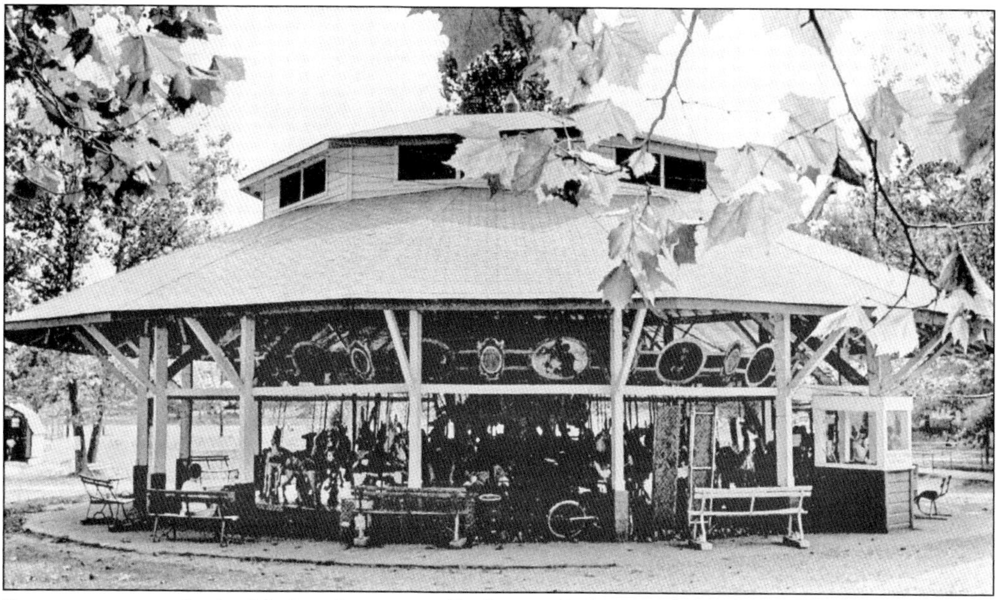

For many years, the highlight of a visit to Burlington's City Park has been the carousel. It was first used in the 1950s. In later years, it was discovered that the carousel was a Dentzel Carousel, made by one of the most famous carousel makers in the world. The carousel has since been restored to its original status, and Burlington has been the site of national conventions for carousel enthusiasts.

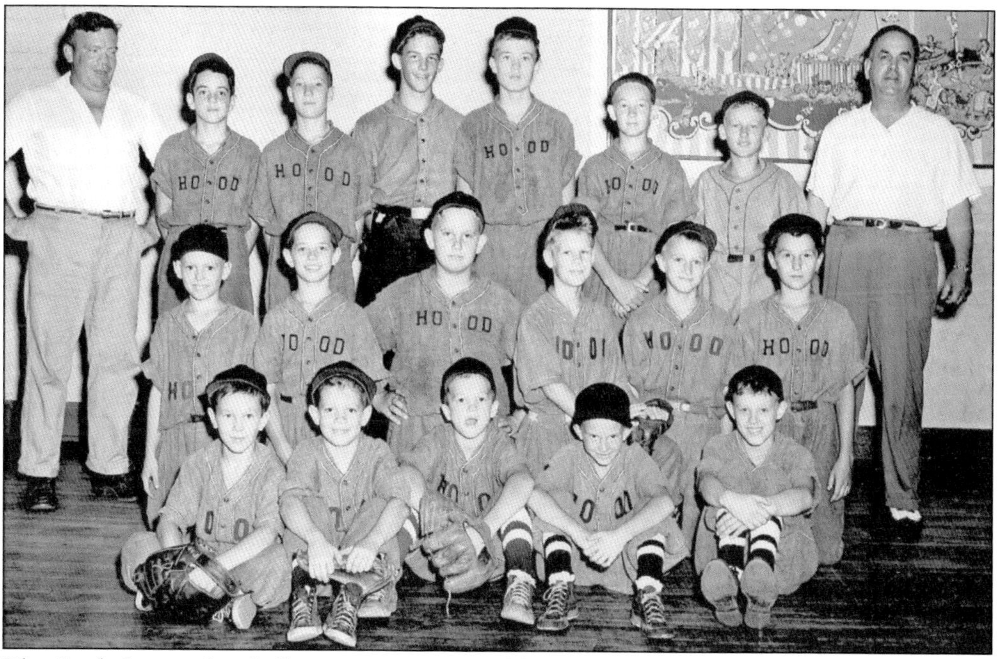

This Little League baseball team was sponsored by Hood's Sporting Goods in the 1950s, one of the early sporting goods stores in Burlington. Brodie Hood (third row, far right) owned the business and supplied area schools with sports equipment for their athletic programs. Assisting him in coaching this team was Daryl Seelinger (third row, far left), an assistant football coach at Williams High School.

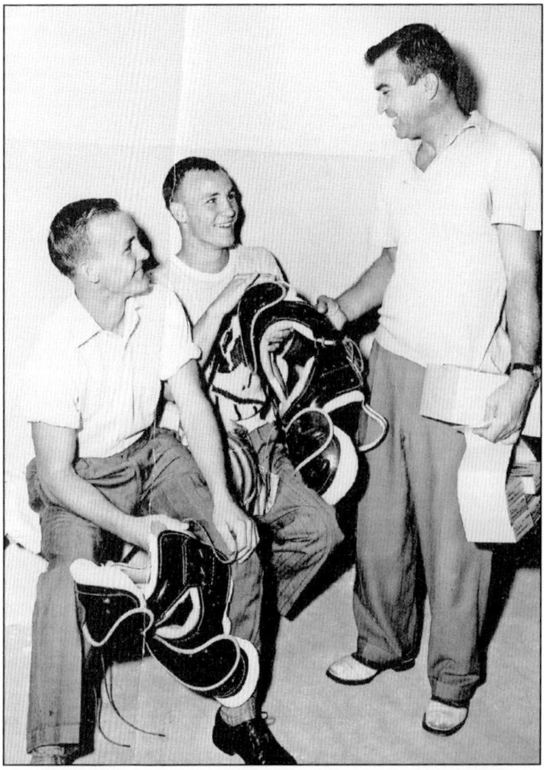

Stan Huffman (right) was the popular football coach at Williams High School for many years. His teams consistently ranked high in the state and were often in the playoffs. Huffman is shown here with two of his key players in the 1950s, Gene Kizziah and Jack Kizziah, twin brothers who were starters for the Williams High School Bulldogs.

When the day ended at Burlington High School in the 1950s, students headed downtown to the Burlington Teenage Club. A jukebox provided music for dancing. The club was also the site of special dance events, and it was a favorite gathering spot for teens for several years. The club was operated by the Burlington Recreation Department.

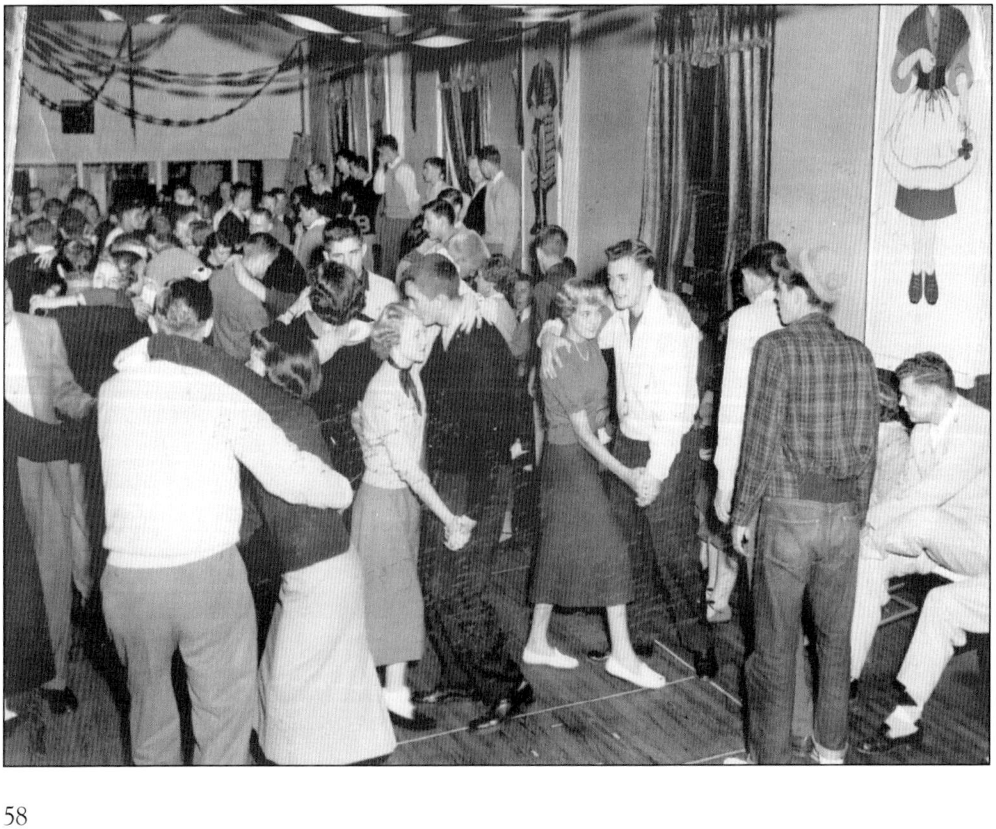

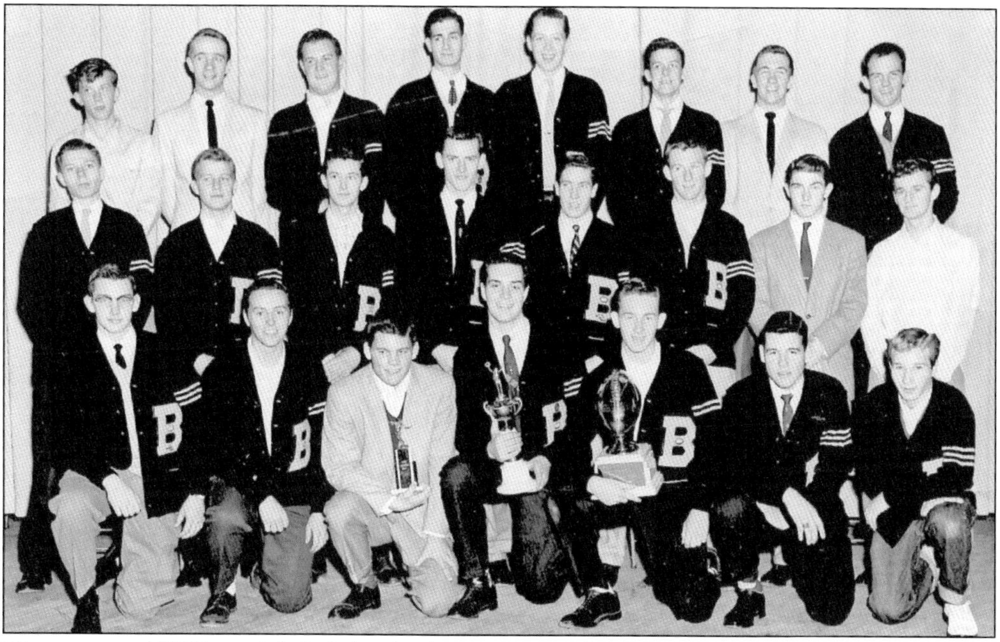

This group of Williams High School athletes received their letters and sweaters for athletic achievement in 1955. The group made up the Monogram Club for that year. The club included members of all school athletic teams who earned letters during the year. They were awarded "B" letters for Burlington rather than "W" for Williams.

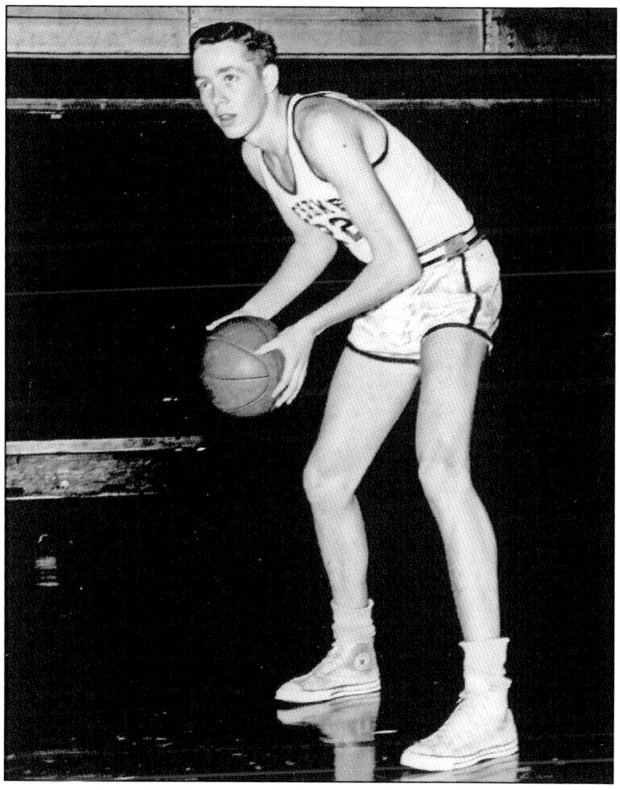

Jerry Robertson was one of the early Williams High School basketball stars. He graduated in 1955 and still holds the school rebounding record. He was team captain in the East-West All-Star game and was one of the most sought-after recruits in state history. He chose Duke University for its excellent academic standards and played basketball for three years. He was cocaptain for the team at Duke University his senior year. (Courtesy of Jeanne Robertson.)

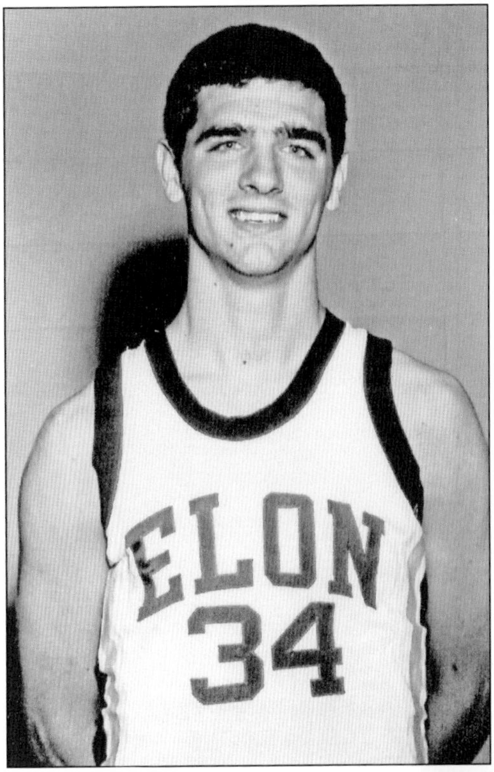

Tommy Cole was another Williams High School graduate who starred in basketball. He went on to Elon College, where he rewrote many of the records there. Then he was drafted by the Boston Celtics. He later returned to Burlington and Williams High School to serve as a basketball coach and golf coach. He is in the Elon Sports Hall of Fame. (Courtesy of Elon University.)

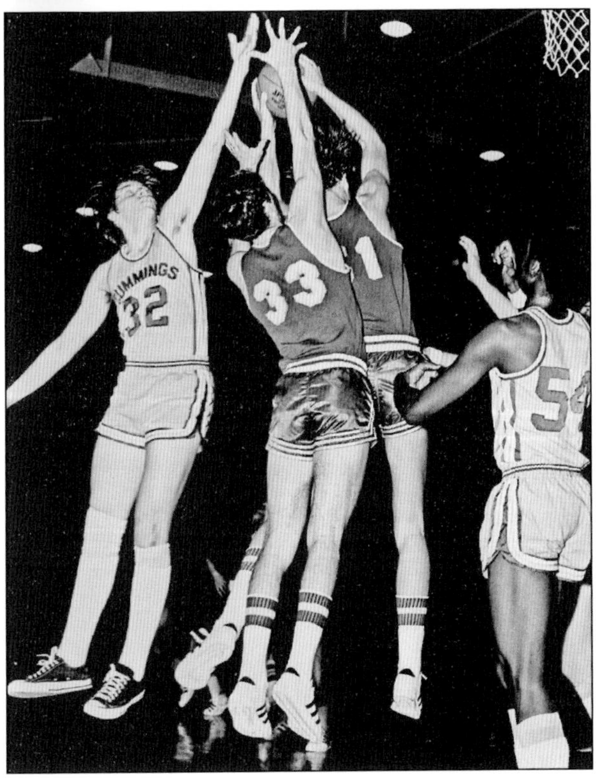

Cummings High School opened in 1970, and it did not take long for the school to produce good athletes. Mike Maness, No. 32 in the photograph, was named to the All-Conference team for the 1971–1972 academic year. Cummings quickly developed strong teams in football and basketball, winning numerous titles. Cummings's athletes have also excelled in track events over the years. (Courtesy of Cummings High School.)

Five

Burlington's Churches

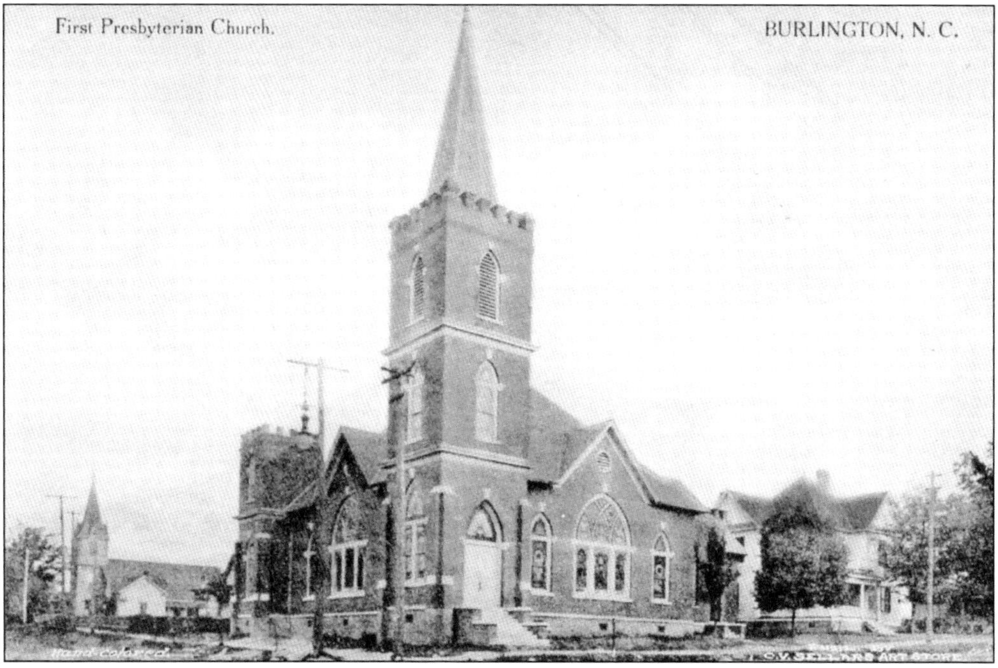

First Presbyterian Church began as Company Shops Presbyterian Church in 1879 when all denominations met in the Union Church built by the railroad company. When Company Shops became Burlington, the church changed its name, and the congregation moved into its own building in 1891. This building sat at Church and Front Streets, the location of today's fire station headquarters. The church later moved to West Davis Street. (Courtesy of Jane Moore.)

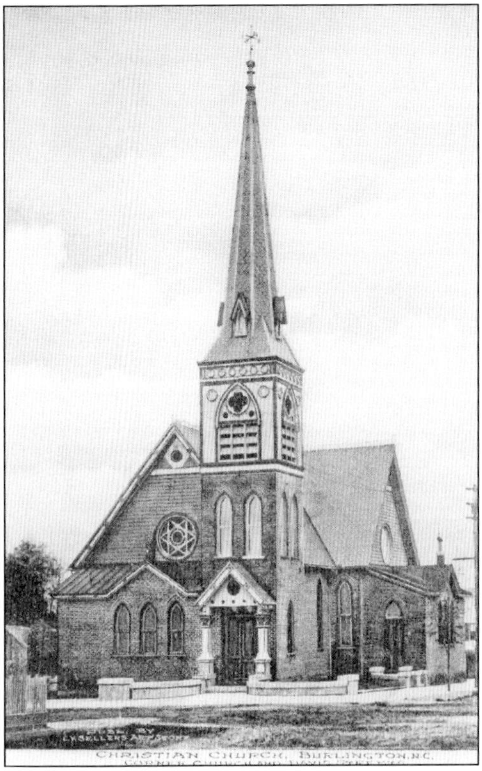

Burlington's First Christian United Church of Christ dedicated this building in December 1893. This is another city church that grew out of the Union Church when it was formed on February 18, 1888. This church was later replaced by a new structure, which is at Church and Davis Streets. (Courtesy of Jane Moore.)

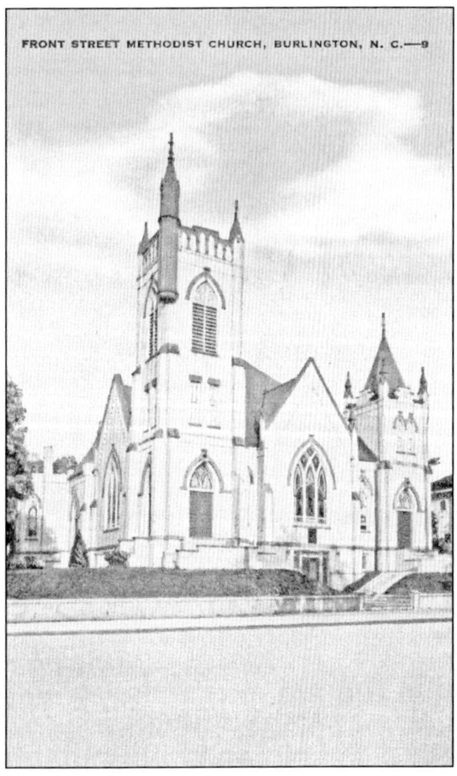

This classic structure, the home of Front Street Methodist Church, was destroyed by fire in 1949. Front Street Methodist Church originated in 1888 and moved into this building in 1912. Following destruction of the church building, a large new church complex was erected on the same site on West Front Street and was occupied for the first time in a special service in 1956. (Courtesy of Jane Moore.)

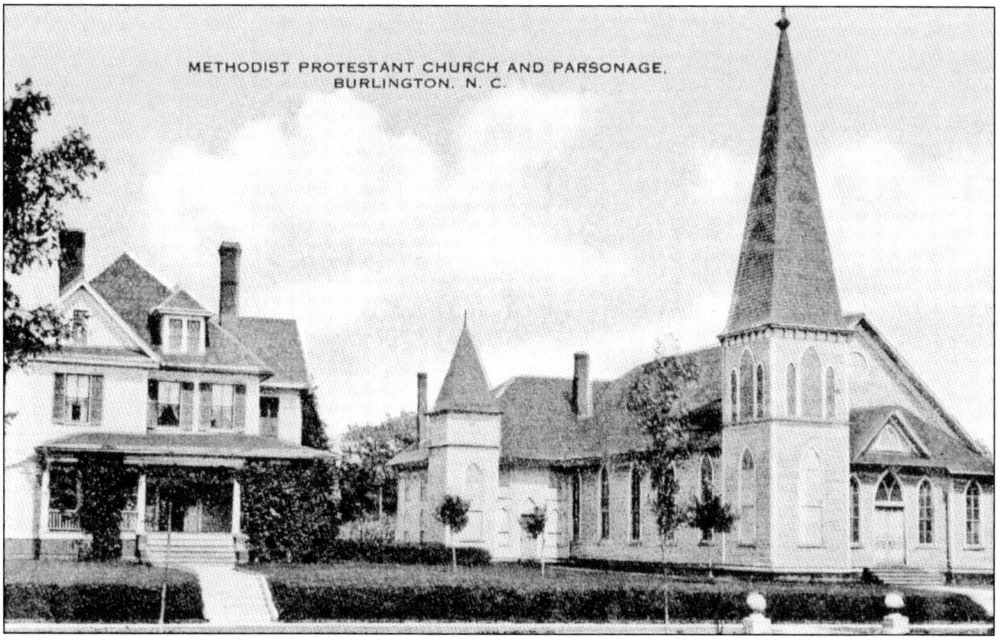

The Methodist Protestant Church on East Davis Street became the Davis Street United Methodist Church after the merger of two wings of the Methodist church in the mid-20th century. The church was founded in 1890 and has occupied the same location since. This view was in 1917, and the house at left was the church parsonage. (Courtesy of Jane Moore.)

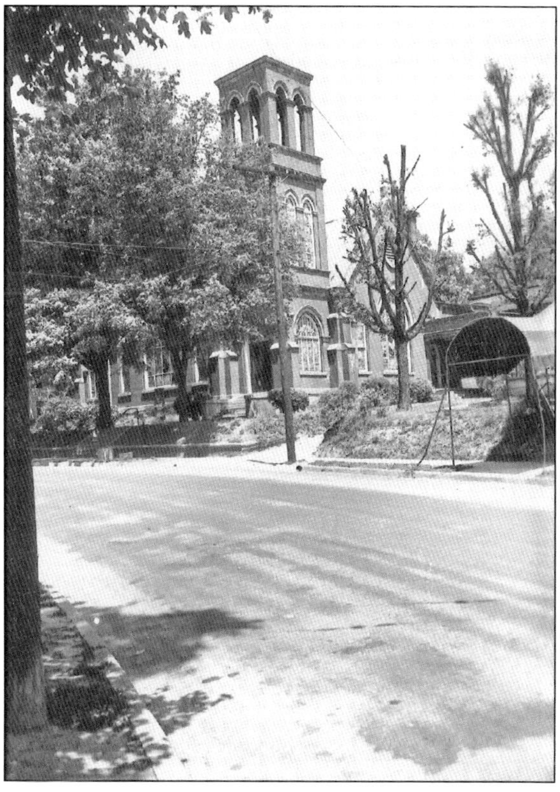

The Macedonia Lutheran Church traces its beginning to 1869 in a brush arbor near the site of the Mayfair Mill in west Burlington. The first sanctuary was opened in 1879 facing Hoke Street. In 1909, the building was turned to face West Front Street and was enlarged, as shown here. This building later was razed and replaced by today's modern church facility.

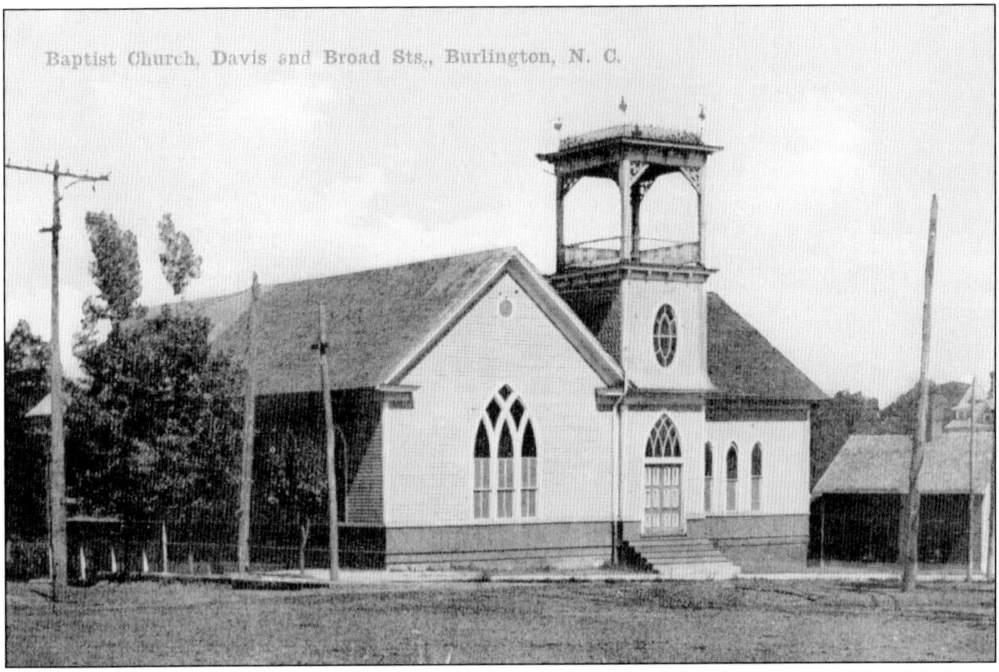

Like the other churches in downtown Burlington, the First Baptist Church grew out of the old Union Church. Various congregations met individually in the church before moving out to build their own sanctuaries. First Baptist Church was formed in 1887, and this was its first building, shown in 1913, at Broad Street and East Davis Street. A new sanctuary was built across the street in 1924.

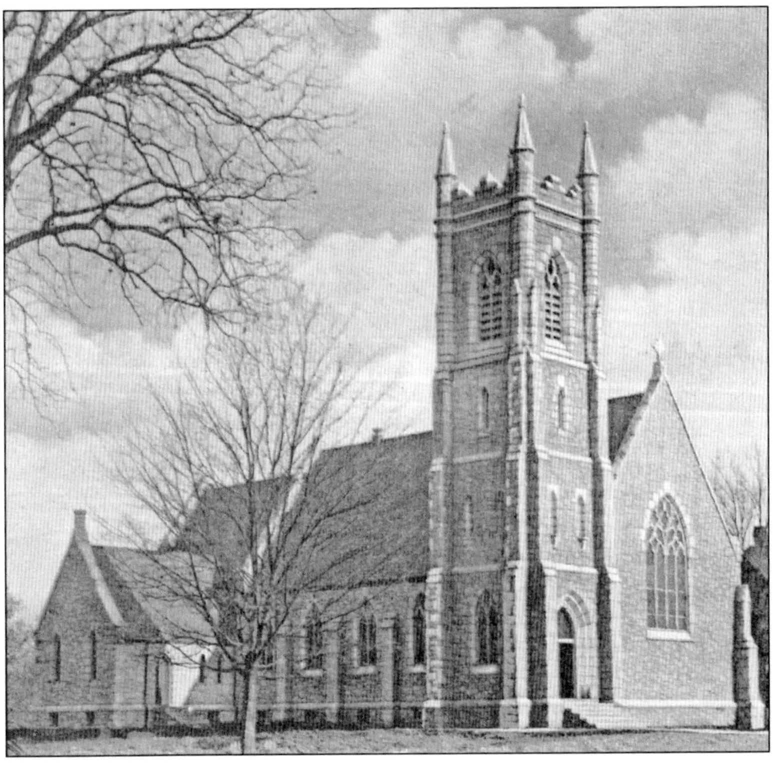

The Episcopal Church of the Holy Comforter originated in the little St. Athanasius Church on Webb Avenue in 1880. The sanctuary (pictured here) was built on the opposite side of the property on Davis Street in 1911. The original church has been maintained, and a small church cemetery lies between the two church sites. (Courtesy of Jane Moore.)

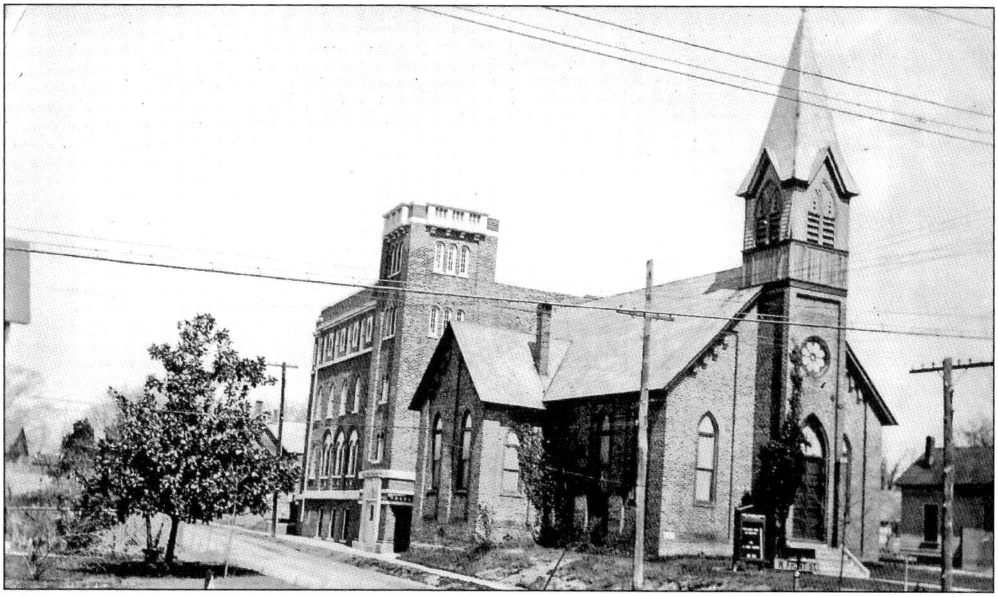

The First Reformed United Church of Christ was born in 1888. This photograph shows the building that was occupied on January 6, 1901. In the background is an addition, which was occupied in 1932. This photograph offers a stark contrast in architectural styles with the old traditional church building from the beginning of the 20th century shown in front and the modern structure in the back of the photograph. (Courtesy of First Reformed United Church of Christ Church.)

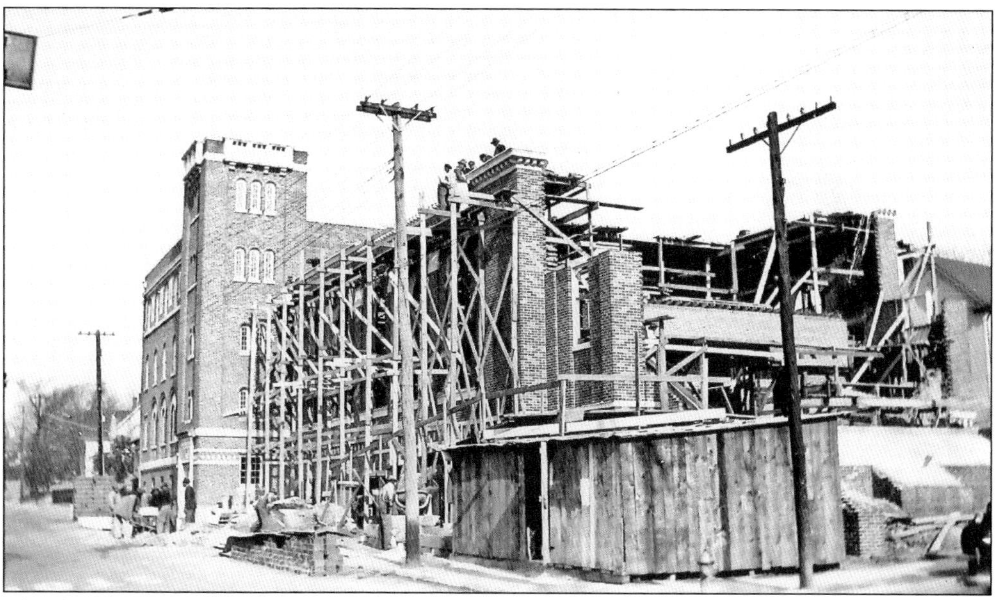

The differences in architectural styles at the First Reformed United Church of Christ changed between 1940 and 1941. The old sanctuary building in front was torn away, and over the period of a year's time, a new, modern church building was erected. The new sanctuary was occupied for the first time on October 12, 1941. (Courtesy of First Reformed United Church of Christ.)

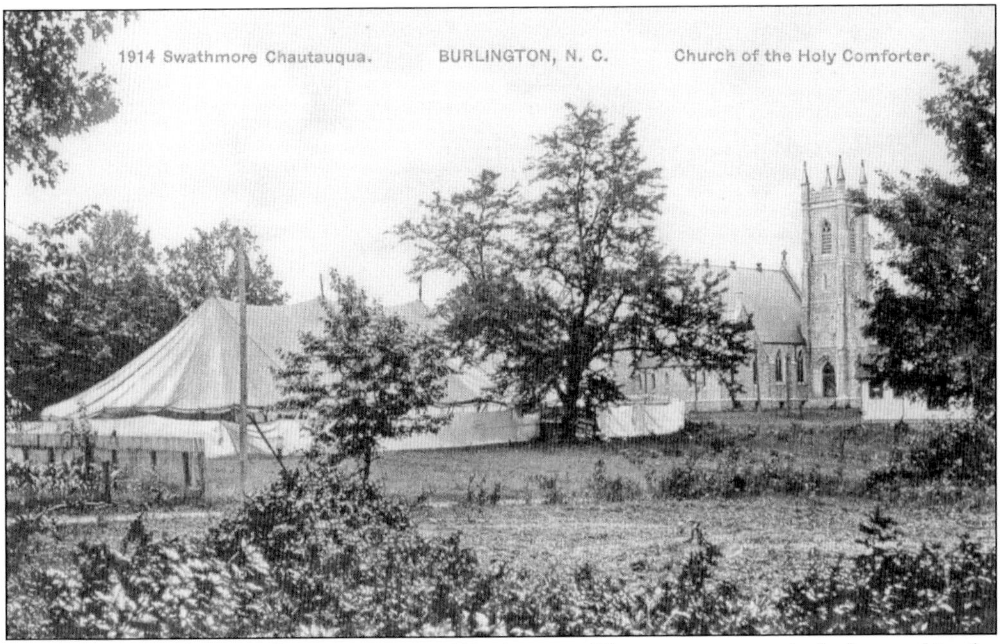

In 1914, the Swathmore Chautauqua visited Burlington. This group was typical of several in the nation, which were highly popular at the time, and its Burlington location was beside the Episcopal Church of the Holy Comforter. The traveling group presented plays, lectures, and concerts, many of which were religious in nature. The large tent attracted many visitors during the Burlington visit. (Courtesy of Jane Moore.)

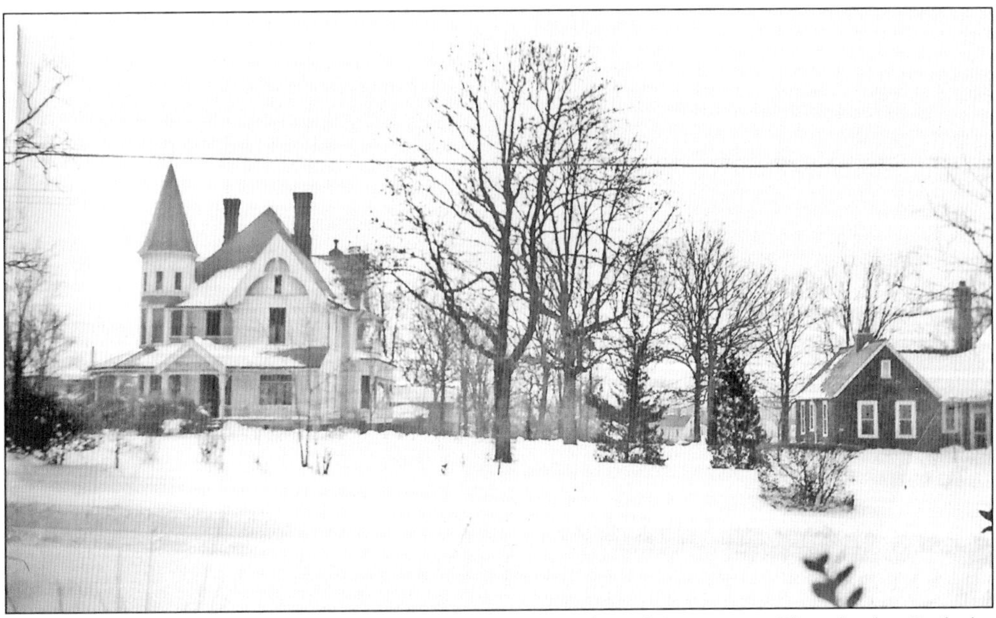

The home of Col. James H. Holt became the site of the Blessed Sacrament Church, the Catholic church in Burlington. The church was built at right, and a school operated in the Holt house. The present church and activities center are still located on this Davis Street site, and offices are in a former medical building across Fisher Street. (Courtesy of Blessed Sacrament Catholic Church.)

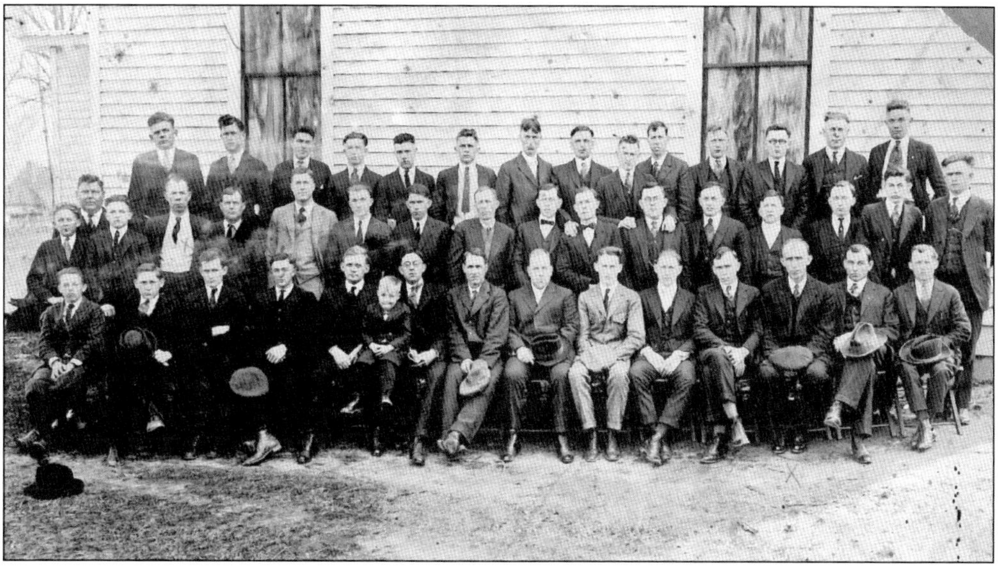

The Hocutt Memorial Baptist Church originated in 1913 and was established with the help of the First Baptist Church of Burlington. Located in northwest Burlington, the church is one of several to have been started through the efforts of the downtown church. This is the men's class at the Hocutt Memorial Baptist Church in 1923.

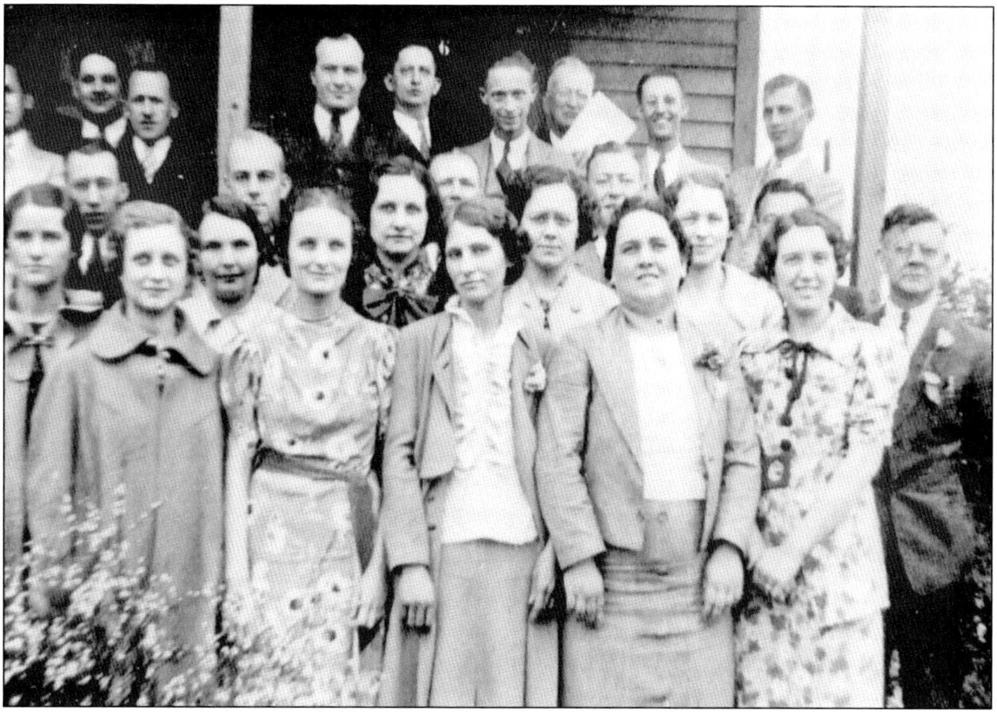

In the late 1920s, residents around the original plant of Burlington Mills saw a need for a church in the community. This group worked with J. Spencer Love, founder of the textile company, to form Glen Hope Baptist Church in 1927. With Love's help, they were able to bring the Reverend George W. Swinney from Greensboro to be the first pastor of the church. (Courtesy of Betty Morin.)

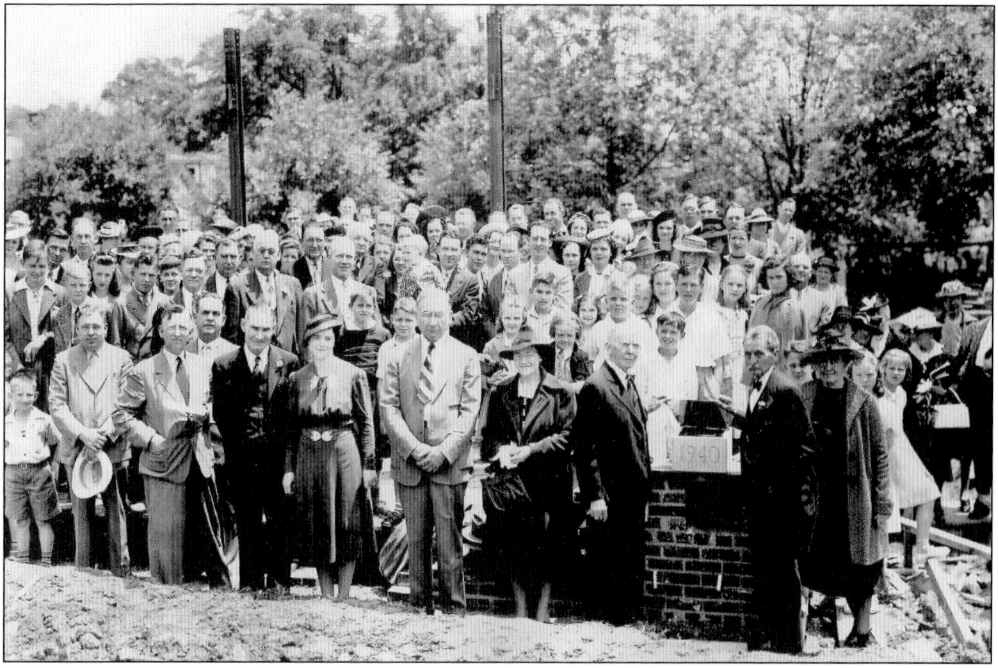

In 1940, the First Baptist Church made the first expansion of its facilities since the 1924 construction of the sanctuary. These church members gathered to lay the cornerstone for a new education building. Dr. Albert Kinnett was pastor of the church then. He is wearing a dark suit and stands to the left in the first row.

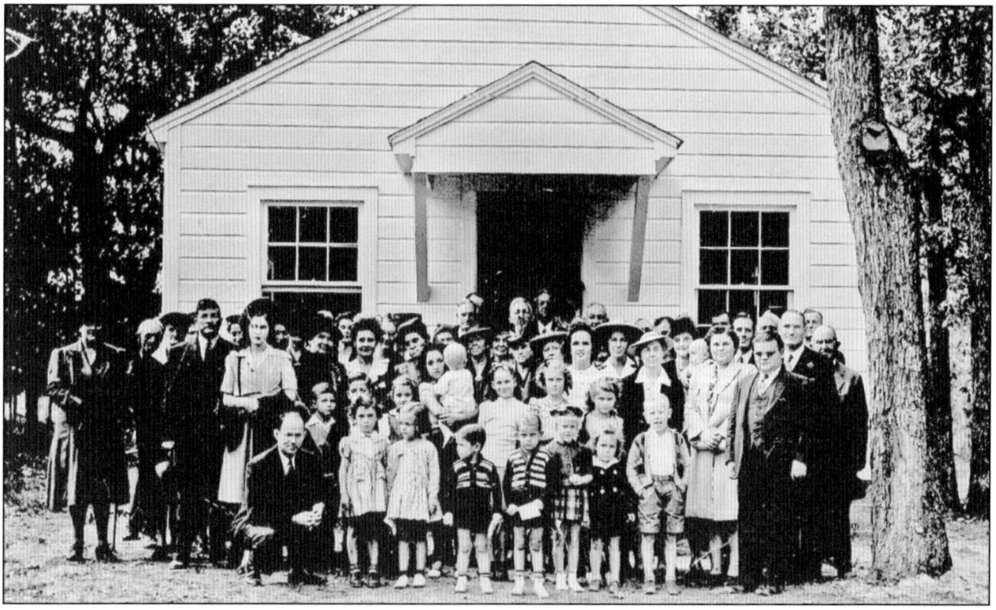

The Grove Park Baptist Church has become one of the larger churches in Burlington, and it grew out of this little building. The church had its first service here on September 26, 1943, with 86 people present. The new church began as one of several mission churches of the First Baptist Church downtown. When Grove Park Baptist Church was formed, it was well outside the city limits of Burlington. (Courtesy of George Hardie.)

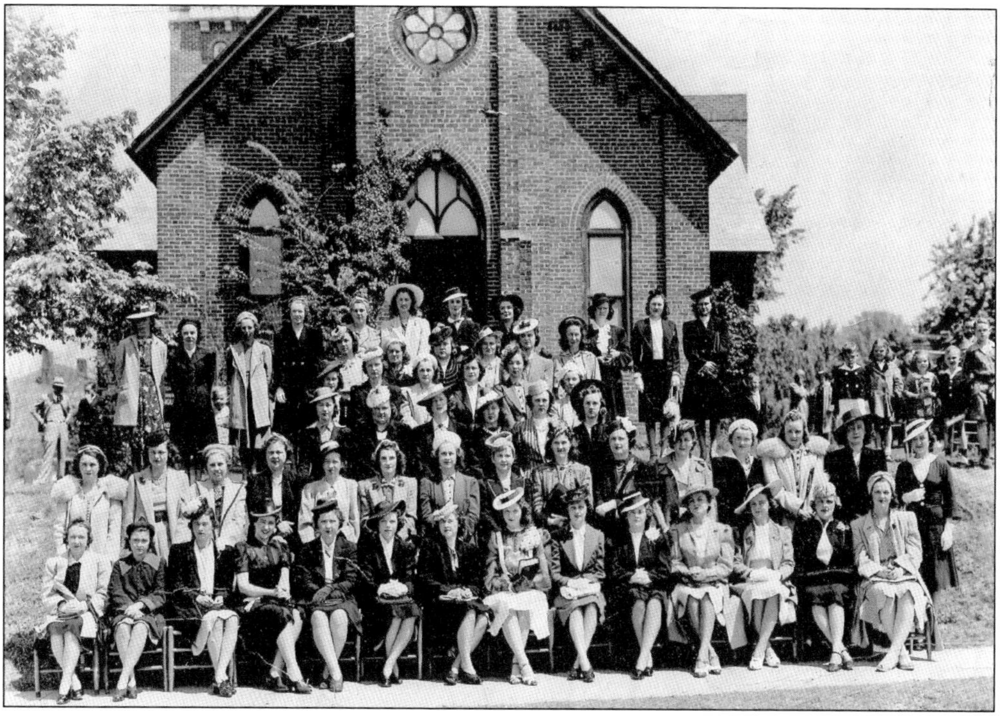

The old building of the First Reformed United Church of Christ formed the backdrop for the ladies group from the church. This picture was made in the late 1930s. This was just prior to the time the building was torn down and replaced with the present sanctuary building, which was first used in 1941. (Courtesy of First Reformed United Church of Christ.)

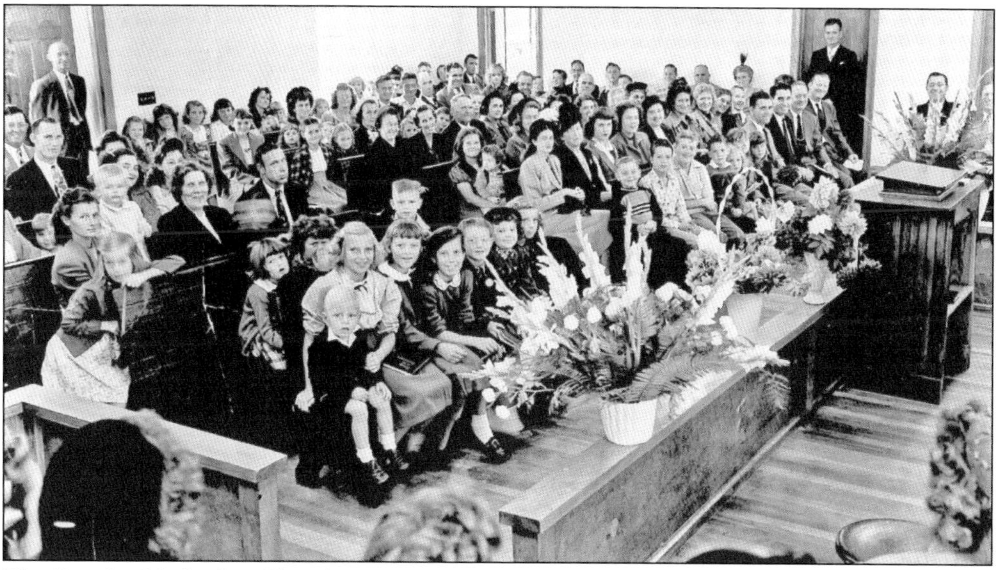

The Peoples Methodist Church on Spence Street is typical of the many small churches that have served Burlington. This photograph was taken around 1950. In the foreground, a girl holds a small boy. To the left and above, looking at the camera, is a young man known to many people who lived in Burlington at the time. He is Charlie Morgan, a regular in the downtown area. (Courtesy of Richard Campbell.)

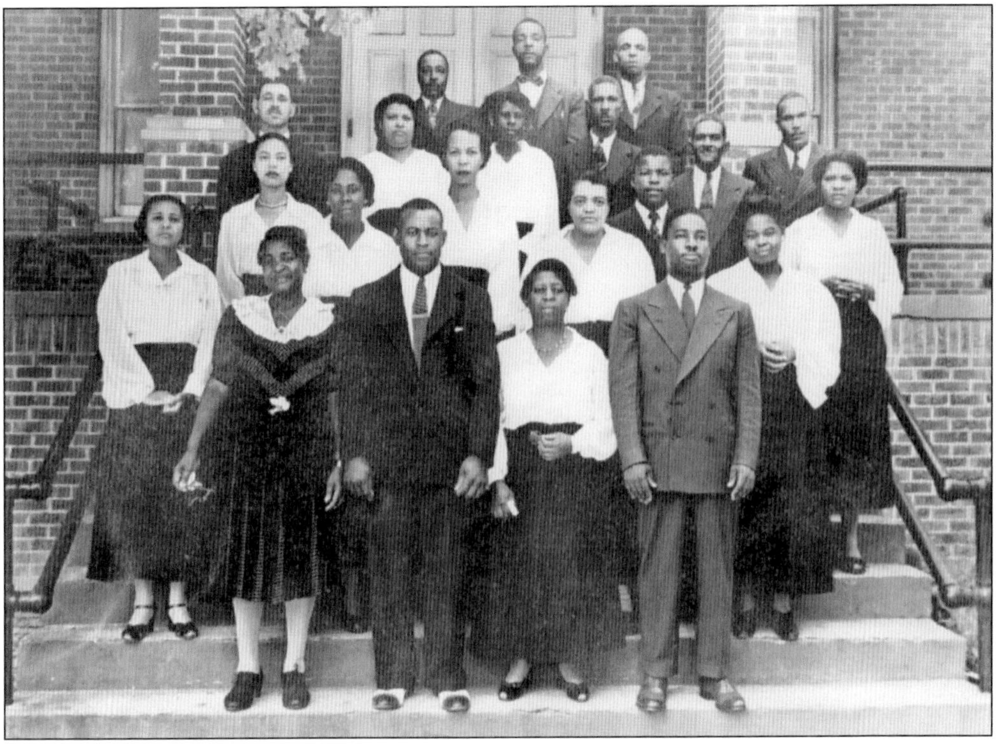

The First Baptist Church on Apple Street has had many well-known singing groups over the years. This is the gospel choir of the church in the 1950s, led by the Reverend Clarence Dortch, the man standing in the first row, second from left. The First Baptist Church was one of the early churches to serve the African American community in Burlington. (Courtesy of Leroy Richardson.)

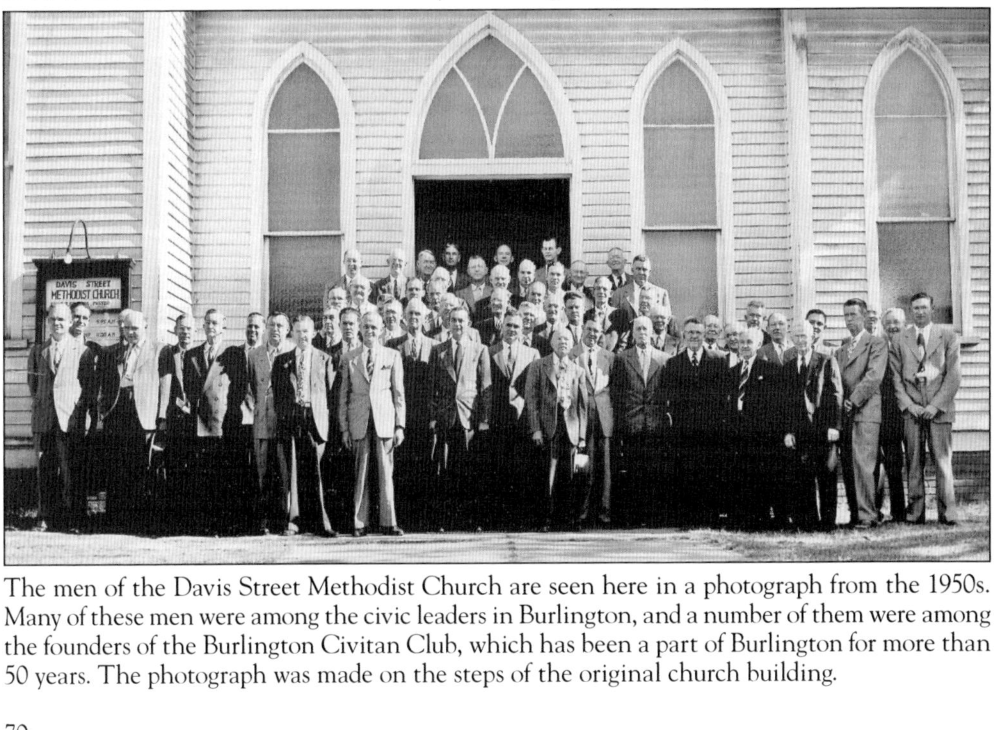

The men of the Davis Street Methodist Church are seen here in a photograph from the 1950s. Many of these men were among the civic leaders in Burlington, and a number of them were among the founders of the Burlington Civitan Club, which has been a part of Burlington for more than 50 years. The photograph was made on the steps of the original church building.

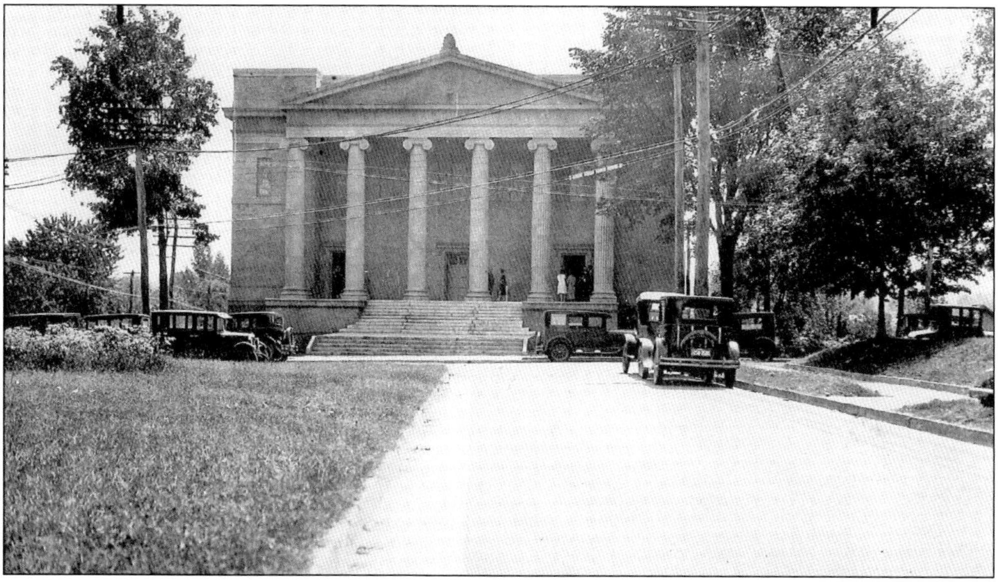

The present sanctuary of the First Baptist Church of Burlington was built on Broad Street in 1924, replacing a small frame building across Davis Street. This building was designed by High Point, North Carolina, architect Herbert Hunter and follows the Greek architectural style, highlighted by the Ionic columns across the front. The church looks directly across the downtown business area of Burlington.

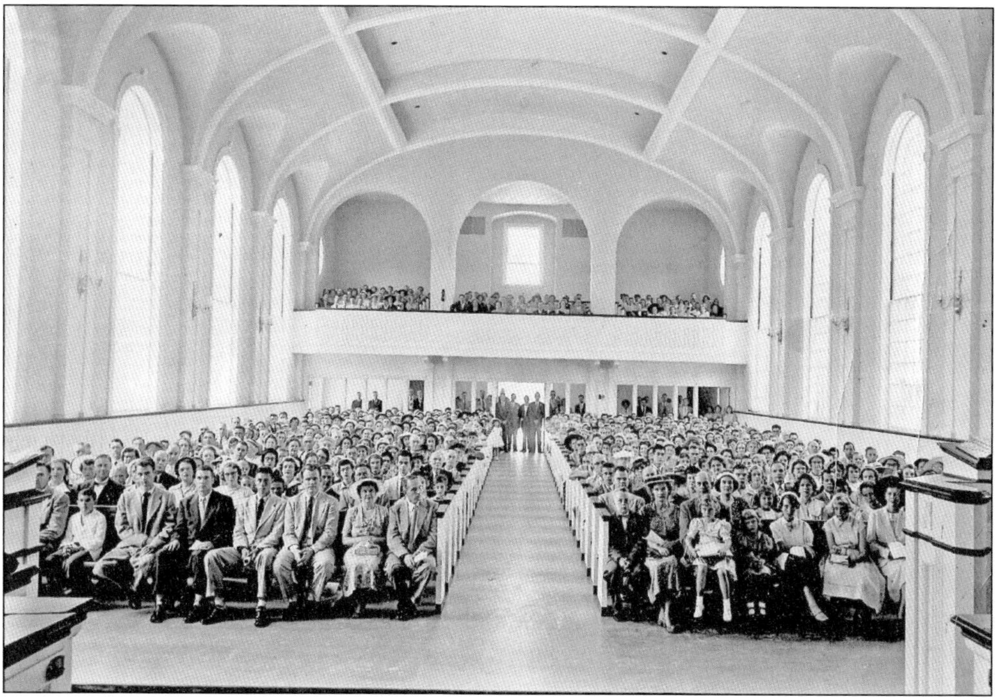

A spectacular fire in 1949 destroyed the Front Street United Methodist Church sanctuary. It took several years to replace that building with the much larger and more modern church facility that stands today. This photograph was made in 1956 when the congregation gathered for the first service in the new sanctuary. (Courtesy of Barbara Hall.)

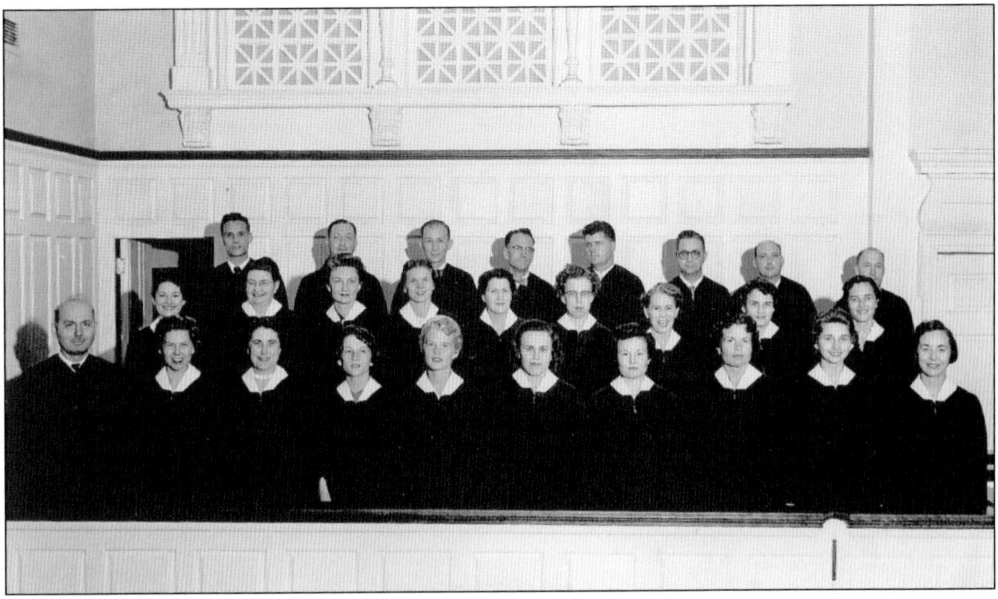

The choir of the Front Street United Methodist Church has included a number of talented musicians over the years, and for many of those years, Clarence Southern (first row, far left) conducted the choir. Southern was a professional musician who, with his wife, Louise, taught private students for many years in their home on West Davis Street. (Courtesy of Barbara Hall.)

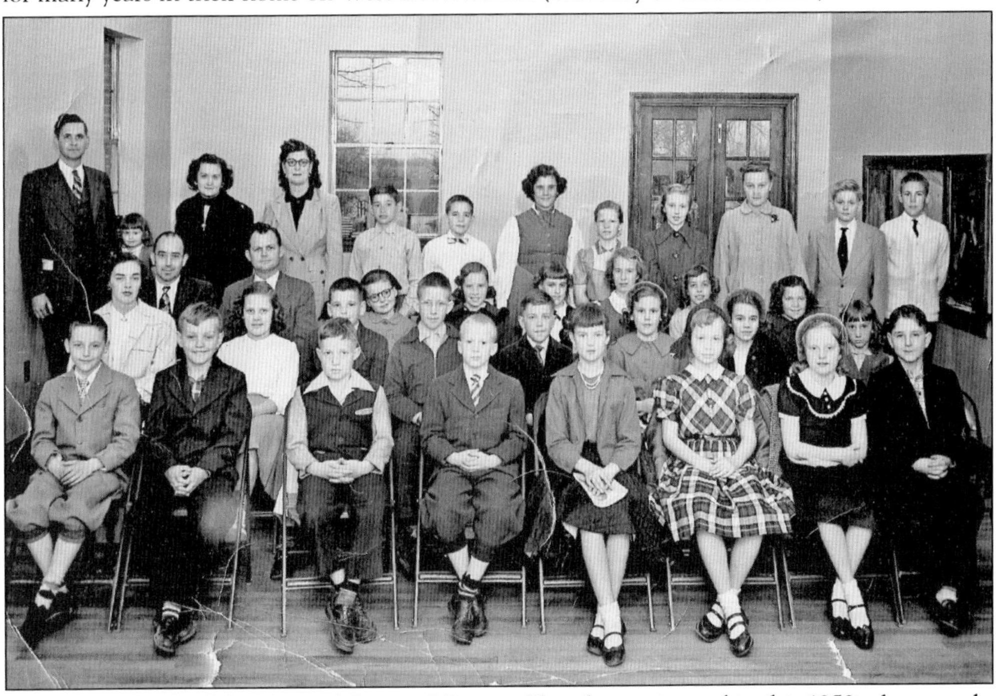

The young people of the Hocutt Memorial Baptist Church are pictured in this 1950s photograph. The church is on Logan Street and has served the west Burlington community since 1913. This community was once the center of a major textile community in the city, with the E. M. Holt Plaid Mill and the Mayfair Mill located nearby, and many served by this church worked in those mills. (Courtesy of John Kinney.)

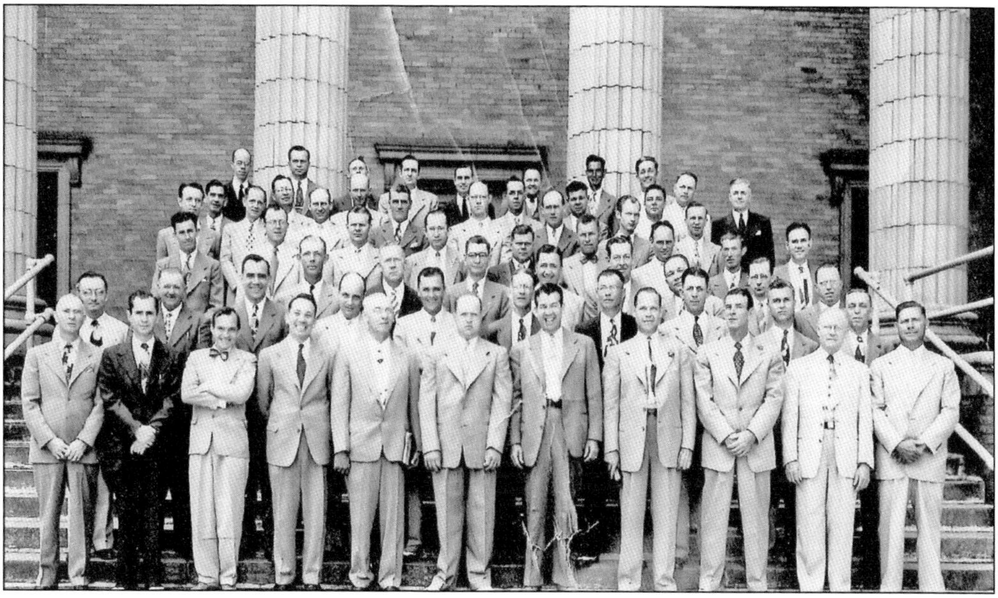

Calvin C. Linnemann was the principal of Burlington High School in the 1950s, but at the First Baptist Church, he is remembered for something other than his role in the city's education program. He is recalled by many as an outstanding Sunday school teacher. This was the C. C. Linnemann Sunday school class at First Baptist in the 1950s. Linnemann is seventh from left on the first row.

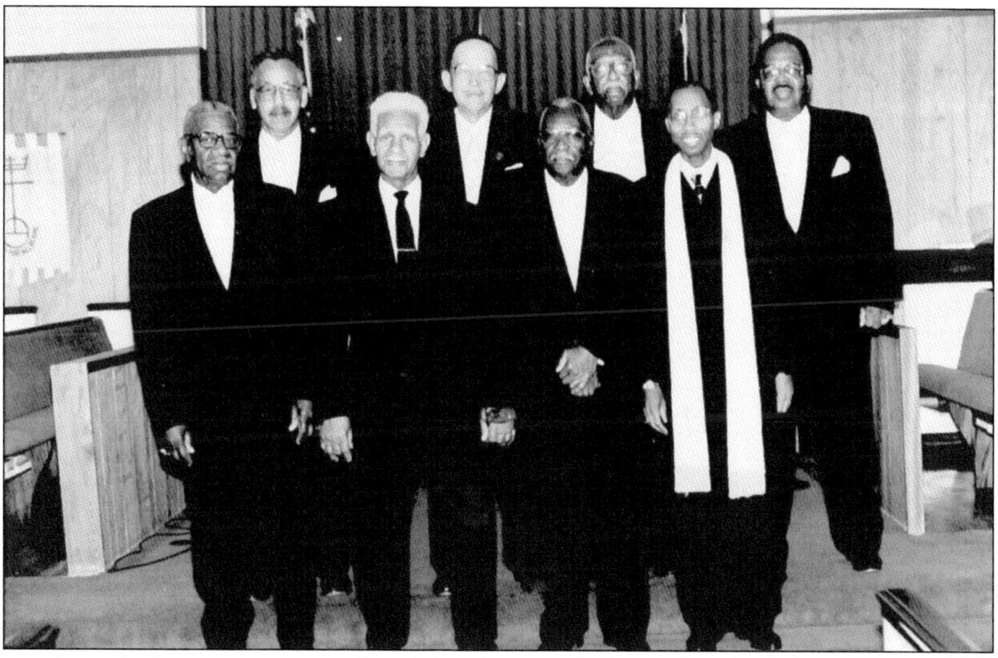

Rev. Larry E. Covington (first row, far right) is shown with church deacons at the Ebenezer United Church of Christ on Apple Street. Ebenezer had its beginning in May 1882. Residents of the area walked a long way to worship at the Arches Grove Christian Church, and they wanted a church closer to their homes, so they came together to form Ebenezer. (Courtesy of Brenda Torain, Ebenezer United Church of Christ.)

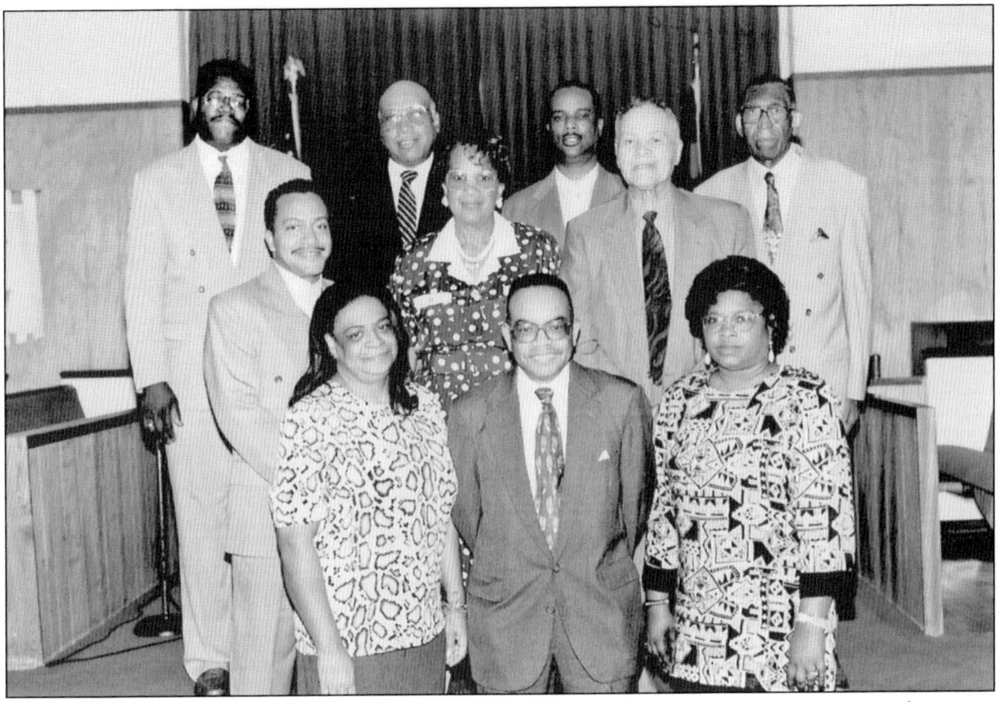

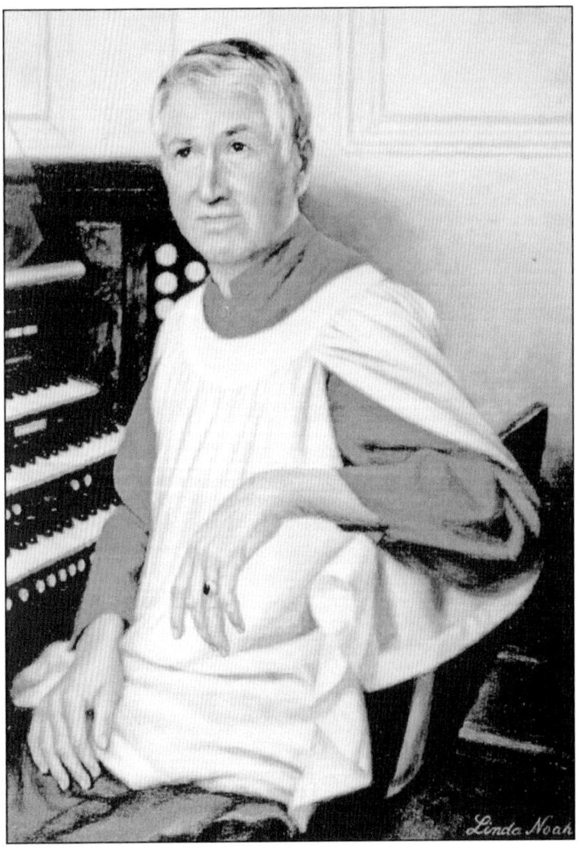

The trustee ministry serves the Ebenezer United Church of Christ, continuing the work of the church that had its earliest meetings in a building formerly used as a cotton gin. There have been several buildings in its history, and the current facility was dedicated in April 1964, seventy-six years after the first meeting of its congregation. (Courtesy of Brenda Torain, Ebenezer United Church of Christ.)

Robert Burns King served as organist-choirmaster at the First Presbyterian Church of Burlington for more than 40 years. His music and his influence carried him far beyond the First Presbyterian Church of Burlington's keyboard. As a Fulbright Scholar, he studied with some of the world's best teachers and has played in most of the world's great churches. (From a portrait by Linda Noah, courtesy of Robert Burns King.)

Six

Business, Industry, and Government

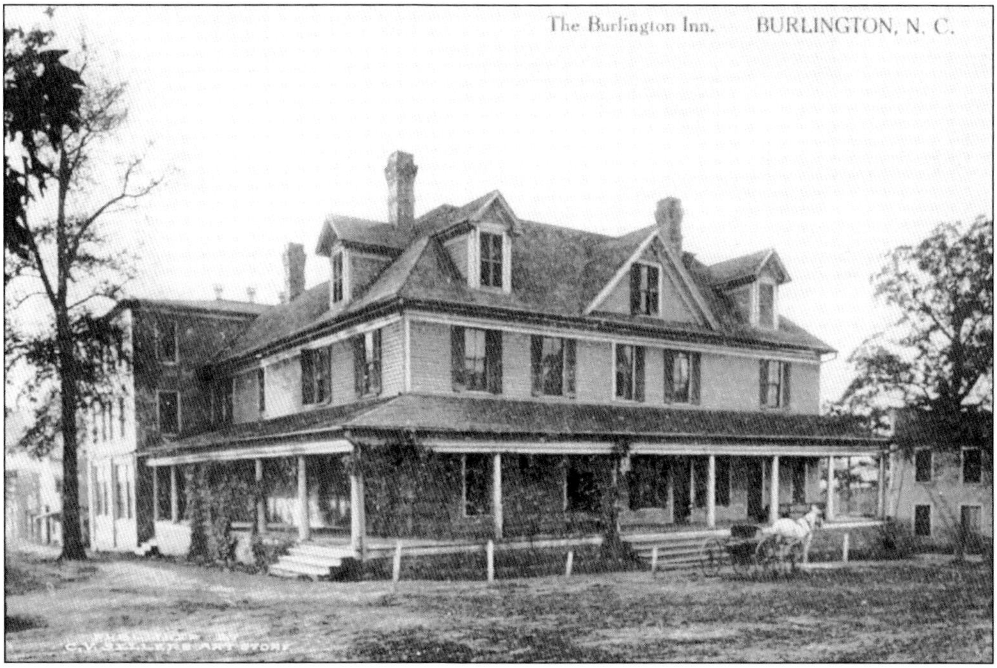

When the old Railroad Hotel burned down in 1904, Jennie Ward took the opportunity to build a new hotel at the corner of Andrews and Church Streets. The structure (pictured here) has been known both as the Burlington Inn and the Ward Hotel. There are actually two buildings on this site, which were a part of the complex. The brick hotel structure is behind the Burlington Inn.

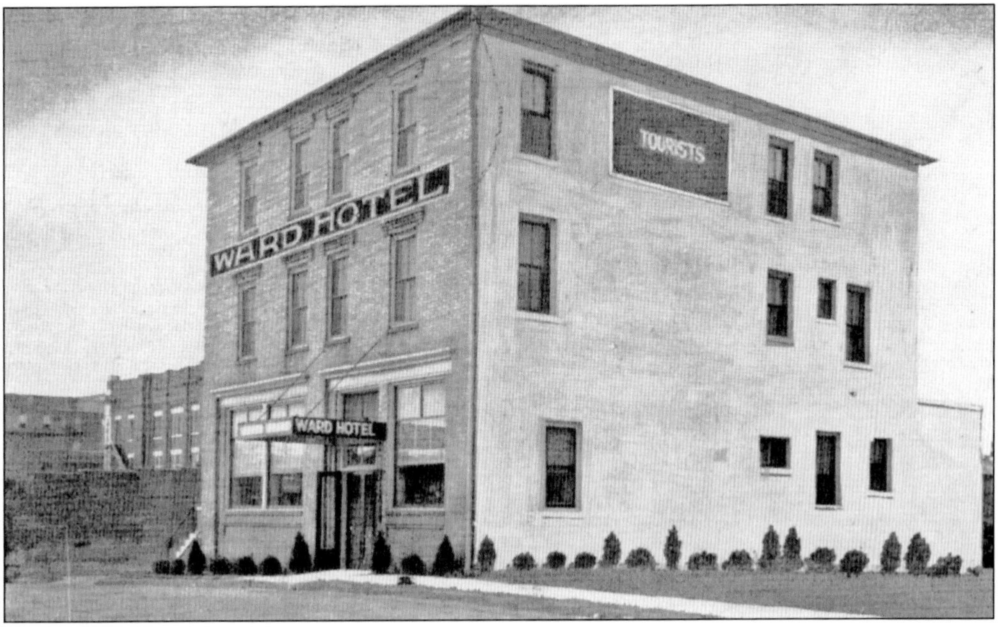

After the old Burlington Inn was torn down, the Ward Hotel survived and remained in service until the 1970s, when many older structures in the city were demolished in a renewal program. The Ward Hotel served the city along with the Piedmont Hotel, built in 1906, and the Alamance Hotel, built in 1925. All were in the business area a few blocks apart. (Courtesy of Jane Moore.)

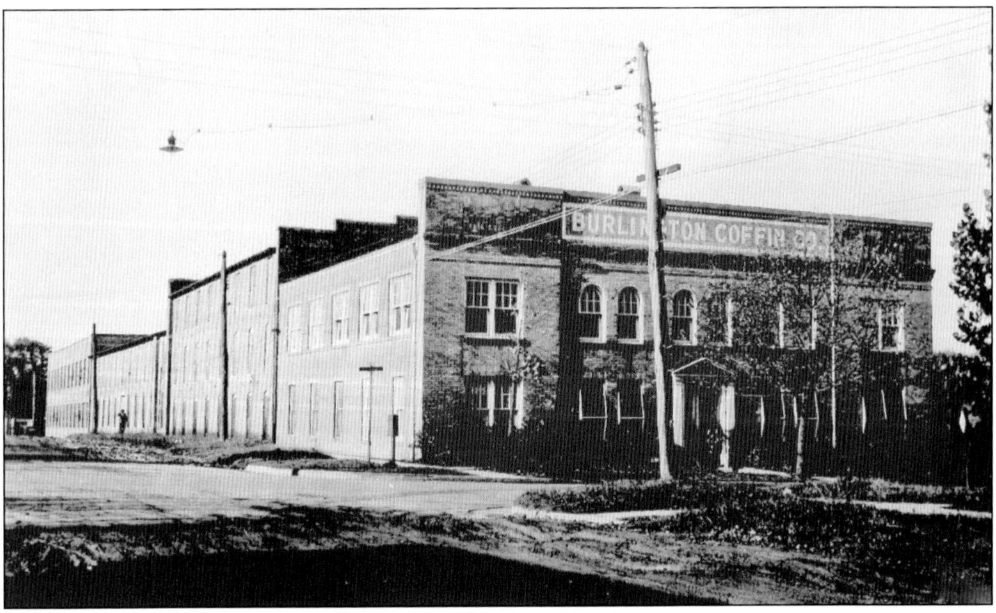
One of Burlington's earliest businesses was the Burlington Coffin Company. The company began in 1884 as the Carolina Coffin Company at Maple Avenue and Tucker Street. It was later reorganized as the Burlington Coffin Company. In 1886, the company was one of the industries providing jobs when the railroad announced it was closing the shops. The business continued until the latter part of the 20th century. (Courtesy of Alamance County Area Chamber of Commerce.)

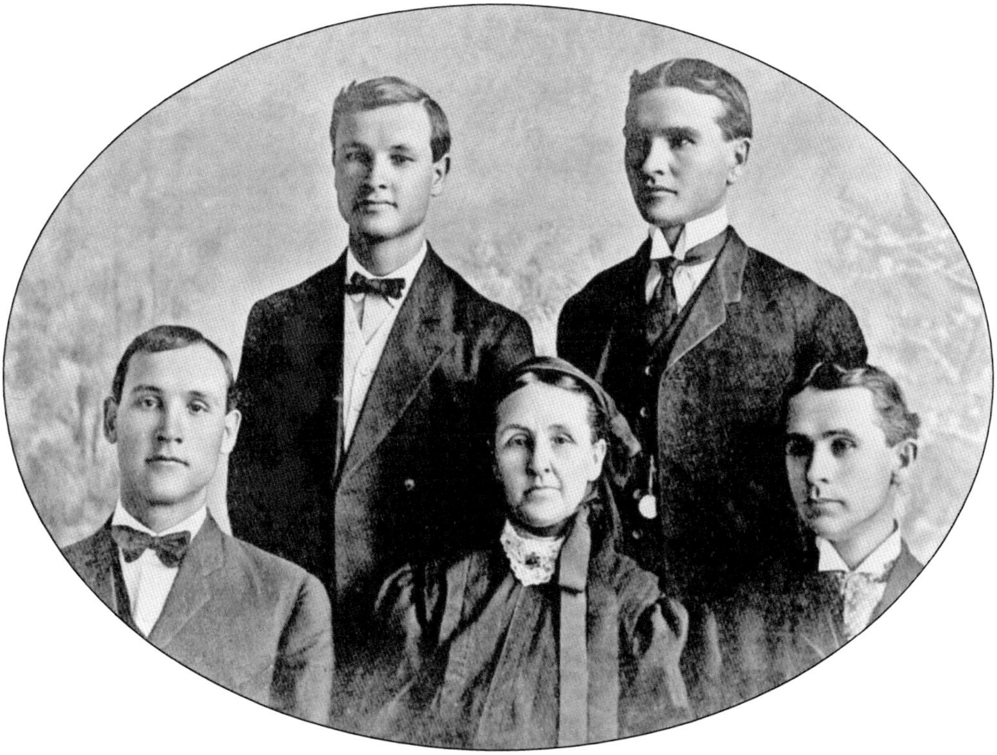

The May family had a major impact on the hosiery industry in Burlington. This photograph shows Ben May (first row, left), Will May (first row, right), Emanuel May (second row, left), and Burton May (second row, right) with their mother, Barbara. The Mays were involved in the Daisy Hosiery Mill on Church Street, then moved to South Main Street and began the May Hosiery Company. They were among the nation's major hosiery producers when Burlington was known as the hosiery center of the South. (Courtesy of Barbara McNeely.)

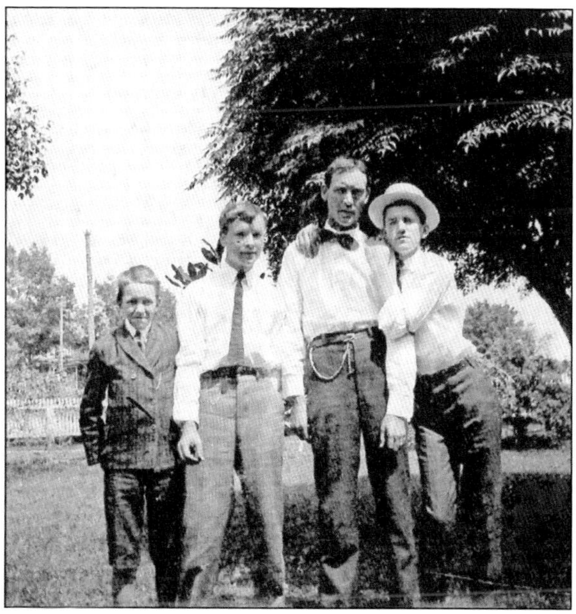

In the early years, the May brothers were like all other teenagers, enjoying themselves without many cares. From left to right, Burton, Ben, and Will May are shown here with friend George Sharpe. Later, however, they would assume major roles in the development of the hosiery industry in Burlington. May Hosiery became the May-McEwen-Kaiser Hosiery Company and then a part of Burlington Industries. (Courtesy of Barbara McNeely.)

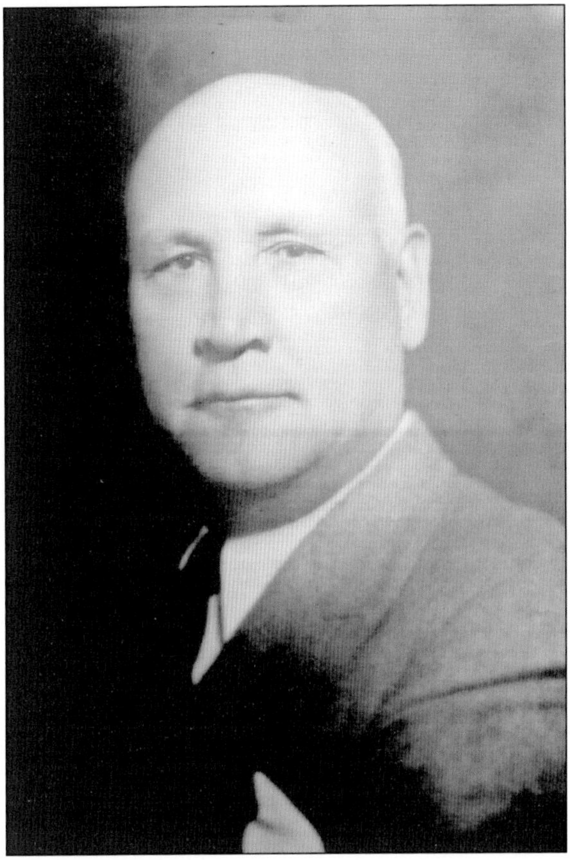

Ben May helped make the May Hosiery Company one of the major hosiery manufacturers in the country in the first half of the 20th century. He and his brother Will were pioneers in the industry, among the first in the nation to use the synthetic fibers nylon and orlon in hosiery. (Courtesy of Barbara McNeely.)

Below, the Daisy Hosiery, at top, was the first step in the May family's history in Burlington's hosiery industry. It was on South Church Street at Fifth Street. The company later became home of the U. S. Rubber Company. The lower image is the first plant of the May Hosiery on Main Street in downtown Burlington. This building was torn down to make way for the national headquarters building of LabCorp. (Courtesy of Jane Moore.)

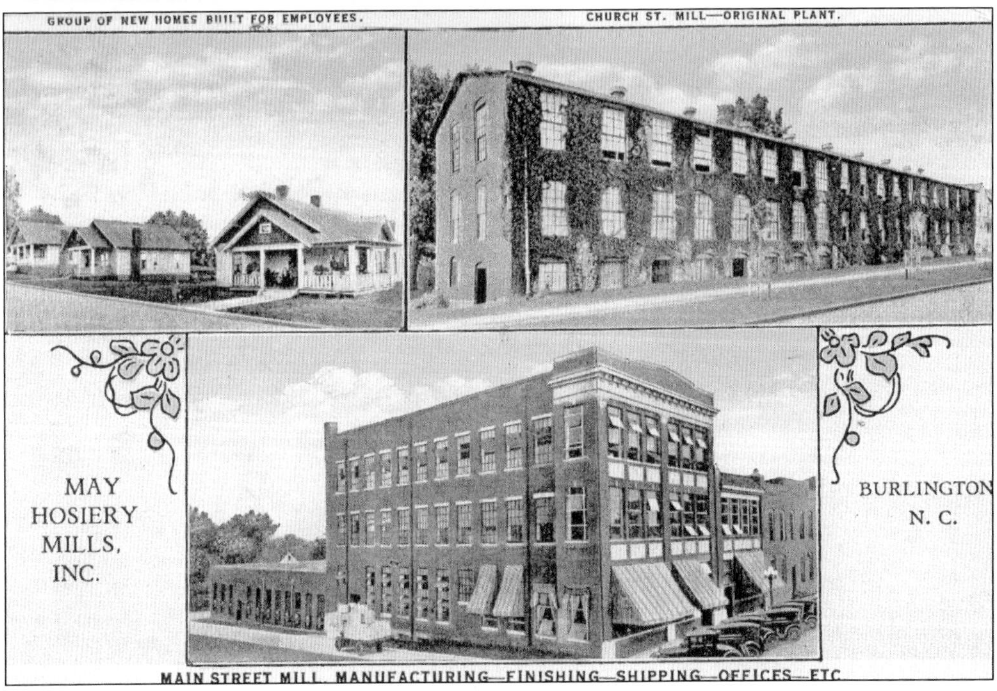

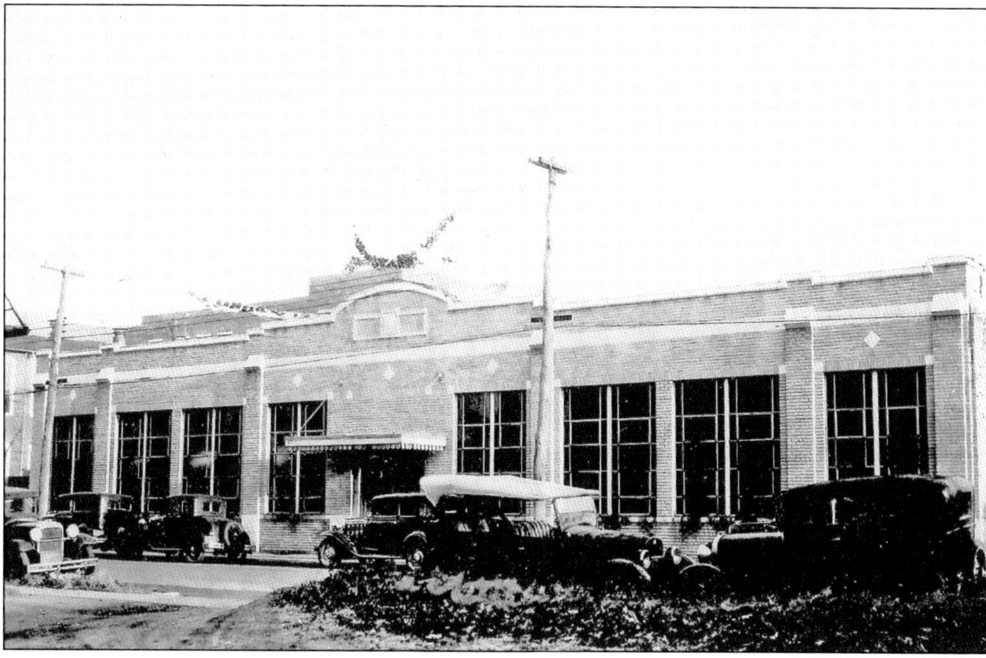

Some years after building on South Main Street, the May Hosiery Company added a finishing plant to its operations. This building is shown in 1934 and is at Main and Morehead Streets across from the original plant's location. This later became the research and development location for Burlington Hosiery and then was occupied by the Kayser-Roth Hosiery Company. (Courtesy of Alamance County Area Chamber of Commerce.)

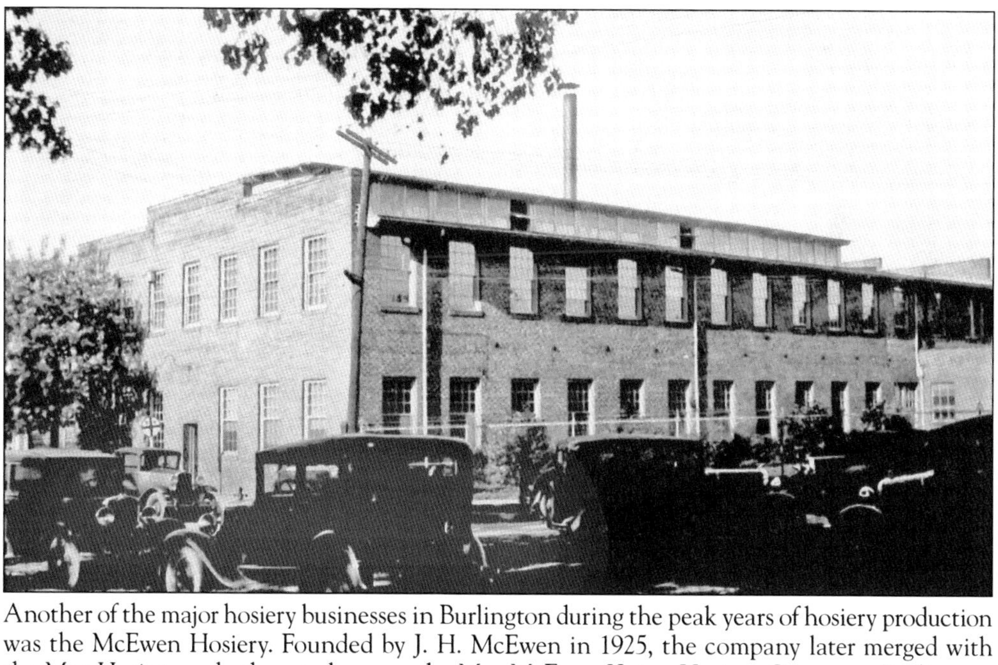

Another of the major hosiery businesses in Burlington during the peak years of hosiery production was the McEwen Hosiery. Founded by J. H. McEwen in 1925, the company later merged with the May Hosiery and others to become the May-McEwen-Kaiser Hosiery Company. Burlington Industries later acquired the firm. The McEwen mill stood on Ireland Street at the railroad tracks. (Courtesy of Alamance County Area Chamber of Commerce.)

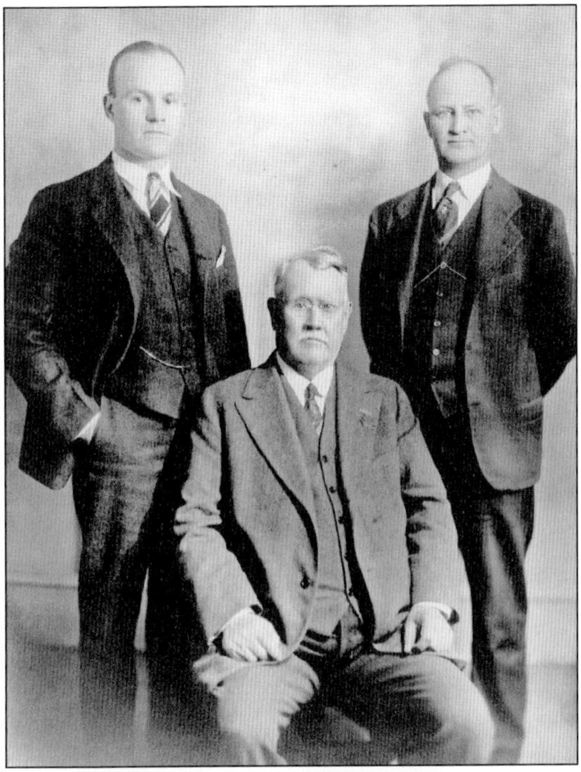

John Q. Gant founded Glen Raven Mills in the late 1800s. The company remains one of Alamance County's oldest industrial operations. Glen Raven Mills has been in a number of fields, including hosiery, and is one of the largest makers of awning fabrics in the world. John Q. Gant (seated) is pictured with sons Allen Gant (left) and Roger Gant, both of whom played roles in the company's success. (Courtesy of Edmund Gant.)

Below, this big desk was first used by John Q. Gant in his office at Glen Raven Mills. Through the years, other officials of the company made use of the desk as well. Seated is Roger Gant Jr., with Edmund Gant (center) and Allen Gant Jr. Each has headed Glen Raven's operations at one time. Glen Raven Mills has continuously been one of the major employers in Alamance County.

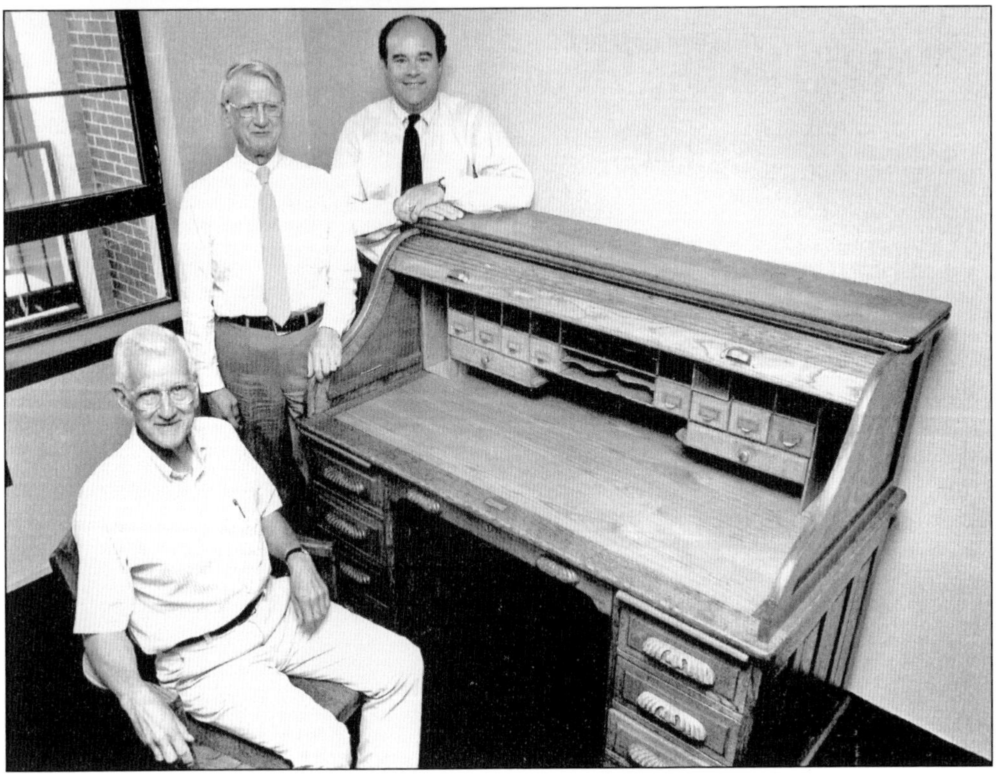

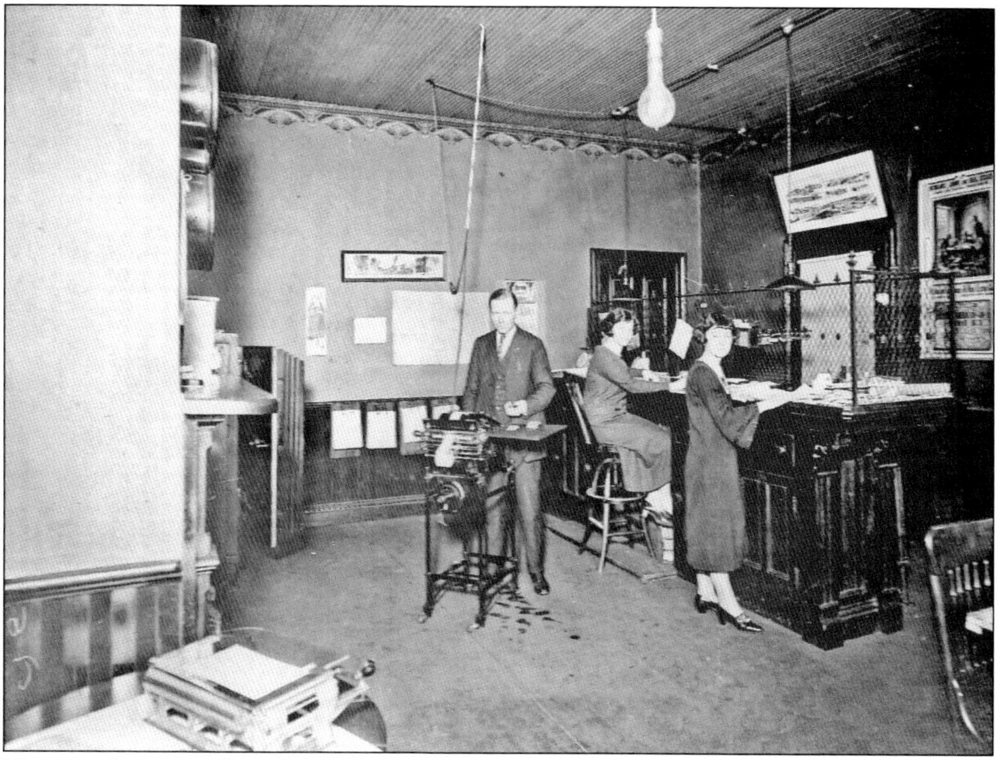

This was the main office of the Whitehead Hosiery Mill, shown in this 1925 photograph. The man pictured and the two clerks at the counter conducted the daily business of the company. The Whitehead Hosiery Mill was a hosiery producer in the 1920s and 1930s when Burlington was a major hosiery center.

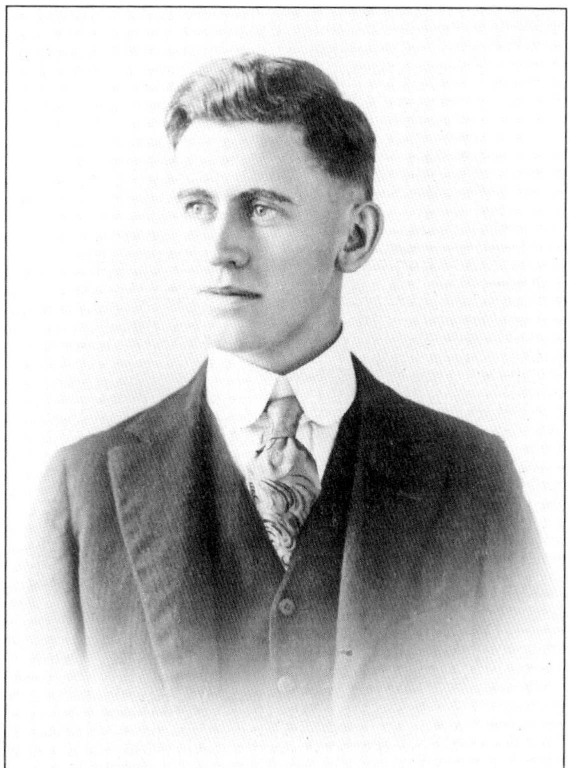

Reid A. Maynard left his position with a Burlington bank and opened the Grace Hosiery Mill in 1927 in east Burlington. Maynard became one of the nation's most prominent hosiery manufacturers, later forming Tower Hosiery and Leath, McCarthy, and Maynard, Inc. He was on the board of trustees at the University of North Carolina and was involved in many local civic and business affairs. (Courtesy of James W. Maynard.)

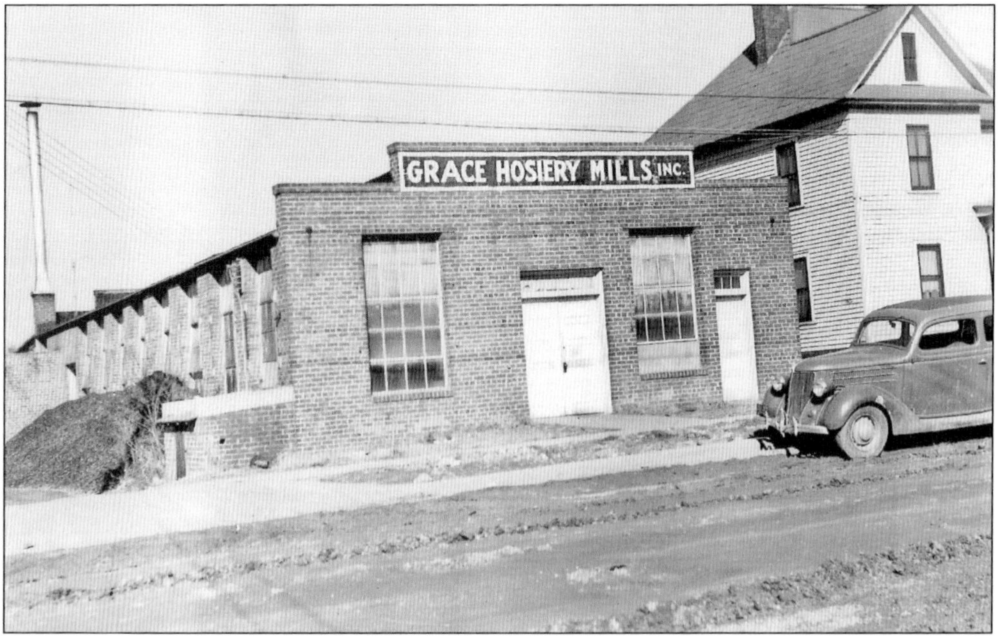

The Grace Hosiery was named for Reid A. Maynard's wife, Grace, and the mill produced socks for children and men. Other incorporators of Grace Hosiery were Maynard's father-in-law, J. E. Moore, and his brothers Grover and Sam. E. H. Moore, the son of J. E. Moore, was also an incorporator, along with J. I. Somers and Grace Maynard. (Courtesy of James W. Maynard.)

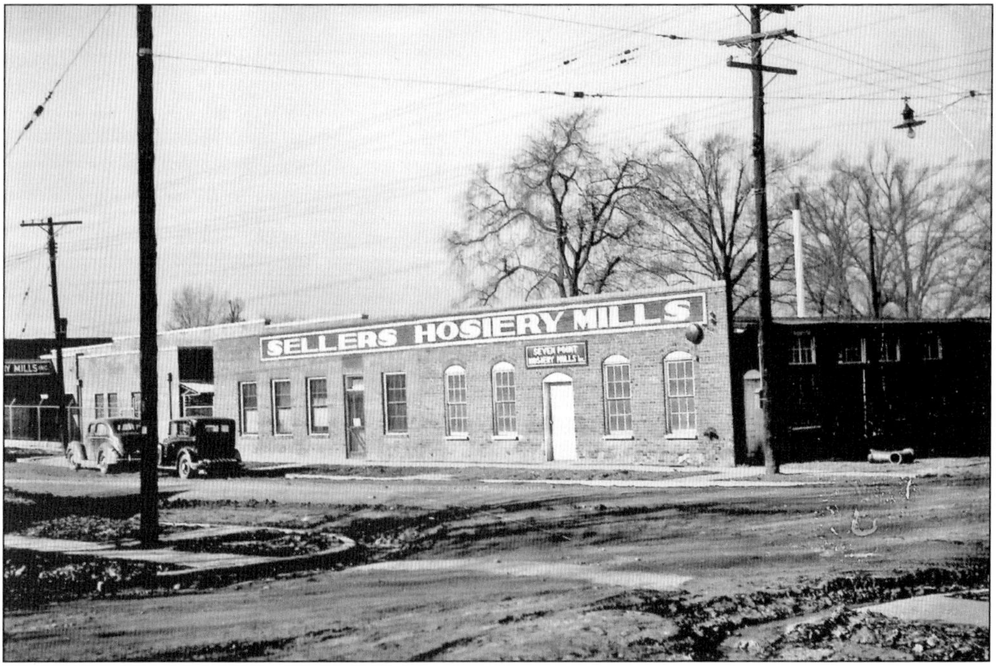

The Sellers Hosiery Mill was organized around 1907, and it was one of the many mills in the community to bear the name of a local family. At one time, there were more than 80 hosiery operations in Burlington, and most of them were family operations. Sellers grew to become one of the largest of the family-owned businesses.

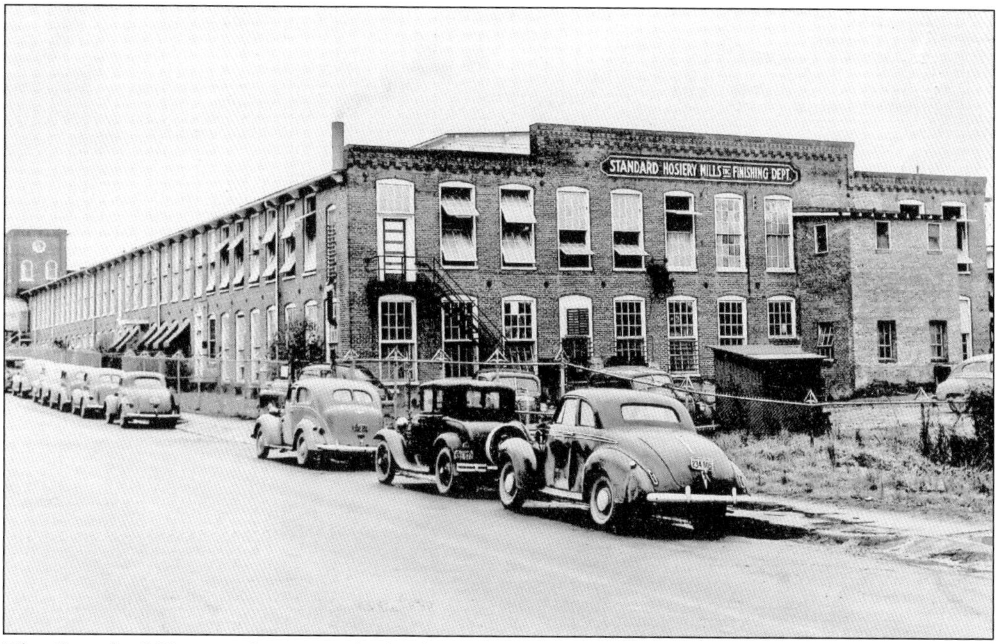

The Standard Hosiery Company had a large operation in this building on East Webb Avenue for many years. John Shoffner founded the company in 1927, and the mill also had operations in the village of Alamance. This plant, the site of one of the earliest textile plants in Burlington, later became a part of the Kayser-Roth Hosiery Company.

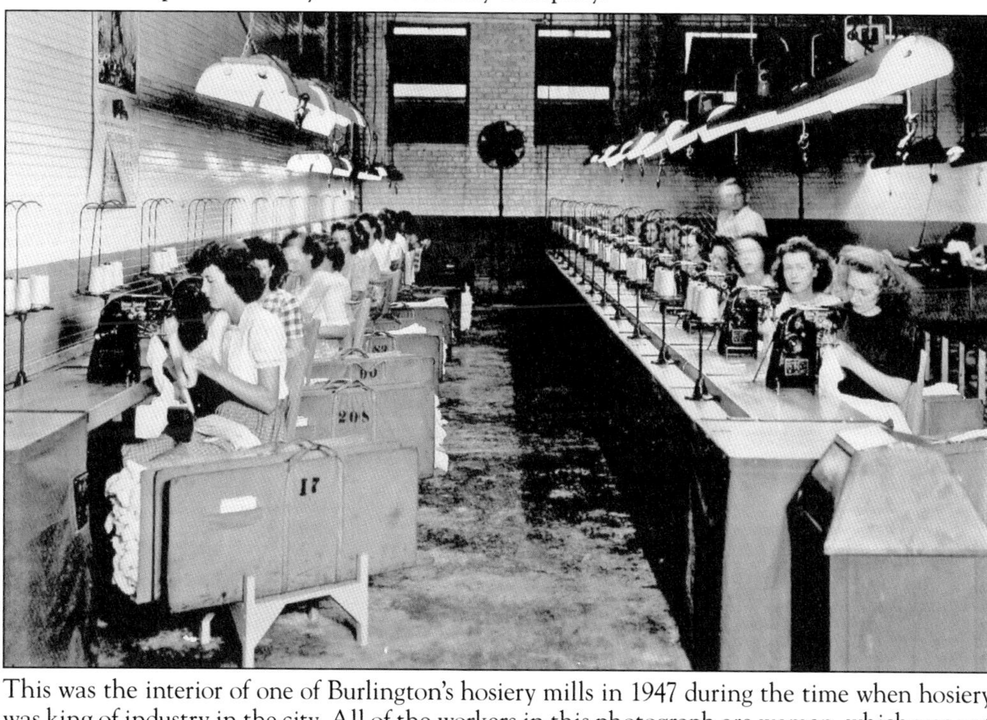

This was the interior of one of Burlington's hosiery mills in 1947 during the time when hosiery was king of industry in the city. All of the workers in this photograph are women, which was not unusual in the hosiery industry. Many women worked in the industry from its beginnings, as was also the case in the area's cotton mills.

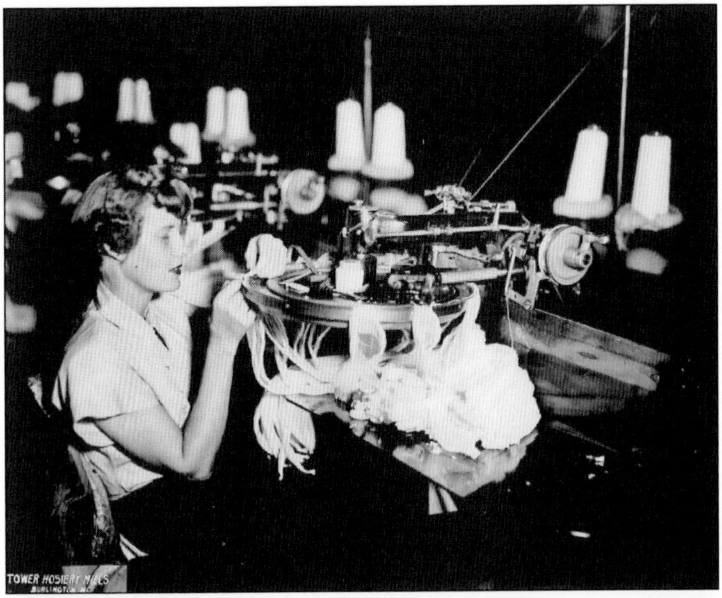

This woman working in the Tower Hosiery Mill was a looper. She looped the toe of the stocking closed before the hosiery was seamed up the back of the leg. This was a highly skilled job in the Tower's production process. The Tower Hosiery Mill was located on Broad Street and was operated by Reid A. Maynard's family. (Courtesy of James W. Maynard.)

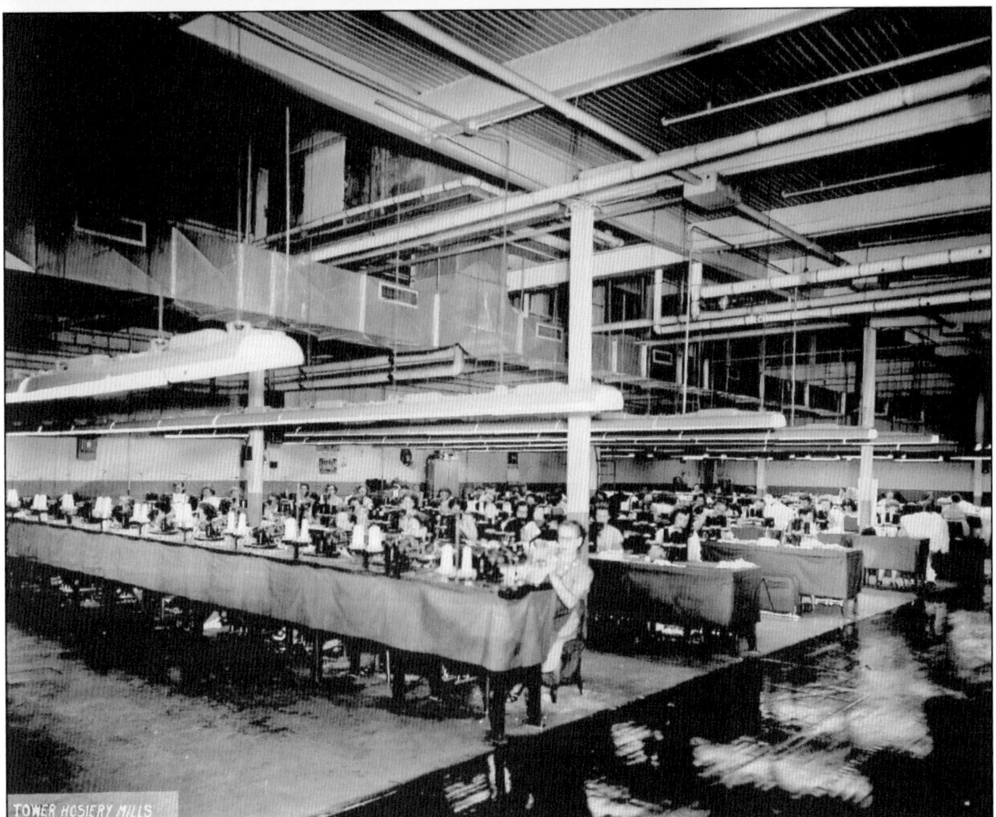

There were up to 60 loopers working on the floor of the Tower Hosiery Mill in Burlington during the peak years of operation. In the early to mid-20th century, hosiery mills ran at full production to meet the demands of customers that included the major department stores of the nation and retail stores around the world. (Courtesy of James W. Maynard.)

In the 1950s while with Chadbourn Hosiery, Bill Leath developed a stretch yarn that revolutionized the ladies' hosiery industry. Previously, hosiery had been sized—6, 6.5, 7, 7.5, etc.—and that required merchants to keep huge inventories. Leath's stretch yarn made it possible to stock small, medium, and large sizes, reducing inventory needs and also making panty hose possible, another development that changed the industry. (Courtesy of James W. Maynard.)

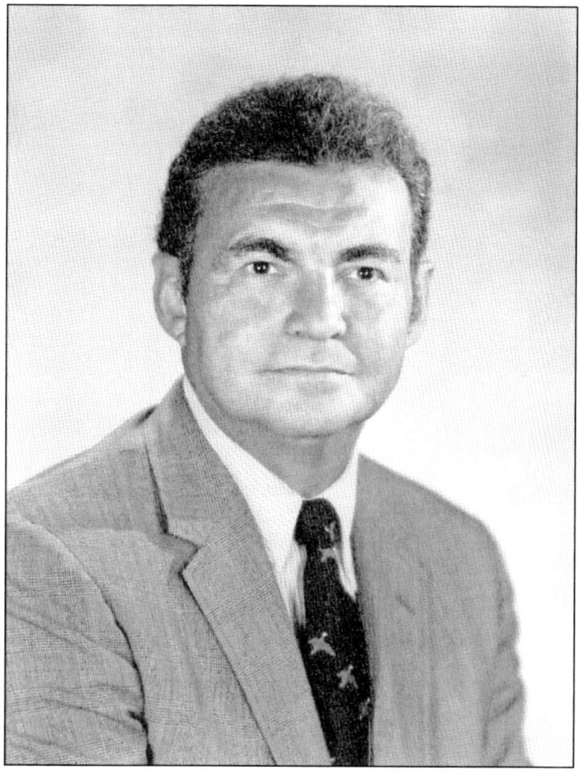

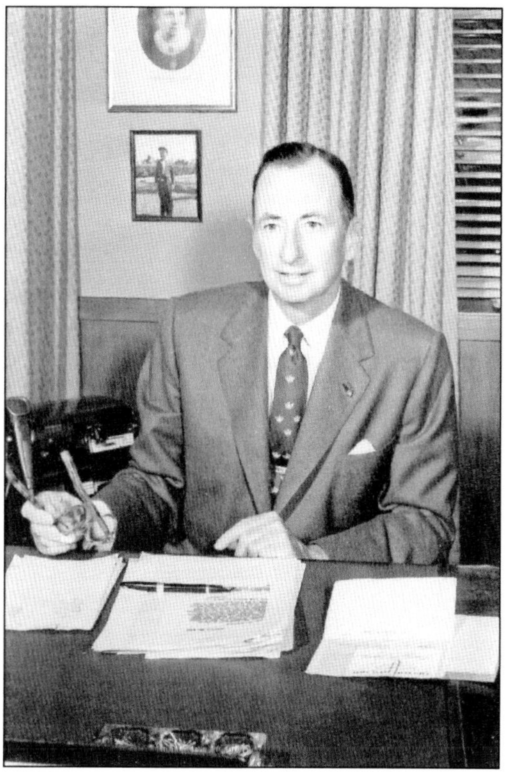

J. Spencer Love came to Burlington in 1923 at the request of local chamber of commerce members to open a new textile operation. Burlington Mills was chartered in November 1923 and began operations in July 1924. The company became Burlington Industries, the largest manufacturer of textile products in the world, with plants in some 25 countries and more than 20,000 employees.

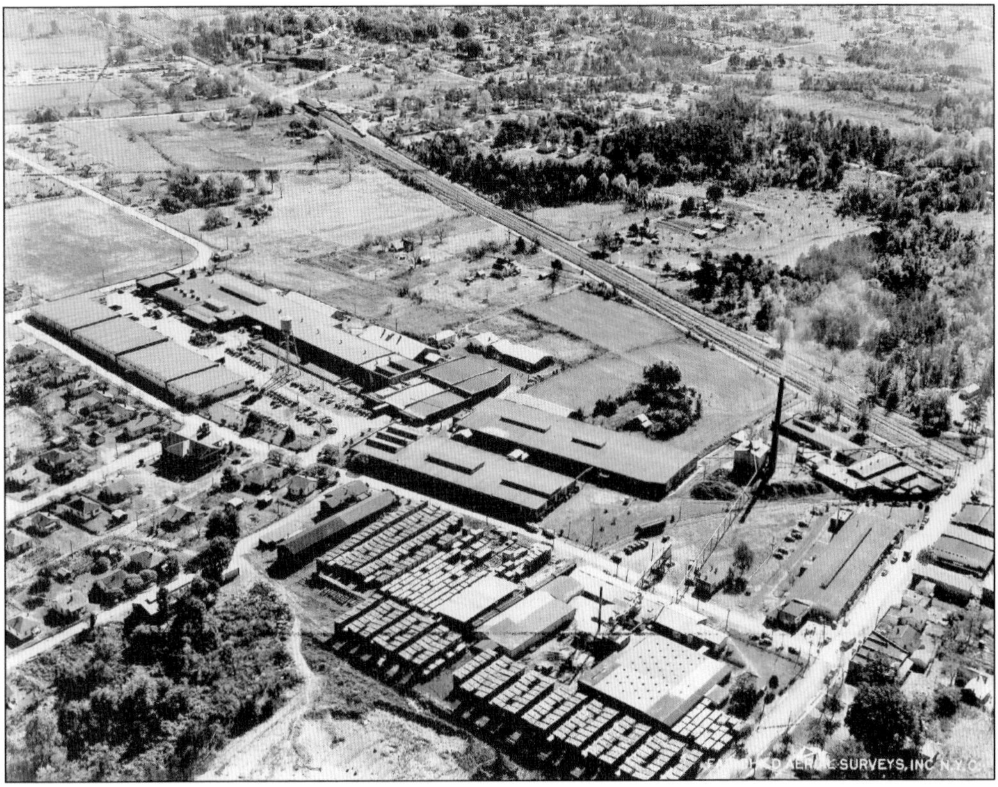

This is an aerial view of Piedmont Heights, the name given to the first plant of Burlington Mills. The mill is surrounded by houses built by the company and rented to employees, giving rise to a mill village known to the present day as the Mill Hill. The first plant later became known as the Pioneer Plant.

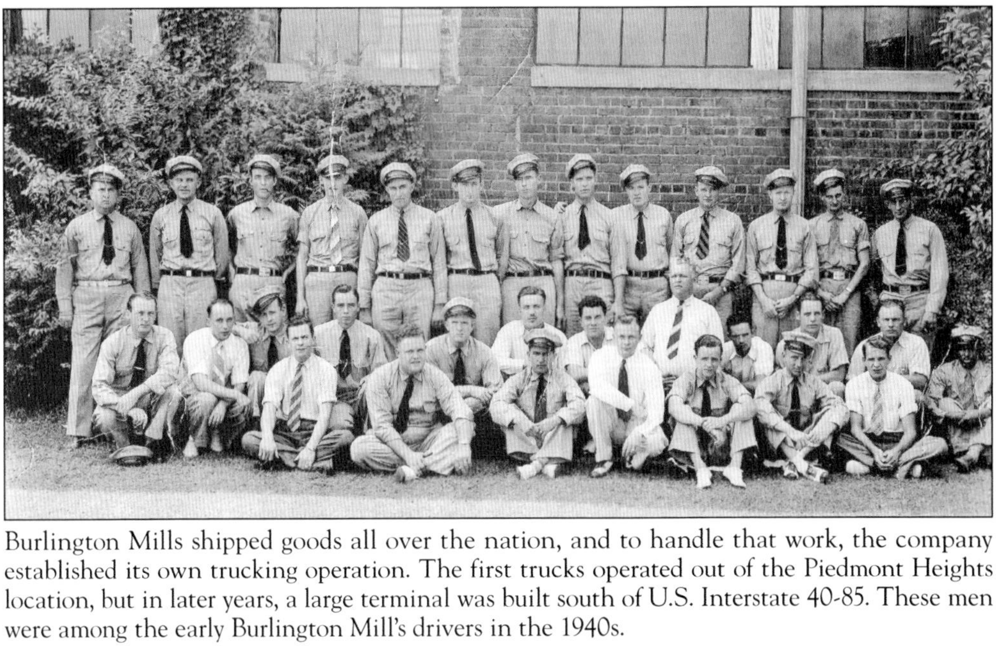

Burlington Mills shipped goods all over the nation, and to handle that work, the company established its own trucking operation. The first trucks operated out of the Piedmont Heights location, but in later years, a large terminal was built south of U.S. Interstate 40-85. These men were among the early Burlington Mill's drivers in the 1940s.

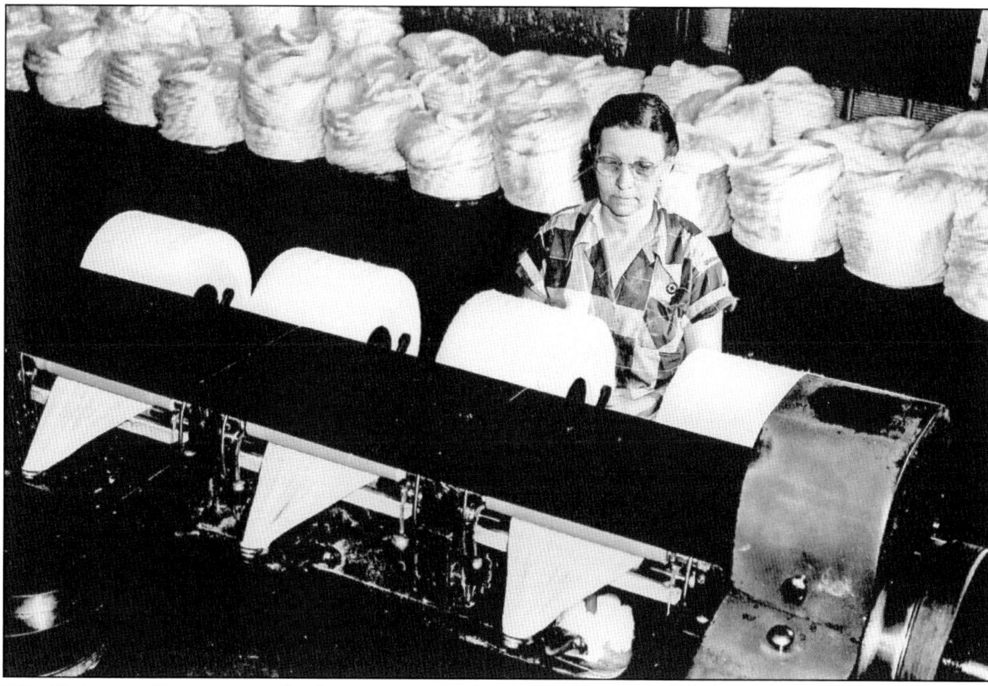

The Celanese Corporation had a major operation in Burlington for many years. The corporation was located on Ireland Street near its junction with East Webb Avenue at the railroad tracks. This lady is seen in one of the mill's large production areas, which again shows that many women were employed in the textile and hosiery industries. (Courtesy of Alamance County Area Chamber of Commerce.)

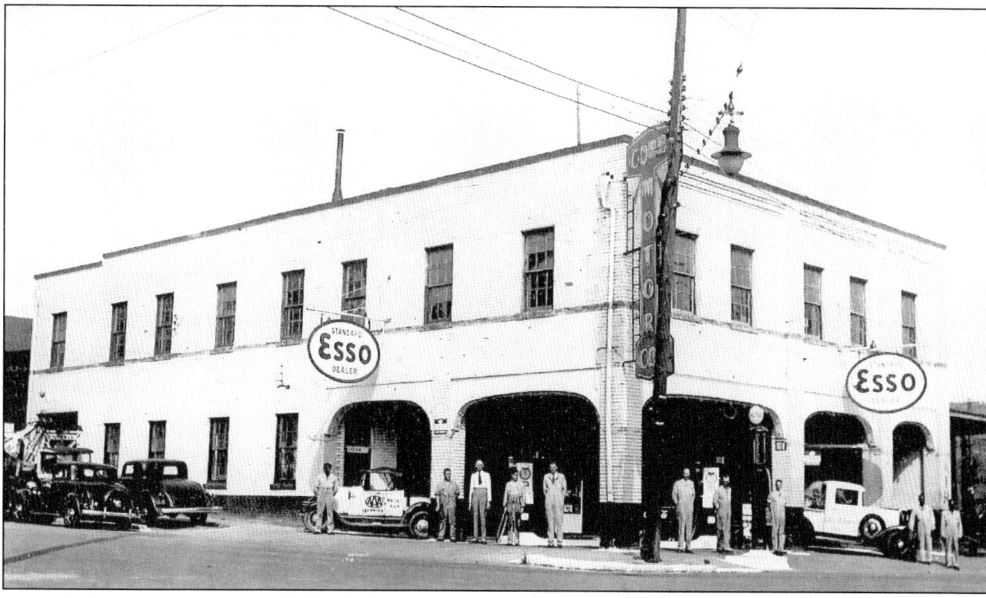

The Cobb Motor Company was a Burlington landmark for several decades. It was home to a service station, an auto repair shop, and a heavy-duty wrecker service. This building stood at the corner of South Church and West Davis Streets. It was torn down in the early 1970s when a number of older buildings in the city were removed. (Courtesy of Paul Cobb.)

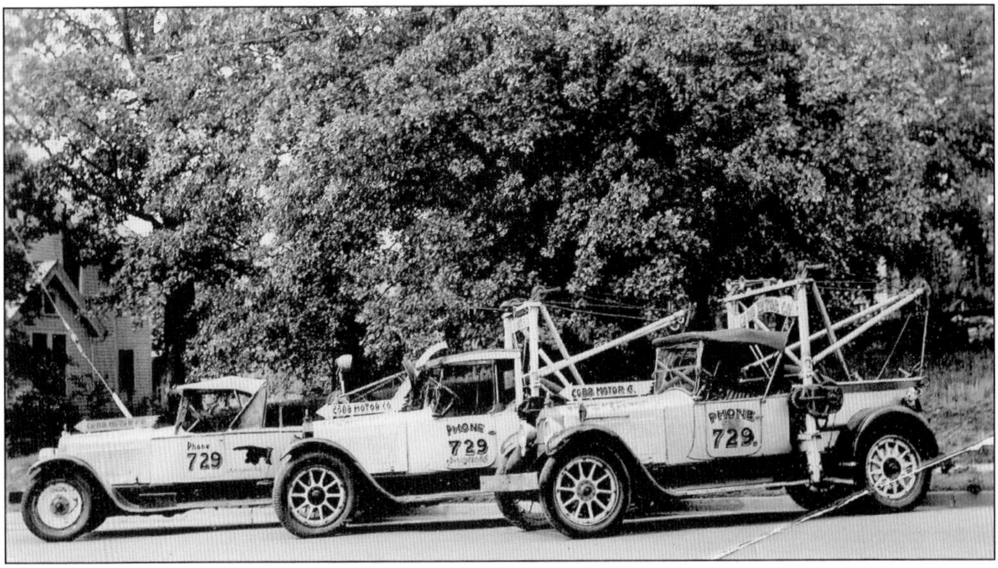

The Cobb Motor Company was the major wrecker and tow service in Burlington for many years. These three wreckers served the community in the company's early years. At one time, the Cobb Motor Company was advertised as the "largest and most complete wrecking service in the South." The company's wreckers were equipped to handle any vehicles that moved on the highways during its years of operations. (Courtesy of Paul Cobb.)

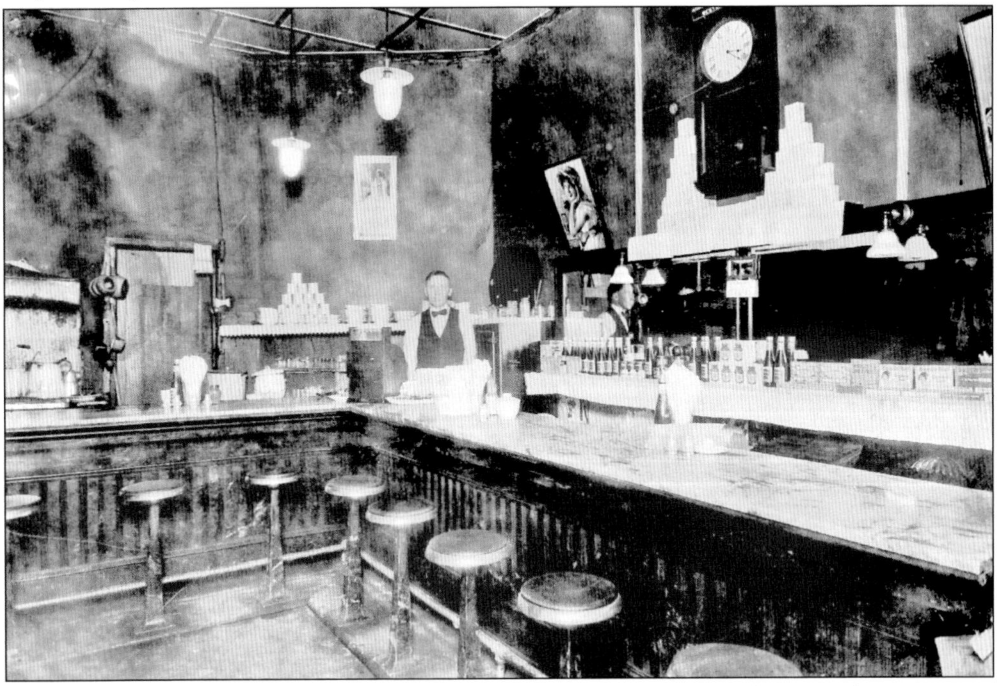

Cole's Dairy Lunch was one of the town's most popular restaurants in the early years. The restaurant's operator, Teeny Cole (pictured above), served a large downtown clientele. Attorneys, dentists, doctors, and other professionals with offices downtown were among his regular customers. In more recent years, Dave Wright and Gary Cole wrote and produced a play about the restaurant, which was performed at the Paramount Theater. (Courtesy of Gary Cole.)

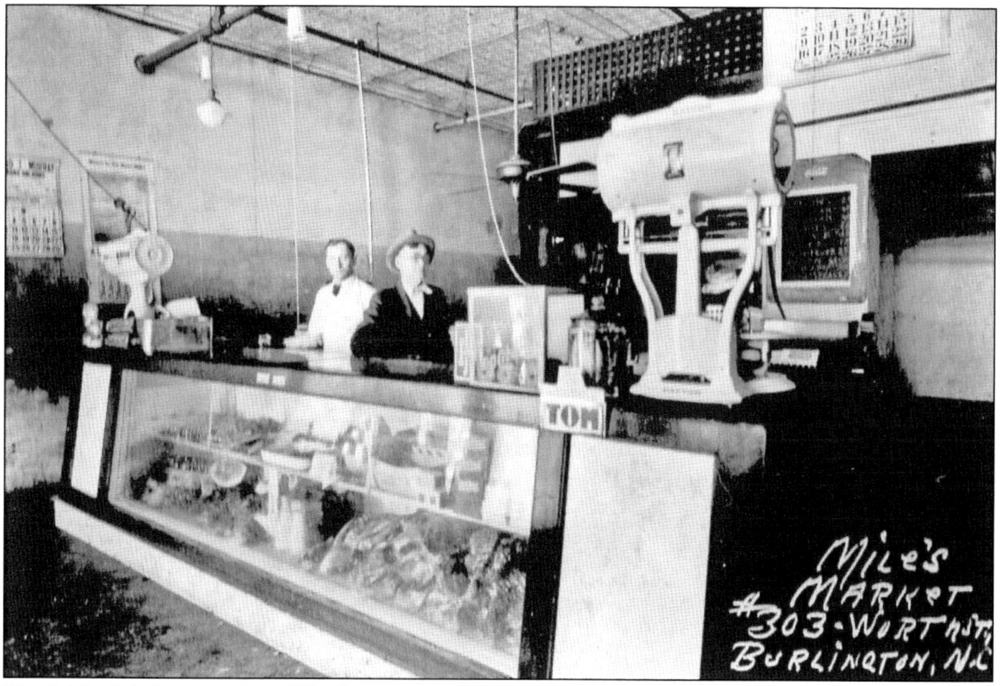

The Miles Market was one of Burlington's early meat markets. This store was located at 303 Worth Street when this photograph was made in 1930. The big counter is filled with meats and bottled drinks, and there are large scales at each end of the counter. Before the big supermarkets came to Burlington, a number of small stores like this one served the community's needs for meats and grocery products.

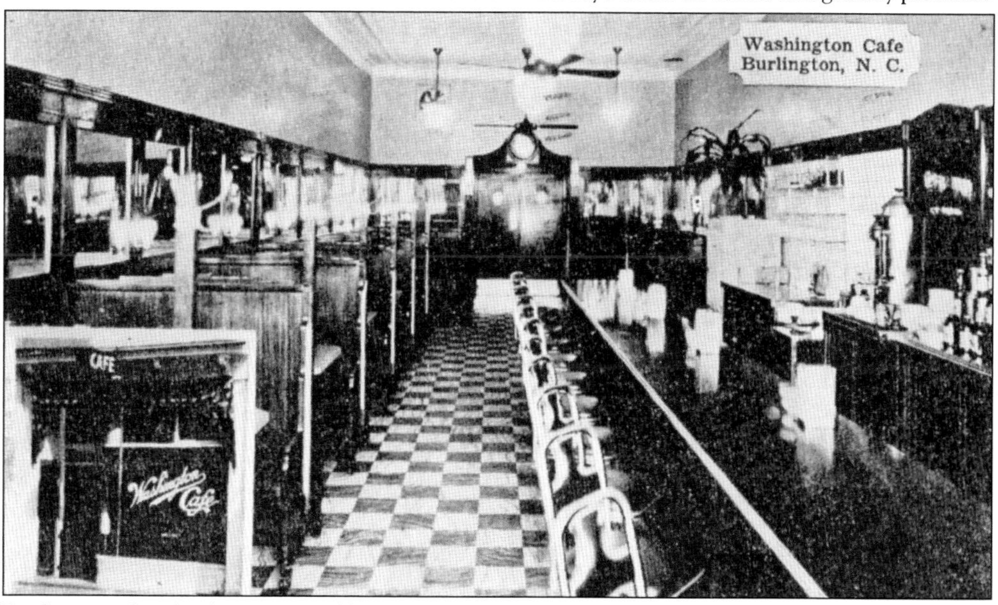

Burlington has had some notable restaurants over the years, and one of the early, upscale establishments was the Washington Café. The café was located in the downtown business area and was one of the largest restaurant locations in the area during the 1930s. The Washington Café had counter stools and featured a number of large booths with individual lighting. (Courtesy of Jane Moore.)

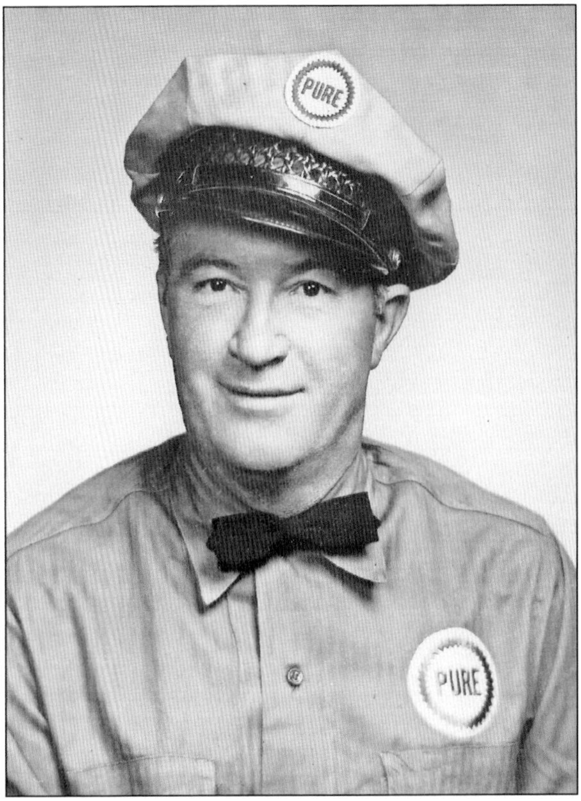

While there were many big industries in Burlington over the years, there have also been many small businessmen who have made successful operations as part of the city's history. One such man was Donnie Medford, a service station owner and operator from 1946 until 1962 in the Burlington Mills community in east Burlington. He was typical of many small service station operators in the mid-20th century. (Courtesy of Betty Morin.)

Donnie Medford operated the Old Hickory Service Station (pictured below) at Graham and Queen Anne Streets. Burlington Mills buildings surrounded the station. Medford leased his location from the mill, and in 1962, he had to move because the mill needed the property for a parking area. Medford moved to a new station on North Church Street. (Courtesy of Betty Morin.)

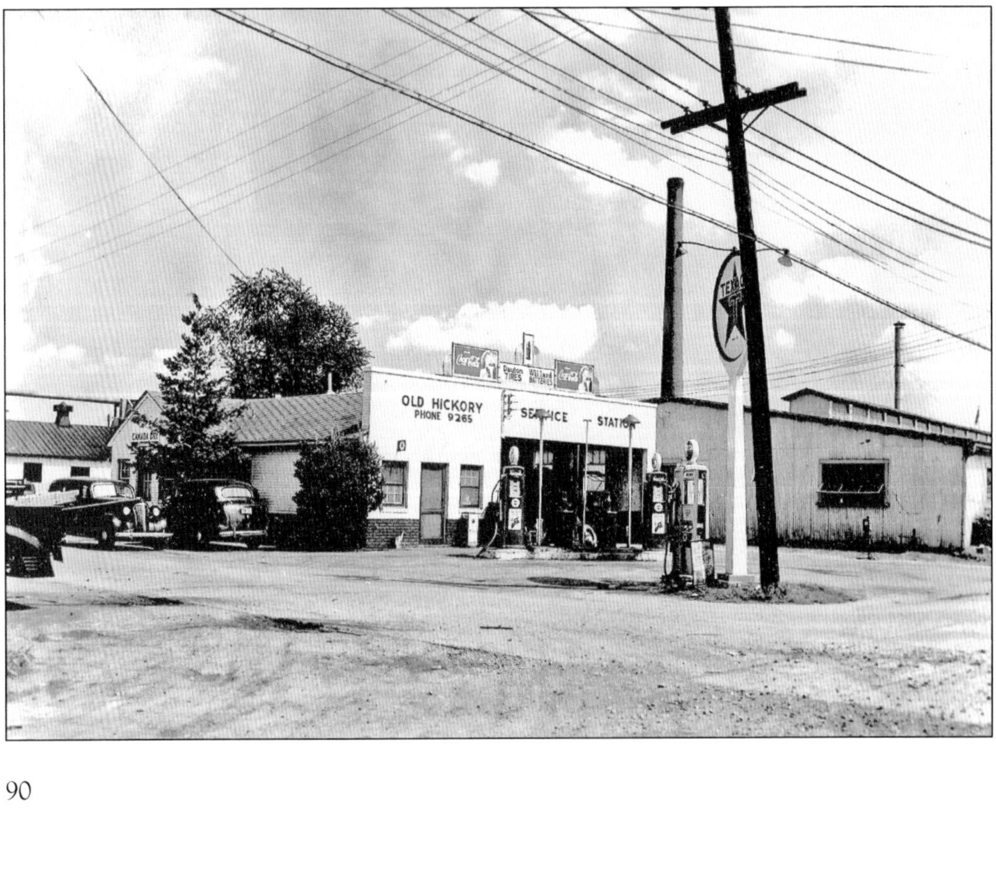

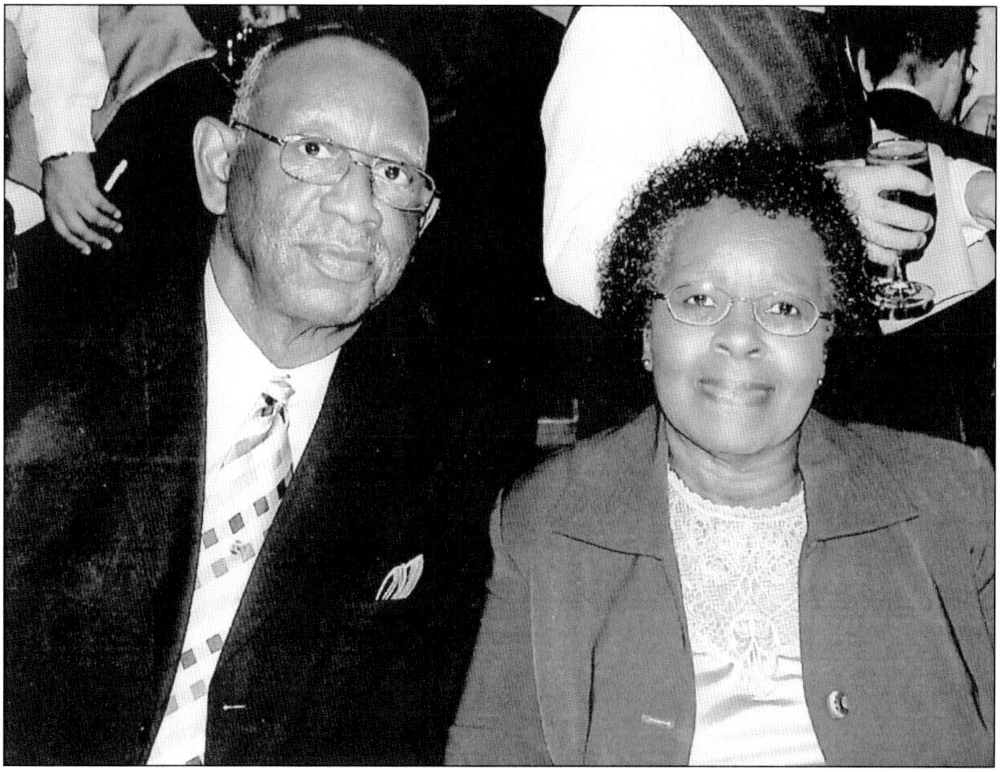

Another person who added to Burlington's economy by operating his own small business is Leroy Richardson. Richardson has operated the Burlington Appliance Service for almost 30 years, providing service for all appliances used in the home and becoming well known in the community. Richardson and his wife, Virginia, are shown above as they celebrated their 50th wedding anniversary. (Courtesy of Leroy Richardson.)

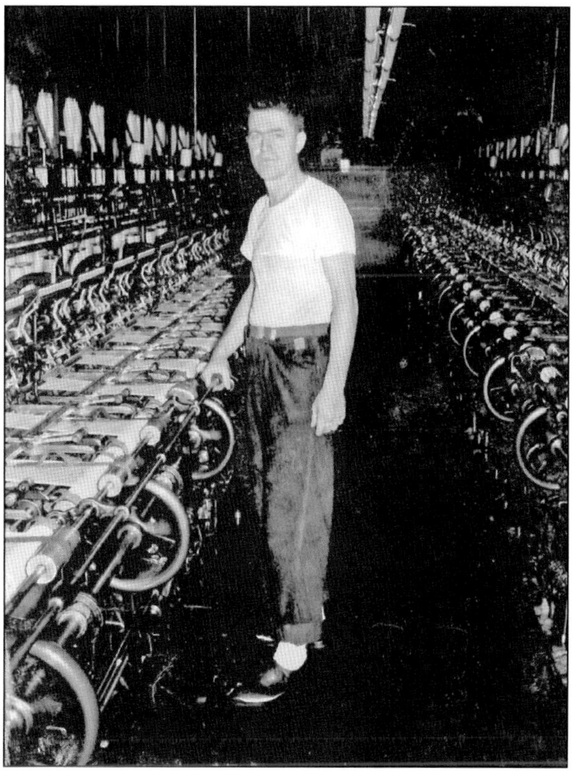

The knitter was a valued employee in Burlington's hosiery mills because the operation of knitting machines was an important process in hosiery production and one that was taught over a period of time. Dexter Austin was a knitter in the Burlington Industries hosiery operations from 1948 to 1958. (Courtesy of Richard Campbell.)

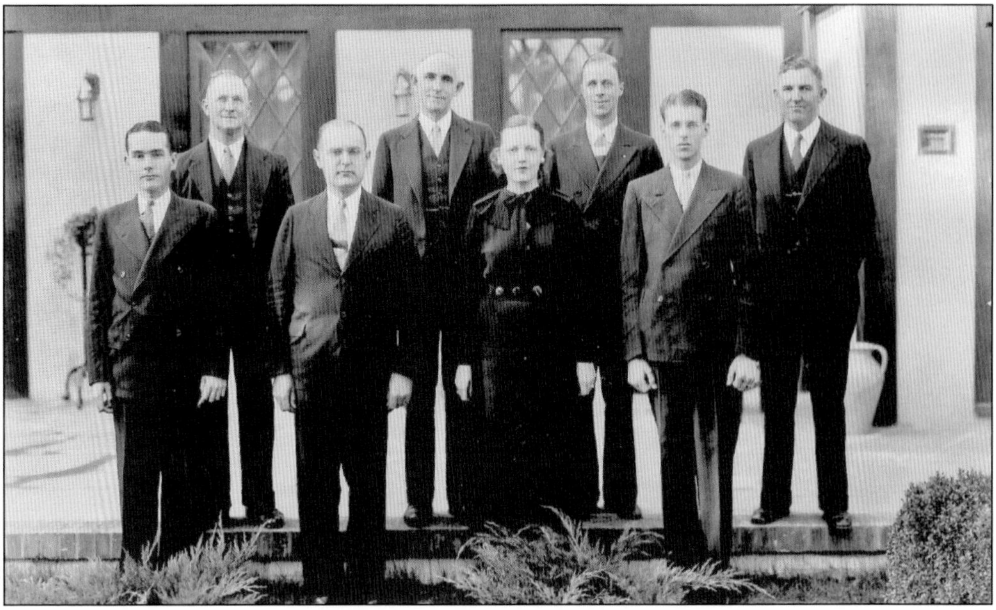

The Rich and Thompson Funeral Service is the area's oldest mortuary establishment. The company opened for business in 1902 and has operations in Burlington and Graham. The staff in 1935 included, from left to right, (first row) W. B. Linens, A. Ray Reitzel, Mrs. Frank Rich, and Frank Rich; (second row) James H. Rich. Charles A. Thompson, Alvis M. Rich and W. Ernest Thompson. (Courtesy of Rich and Thompson Funeral Service.)

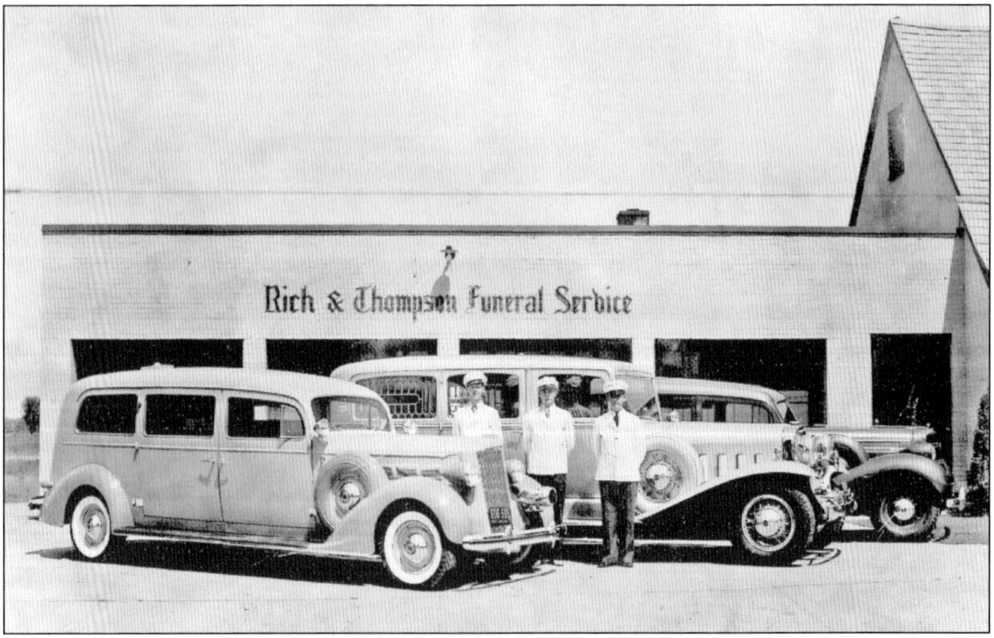

Funeral homes provided ambulance service in Alamance County until 1967. Members of the funeral home staff not only provided funeral services, but also responded to emergency calls with their ambulances. Staff stayed on-call in the funeral home at night to provide round-the-clock ambulance service. Pictured are Rich and Thompson Funeral Service vehicles in the 1940s. (Courtesy Rich and Thompson Funeral Service.)

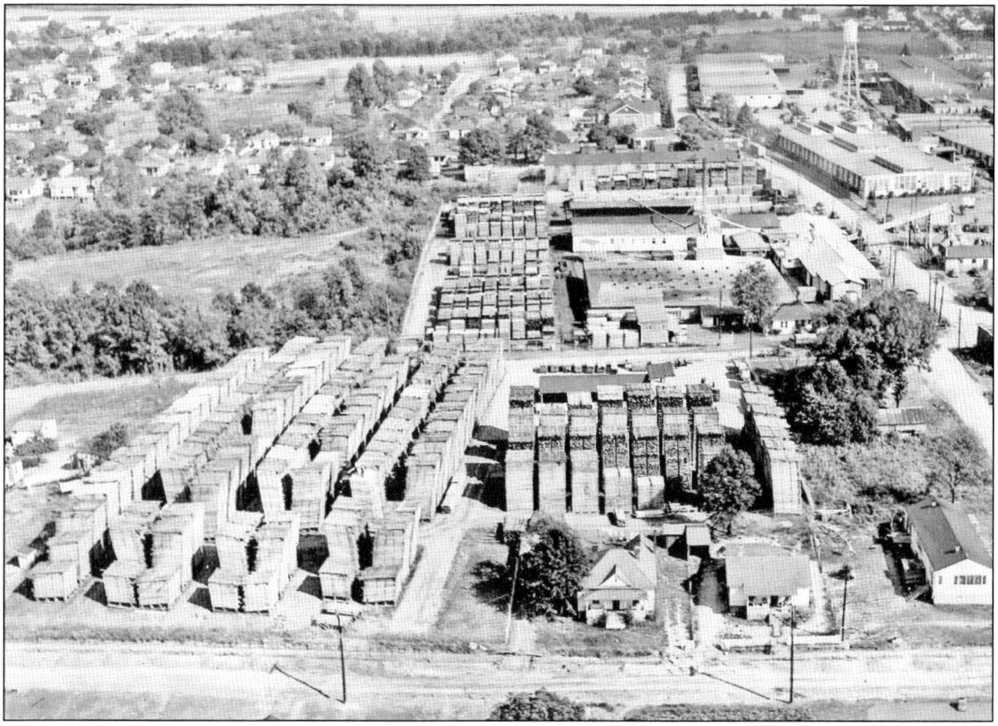

The Cherokee Flooring Company was a major business in east Burlington for many years, providing lumber products for the Alamance County area. The company was located at Graham and Queen Ann Streets. This photograph is from the 1950s. Burlington Mills is located at top right in the photograph, and the mill village is across the top.

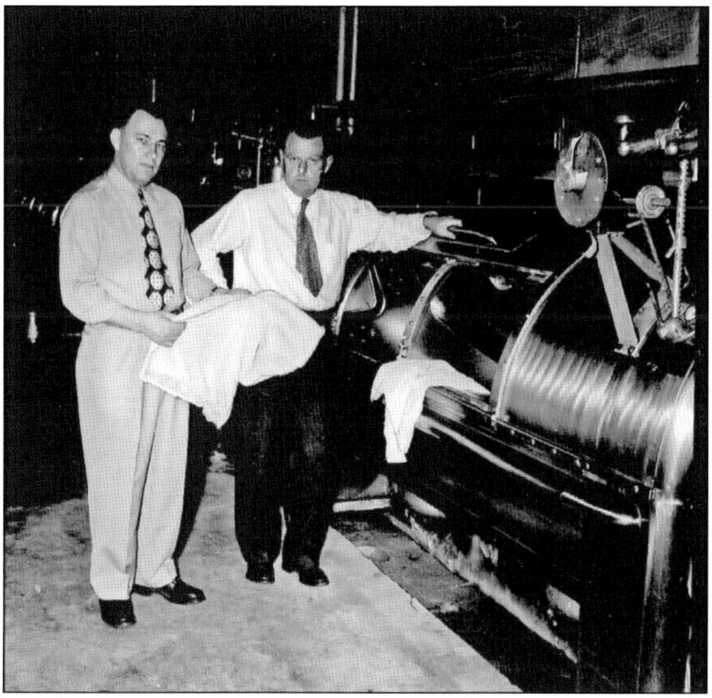

Jesse Kingsland (left) and Wilton Lane were pioneers in the laundry and dry-cleaning business in Burlington. Lane owned Alamance Laundry, which was located for many years in downtown Burlington at Main and Morehead Streets, and Kingsland directed the operations. The laundry was one of the earliest establishments to have a drive-through window.

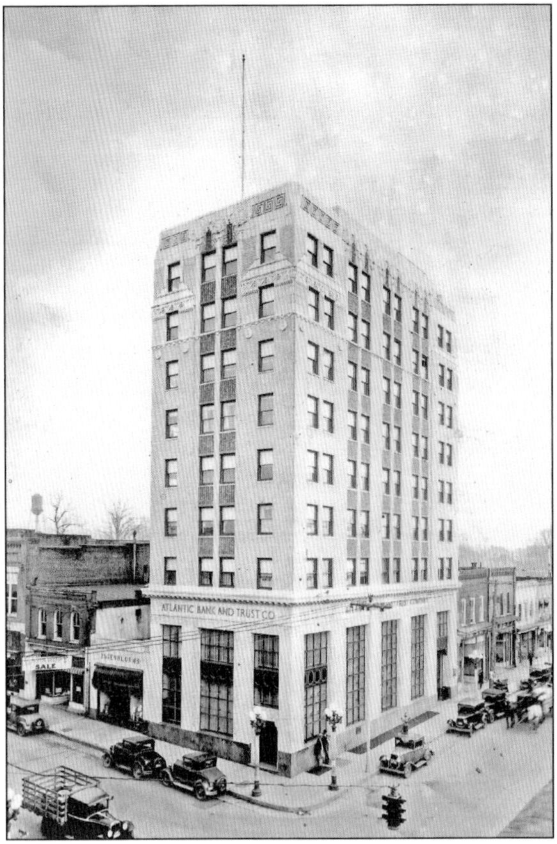

Burlington's tallest building was constructed in 1929 for the Atlantic Bank and Trust Company. Greensboro architect Charles C. Hartmann designed the building in the art deco style. Hartmann also designed the Alamance Hotel, which was built in 1925. The bank tower has been home to several banks, but LabCorp now occupies this building. One floor has been left in its original 1929 state with the architectural plans displayed in frames.

Roy's Bowling Center was a familiar landmark in Burlington in the 1950s and 1960s. For many years, the center was a favorite meeting spot for teenagers, and many young men picked up extra money by working as pin boys, setting up the pins before the era of automatic pin machines. This building at Church and Andrews Streets was torn down during the redevelopment era of the 1970s.

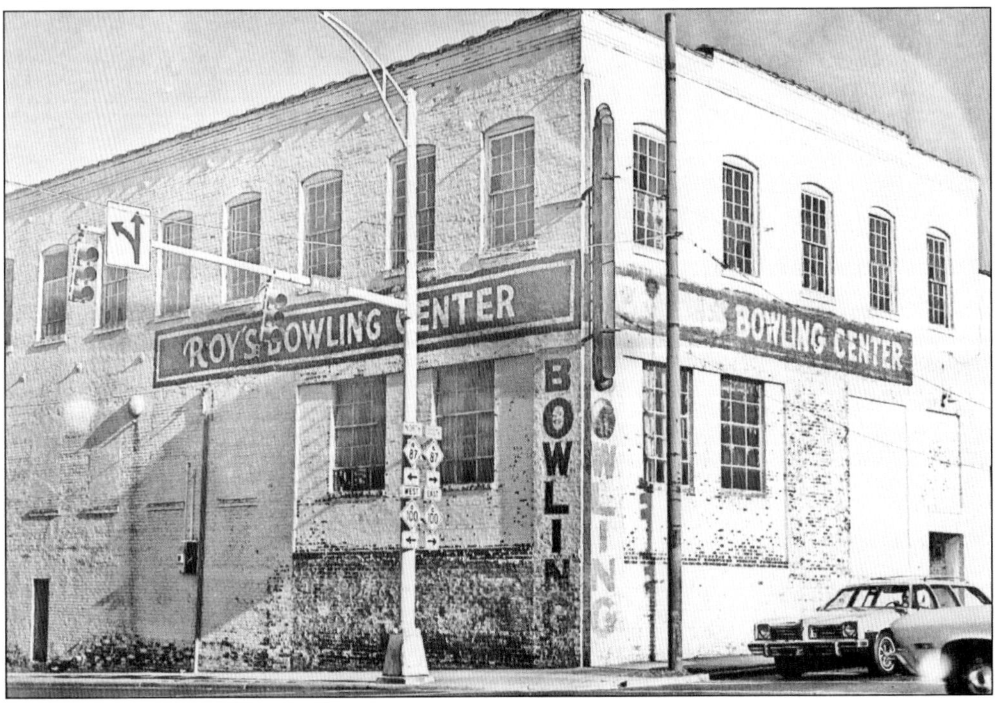

Members of the chamber of commerce decided Burlington needed a new and modern hotel in the early 1920s. They raised money to build the Alamance Hotel at South Main Street and Maple Avenue. The hotel not only provided bedrooms, but also had elegant ballroom space and dining facilities for local meetings and convention groups. It closed in 1974 but later reopened as a residence for the disabled and elderly.

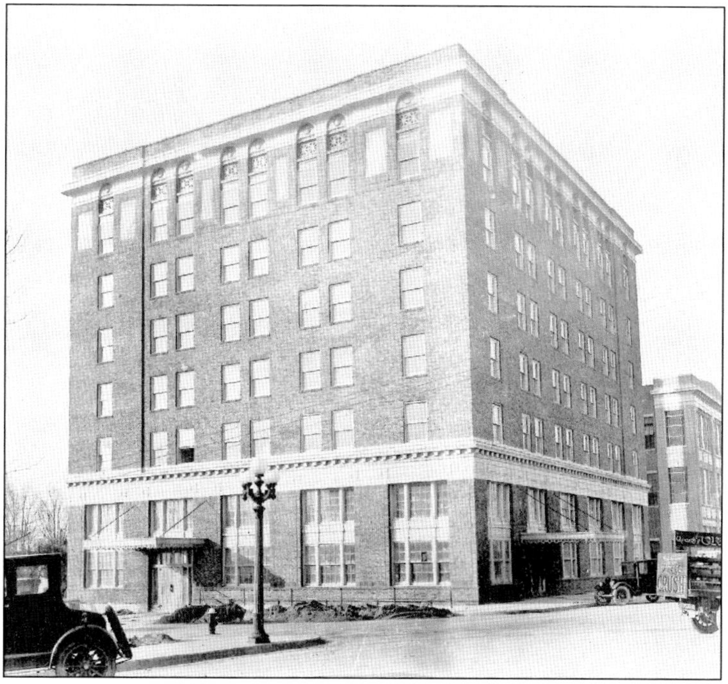

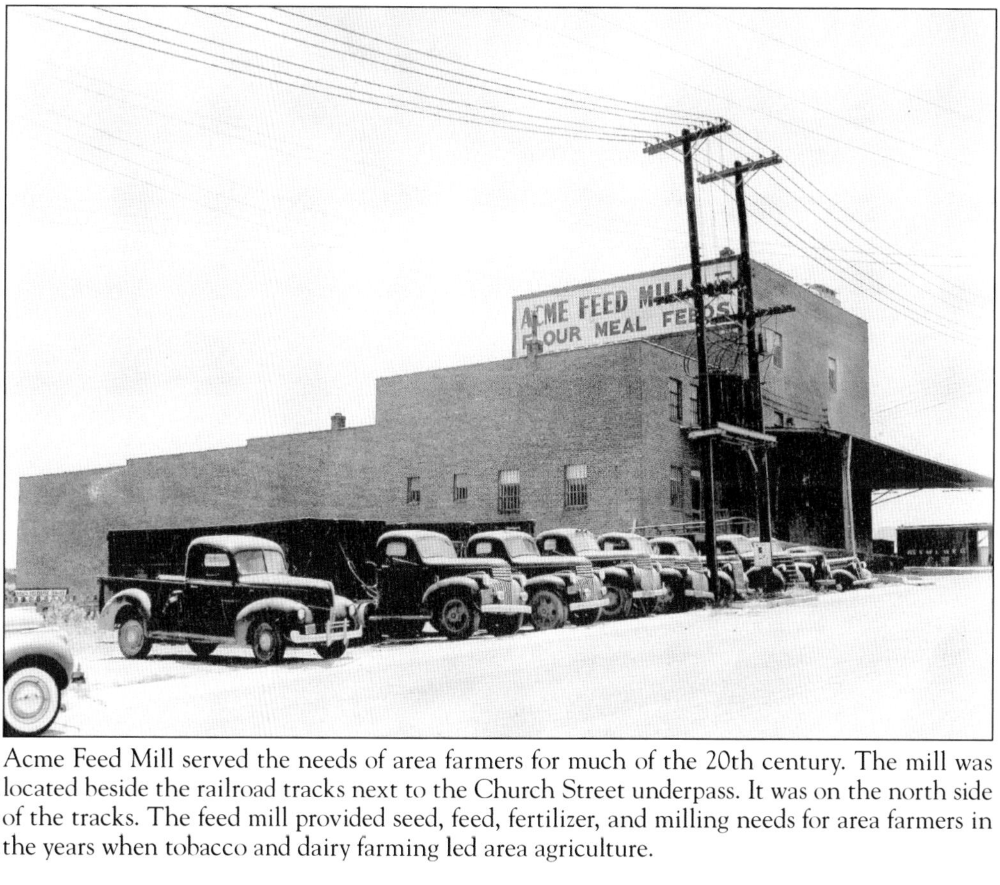

Acme Feed Mill served the needs of area farmers for much of the 20th century. The mill was located beside the railroad tracks next to the Church Street underpass. It was on the north side of the tracks. The feed mill provided seed, feed, fertilizer, and milling needs for area farmers in the years when tobacco and dairy farming led area agriculture.

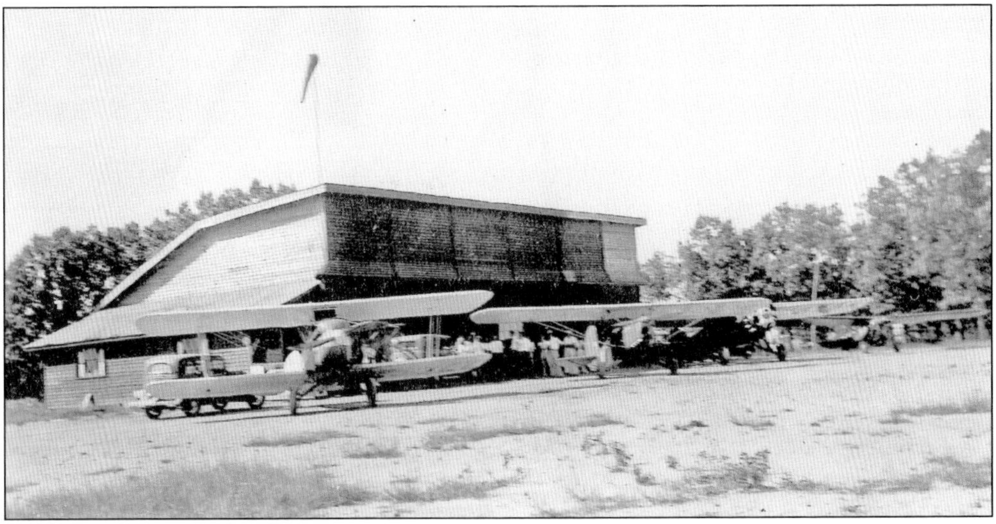

Before World War II, Dover Fogleman operated Huffman Field between Burlington and Haw River, a location now occupied by Wal-Mart Stores, Inc. In 1942, the federal government took the airport as a test site when Fairchild Aircraft moved into the old rayon plant to build training airplanes for the U.S. Army Air Corps. Huffman Field moved near Alamance, site the present Burlington-Alamance County airport operation. (Courtesy of Alamance County Area Chamber of Commerce.)

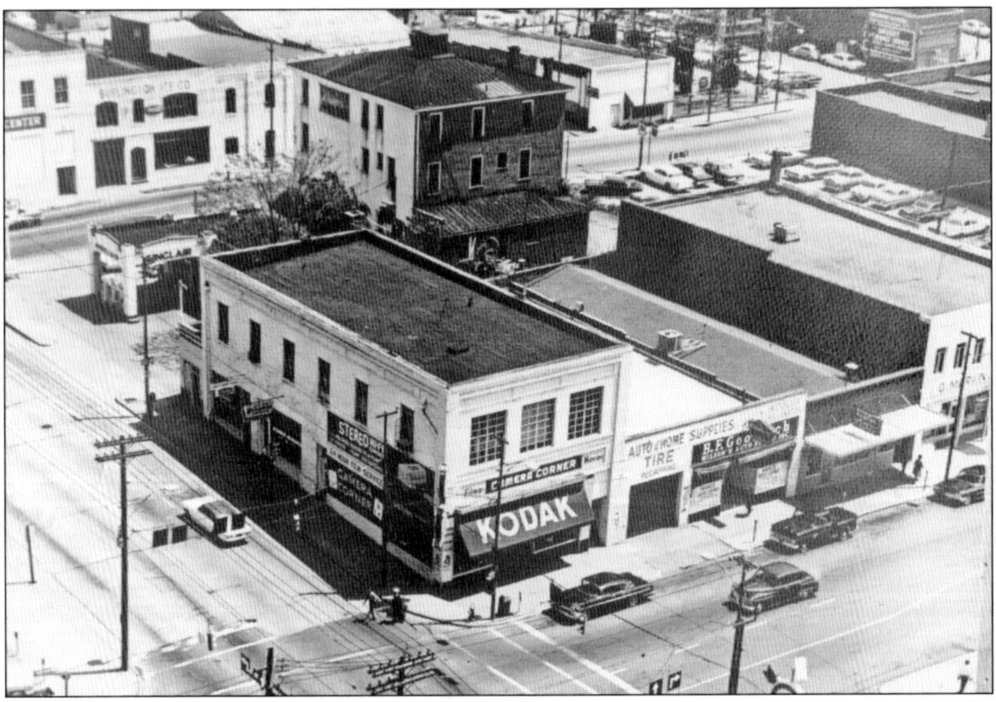

Camera Corner was located at Front and Church Streets when this photograph was made in the 1950s. Dick and Millie Thomas started the little camera store and soda shop, which grew into a major camera and electronics business in Burlington. The store was moved in the 1970s to South Church Street at Gurney Street, where it continues as a part of the area business community. (Courtesy of the Camera Corner.)

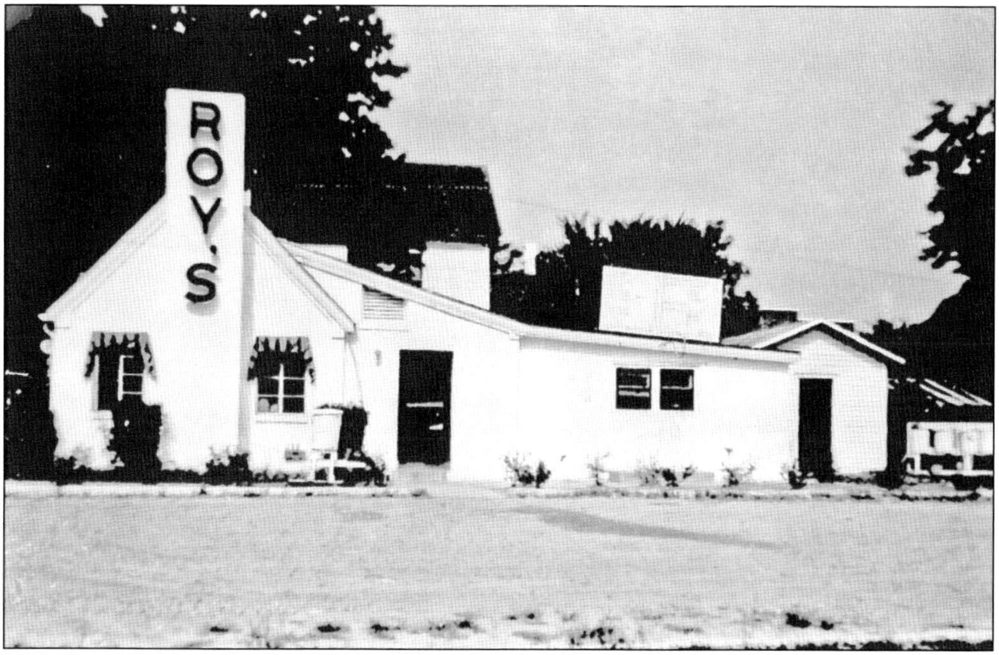

Roy's Drive-In was one of the early local drive-in restaurants. The restaurant was located on South Church Street and was a favorite of the teenage crowd for several years in the 1940s and later. Steve Douglas built the site as the Douglas House. After Douglas died in an airplane crash, the drive-in was sold to Roy Pinion. Another owner later made it the DoNut Shop and Grille.

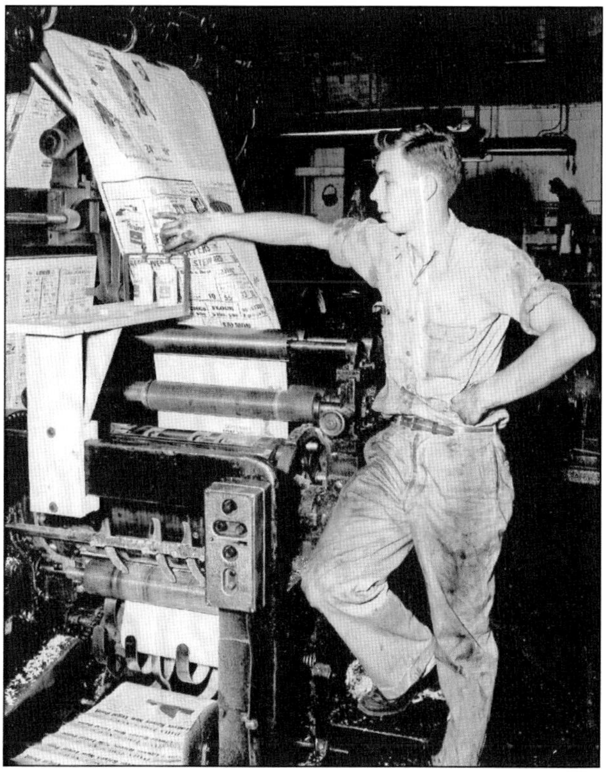

Dan Boswell adjusts the newsprint as it roars off the press at the *Times-News* in the 1950s. The newspaper was founded in 1887 and continues operations as Alamance County's only daily newspaper. The business has been on South Main Street since 1949. It is one of Burlington's oldest businesses, having been started in the same year in which the town's name was changed to Burlington from Company Shops.

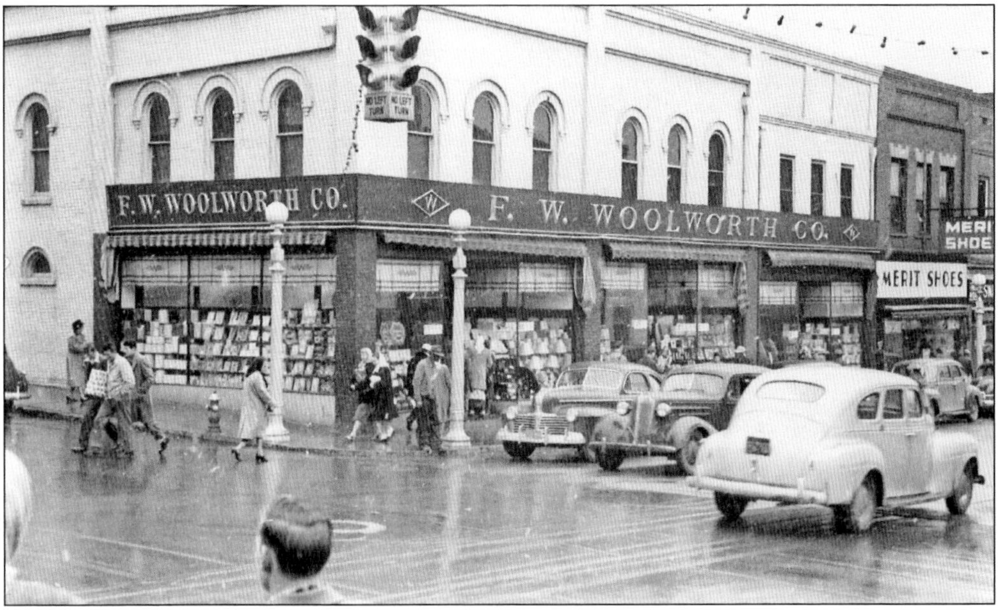

One of the most familiar sights in downtown Burlington for several decades was the Woolworth corner of Main and Davis Streets. Woolworth was one of three 5- and 10-cent stores in the city at the time. Rose's and McClellan's both operated on Main Street in the block just north of Woolworth. Woolworth's lunch counter was a favorite downtown lunch spot for many years.

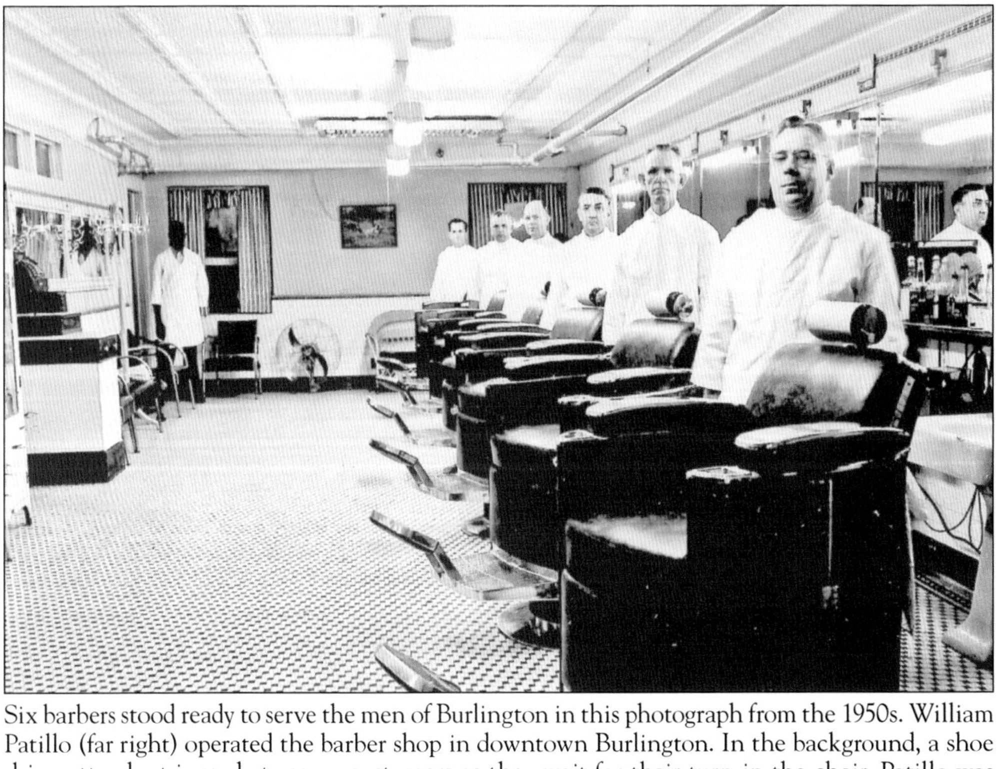

Six barbers stood ready to serve the men of Burlington in this photograph from the 1950s. William Patillo (far right) operated the barber shop in downtown Burlington. In the background, a shoe shine attendant is ready to serve customers as they wait for their turn in the chair. Patillo was well known in the community and plied his barbering trade for several decades.

C. B. Ellis was one of Burlington's best-known merchants throughout its early history. He opened a shop to sell sewing machines before 1900. He later moved into the music business, and the C. B. Ellis Music Company became a fixture in the business community, selling instruments as well as sheet music, records, and other music materials. Ellis worked in his store until he was in his late 80s.

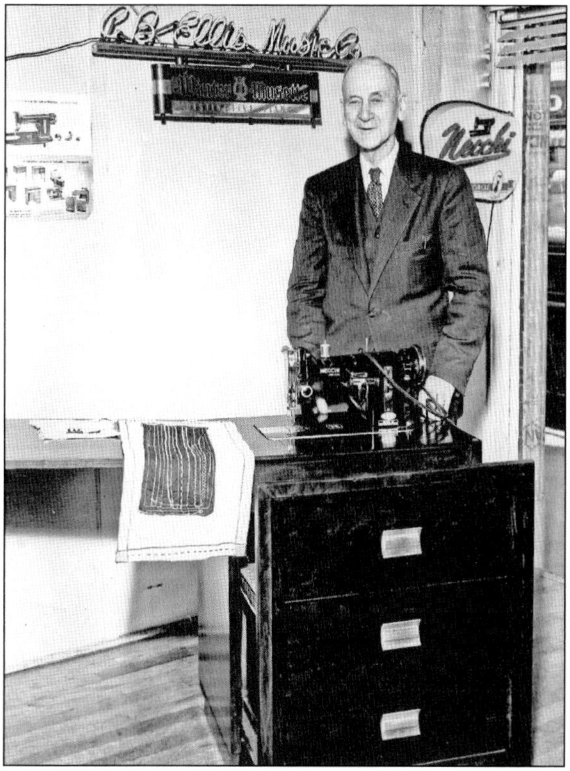

The Western Electric Company came to Burlington after World War II, occupying the property used during the war by Fairchild Aircraft. Western Electric grew to be one of Alamance County's leading employers, with more than 3,000 people working there by the early 1970s. At first, telephone equipment was made there, but later much of the company's production was for the government. (Courtesy of the Alamance County Area Chamber of Commerce.)

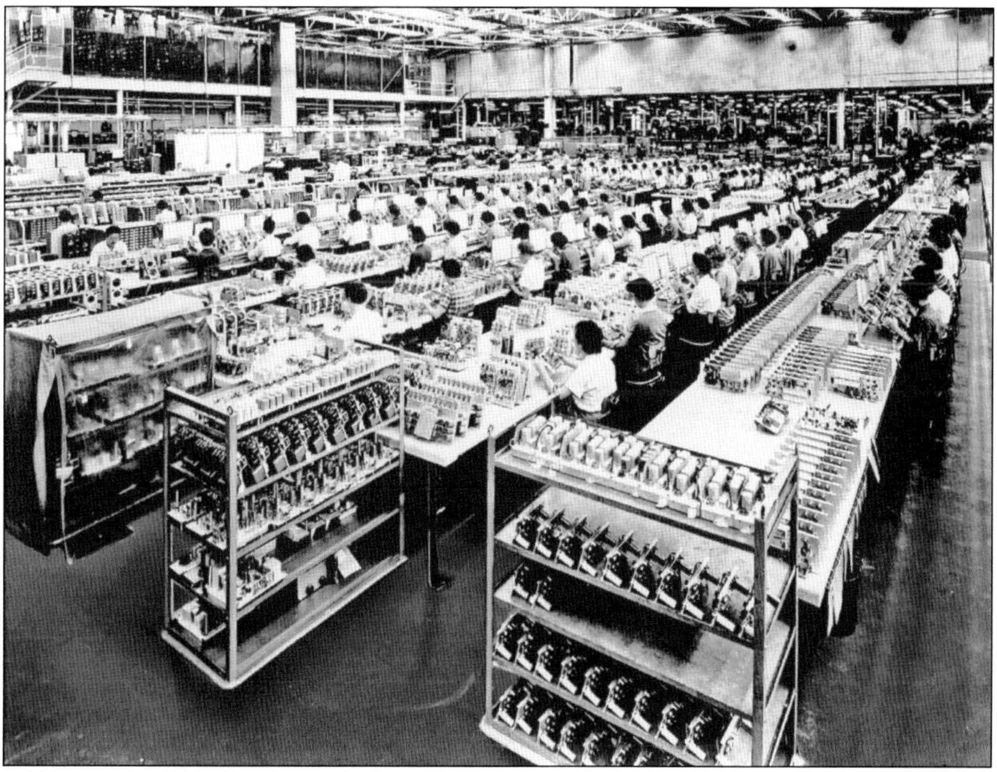

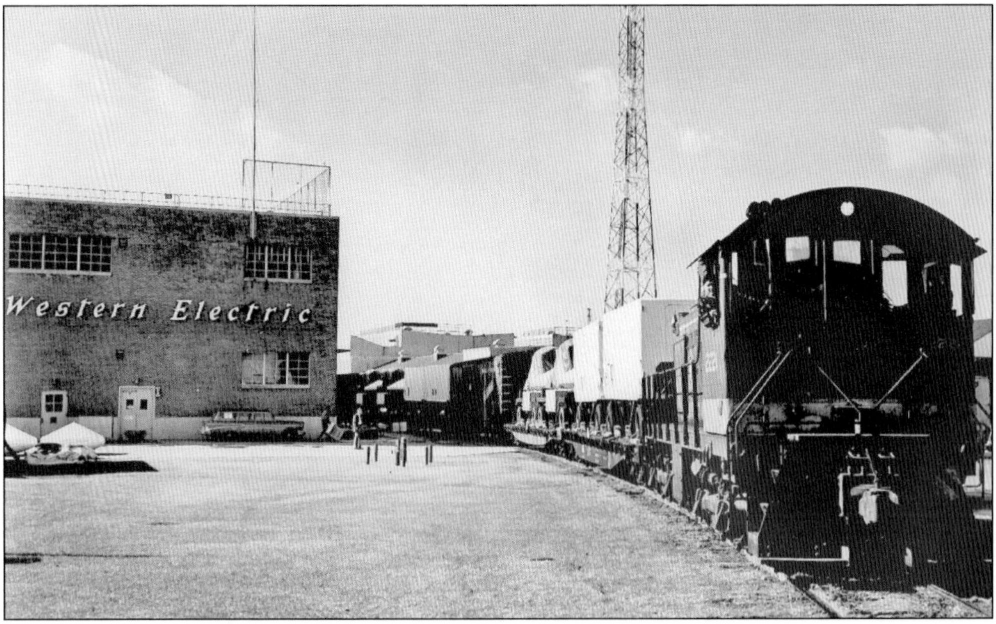

A train leaves the Western Electric Company plant with equipment for the nation's military forces. The company made components for the Nike antimissile system, and it became known as the Tarheel Army Missile Plant. When the United States entered a treaty with the Soviet Union reducing missiles and antimissile systems, work at the plant was severely curtailed. The plant later became a part of AT&T and eventually closed in the 1990s.

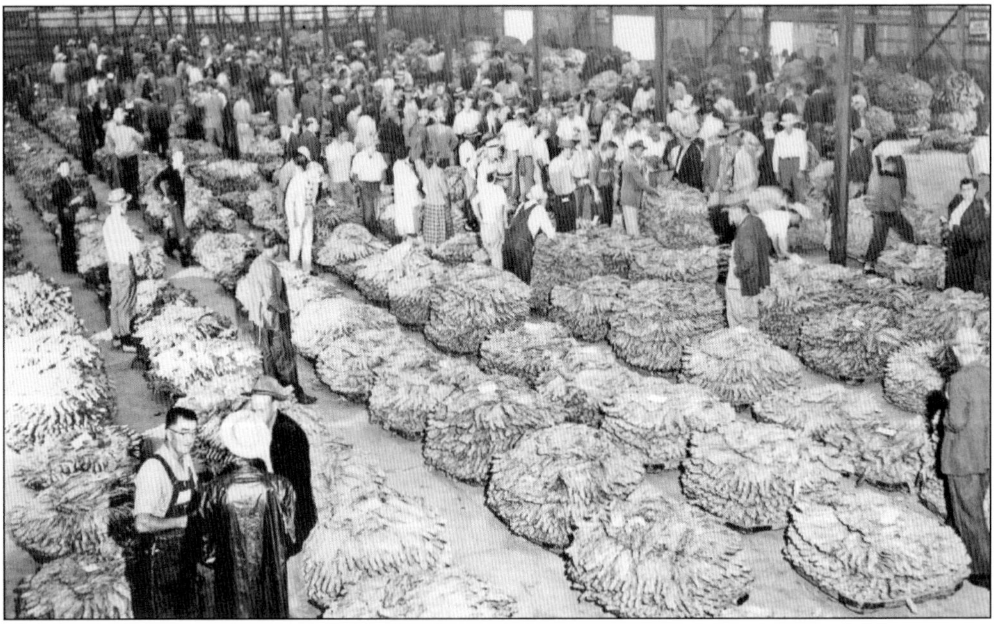

Tobacco was once king of Alamance County agriculture, and Burlington was a major market for many years. Several warehouses operated in Burlington daily throughout the tobacco season. This is a warehouse on sale day in the 1960s. Sale day was a once-a-year payday for area tobacco growers, and the area economy had a major gain every summer, when much of the money was spent in the Burlington area.

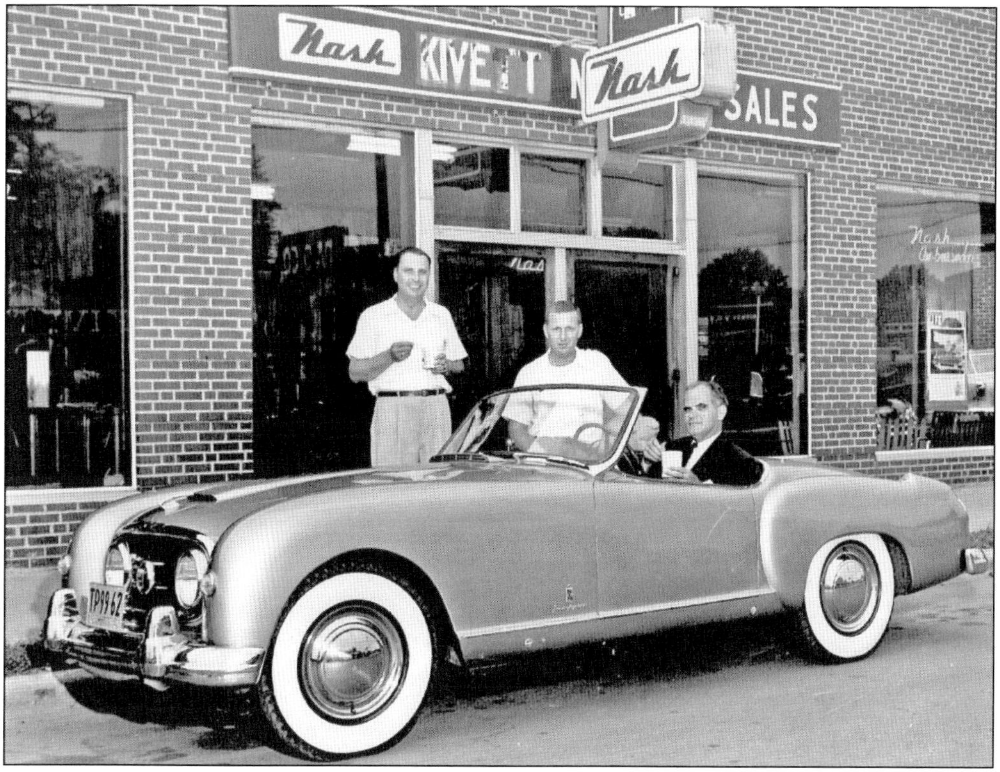

Newspaper and communications executive Roy Park (right) helped promote Melville Dairy ice cream and Nash automobiles in a promotion in the 1950s. George Kivett (left) operated Kivett Nash Sales, and Otis Lackey (center) was an official with Melville Dairy. Melville Dairy began in 1925 and operated on Worth Street. For many years, the dairy's trucks provided front door delivery for customers every morning.

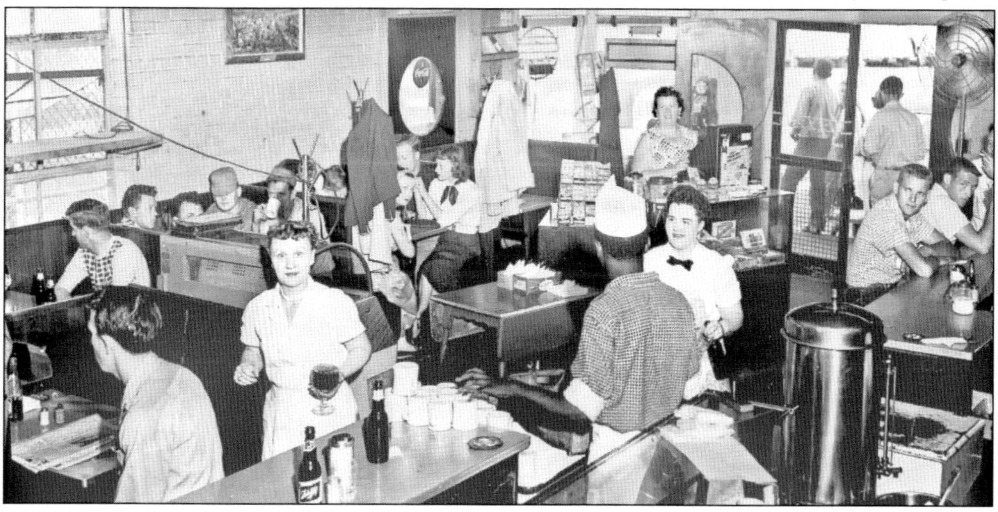
This is the interior of the S and M Café in 1953. It was a busy restaurant outside the gate of the Western Electric Company. The café was operated by S. R. "Shinny" Mansfield. Mansfield's wife, Lavona, is at the cash register. Nick Philson also owned the restaurant at one time, but for many years, it has been the home of the Western Steak House, one of Burlington's most popular restaurants, owned by Johnny Bakatasias.

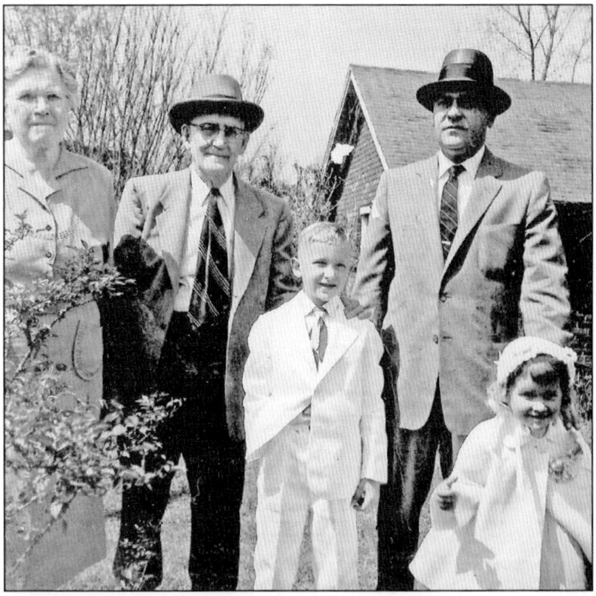

J. R. Qualls was a pioneer in Burlington's movie industry, owning several theaters and bringing the first talking movie to the city. He is pictured (center) with his family in 1956. His wife, Jessie is at left, and E. C. Qualls Jr. is at far right. Ruffin Qualls II and sister Lorah Louise Qualls are in front. E. C. Qualls Jr. managed the State Theater for many years. (Courtesy of Ruffin Qualls II.)

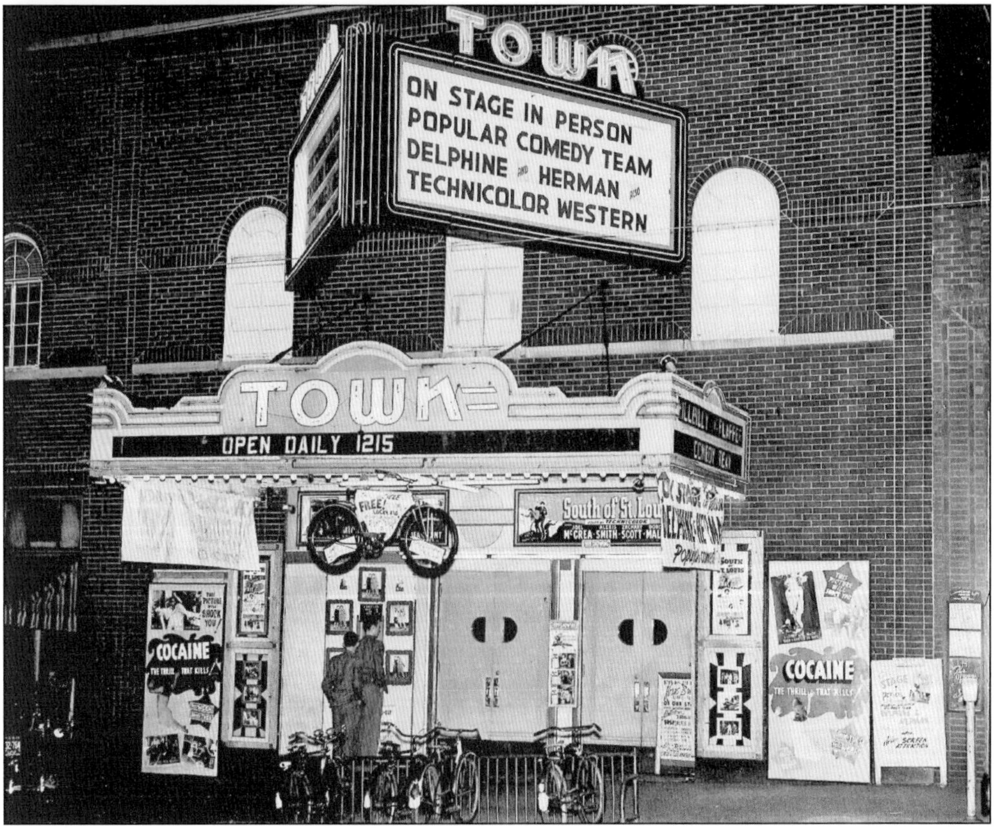

The Town Theater was one of four movie houses in Burlington when downtown was the main business district. The theater had been known as the Alamance in earlier years, and older films were shown at the location. The Town Theater was on West Front Street between Main and Worth Streets. Frank Bruton operated the theater for several years. (Courtesy of Tommy Bruton.)

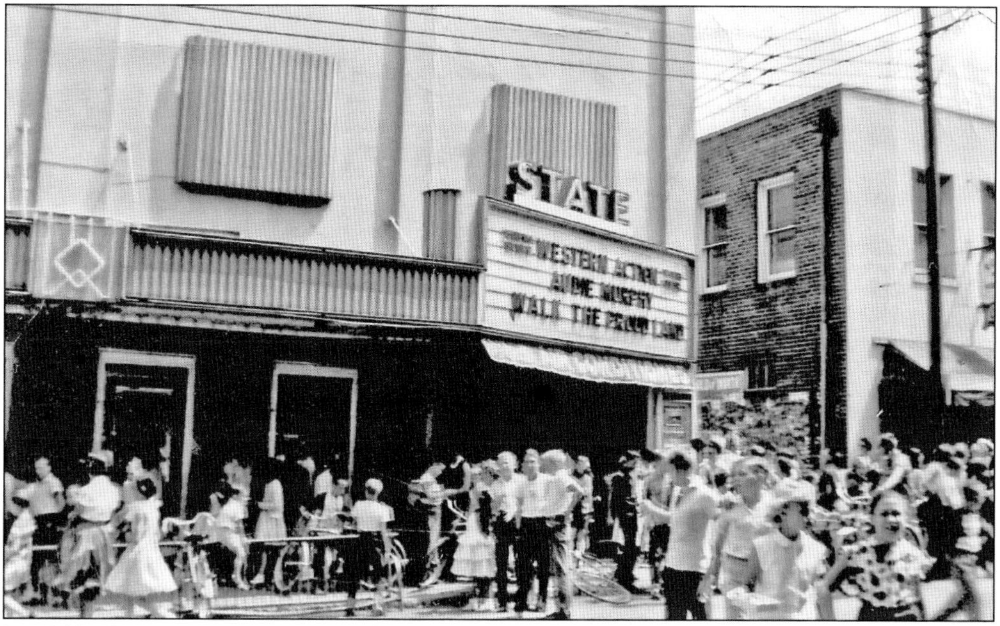

In 1956, "Western Action" was on the marquee of the State Theater on this day. Kids clamored to see an Audie Murphy movie. The Qualls family operated the theater for many years. It was on Andrews Street and showed first-run movies in competition with the Paramount. The theater was torn down as redevelopment eliminated Andrews Street and rerouted several downtown streets in the 1970s. (Courtesy of Tommy Bruton.)

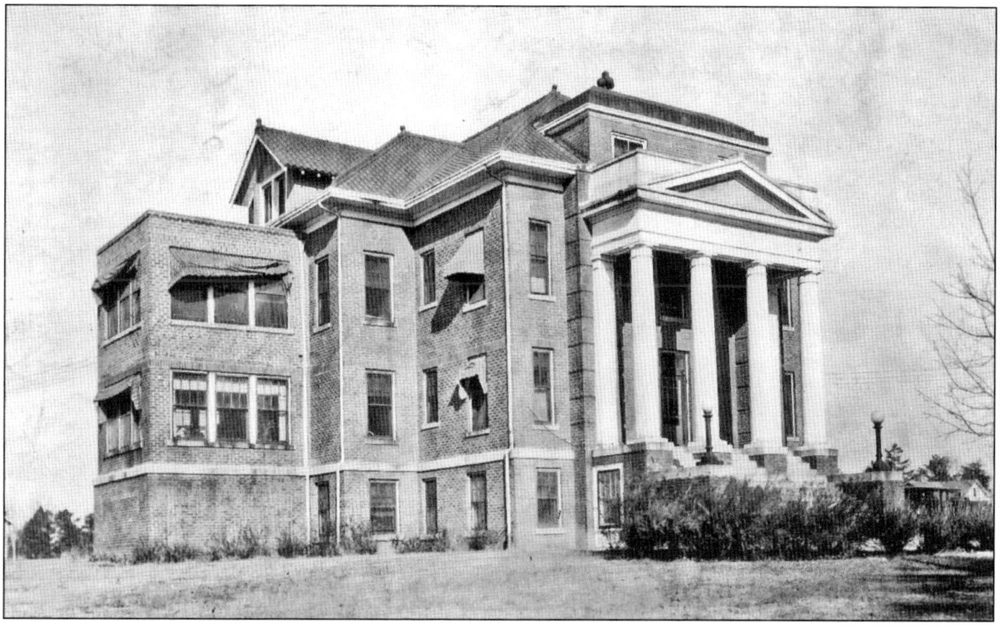

The Alamance General Hospital was built in 1916 and was first known as Rainey Hospital. It was the city's only major hospital until 1954, when the Alamance County Hospital was constructed. Alamance General, on Rainey Street in East Burlington, closed in 1961 when Alamance Memorial Hospital was opened. In later years, Alamance County and Alamance Memorial joined to form the Alamance Regional Medical Center.

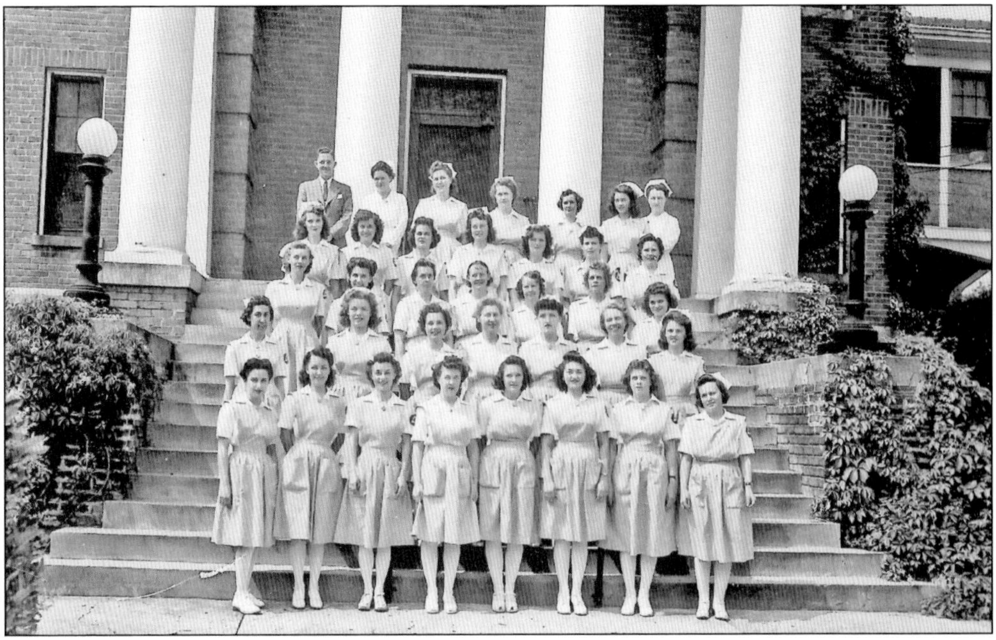

This group poses on the steps of the Alamance General Hospital on Rainey Street. The photograph is likely from the 1950s and appears to be a class of nursing students. The two doctors who headed the hospital's operation for many years were Dr. George Carrington and Dr. Ralph Brooks. Both lived across the street from the hospital. This hospital operated from 1916 to 1961.

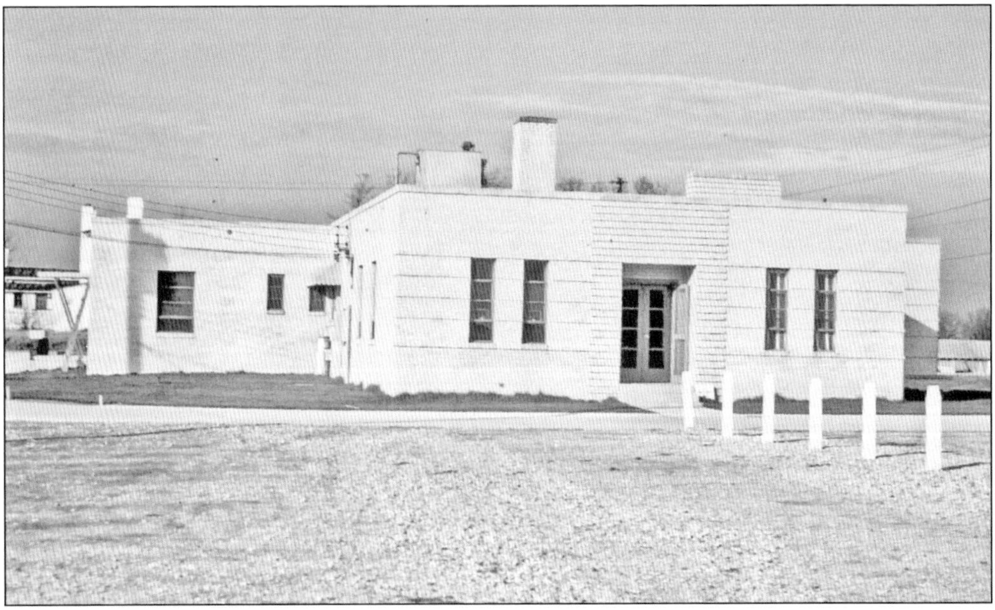

The Kernodle Clinic is a major Burlington medical center with several locations. In 1949, two brothers, Dr. Harold Kernodle Sr. and Dr. Charlie Kernodle, and a cousin, Dr. John Robert Kernodle, joined their Burlington medical practices to form the Kernodle Clinic. This is an early photograph of the first location on Graham-Hopedale Road. This became the Kernodle Clinic Easttown when a new clinic opened at the Alamance Regional Medical Center. (Courtesy of Kernodle Clinic.)

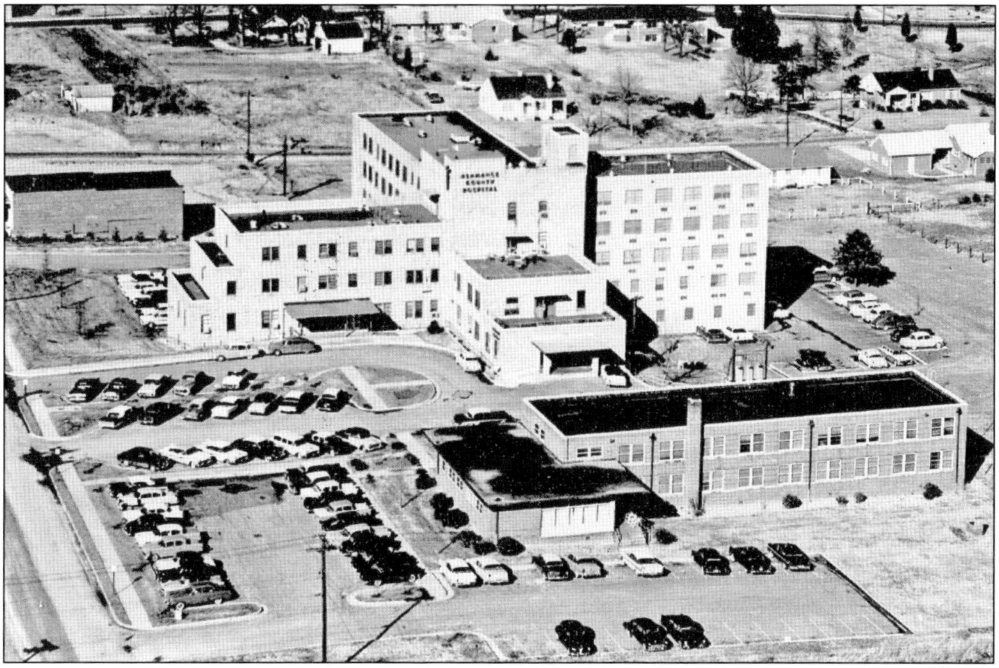

The Alamance County Hospital was built on Graham-Hopedale Road in 1954. It was a county-related facility and was the second built in Burlington, following the Alamance General Hospital. A local board of directors led the hospital, headed for many years by B. Everett Jordan, later a United States senator. The Alamance County Hospital later joined with Memorial Hospital to form the Alamance Regional Medical Center. (Courtesy of the Alamance County Area Chamber of Commerce.)

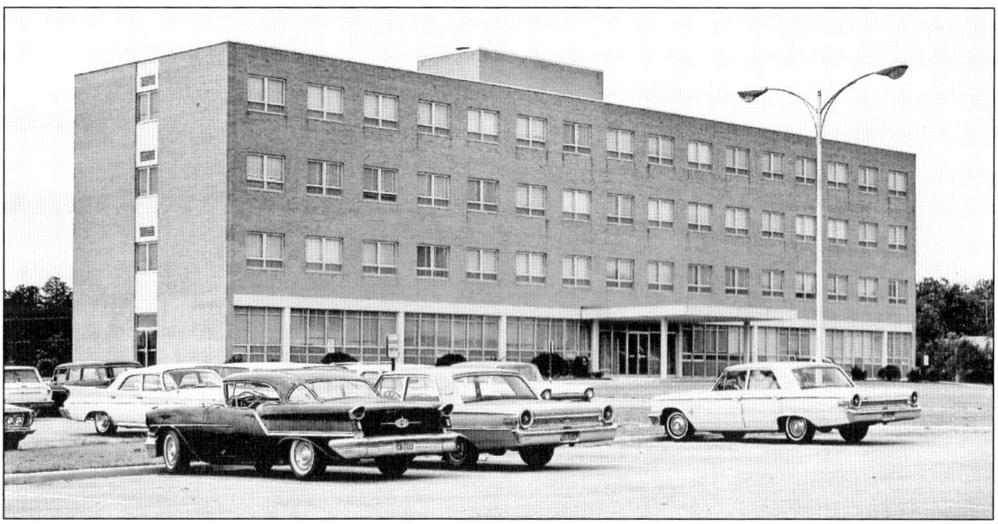

In 1961, the Alamance Memorial Hospital replaced the old Alamance General Hospital, which had been in operation since 1916. Hosiery executive Ralph M. Holt Sr. headed the board for the Alamance Memorial Hospital for many years. When the Alamance Memorial Hospital and the Alamance County Hospital joined to form the Alamance Regional Medical Center, Ralph M. Holt Jr. continued his father's work by serving as board cochair with Earl Pardue. (Courtesy of the Alamance County Area Chamber of Commerce.)

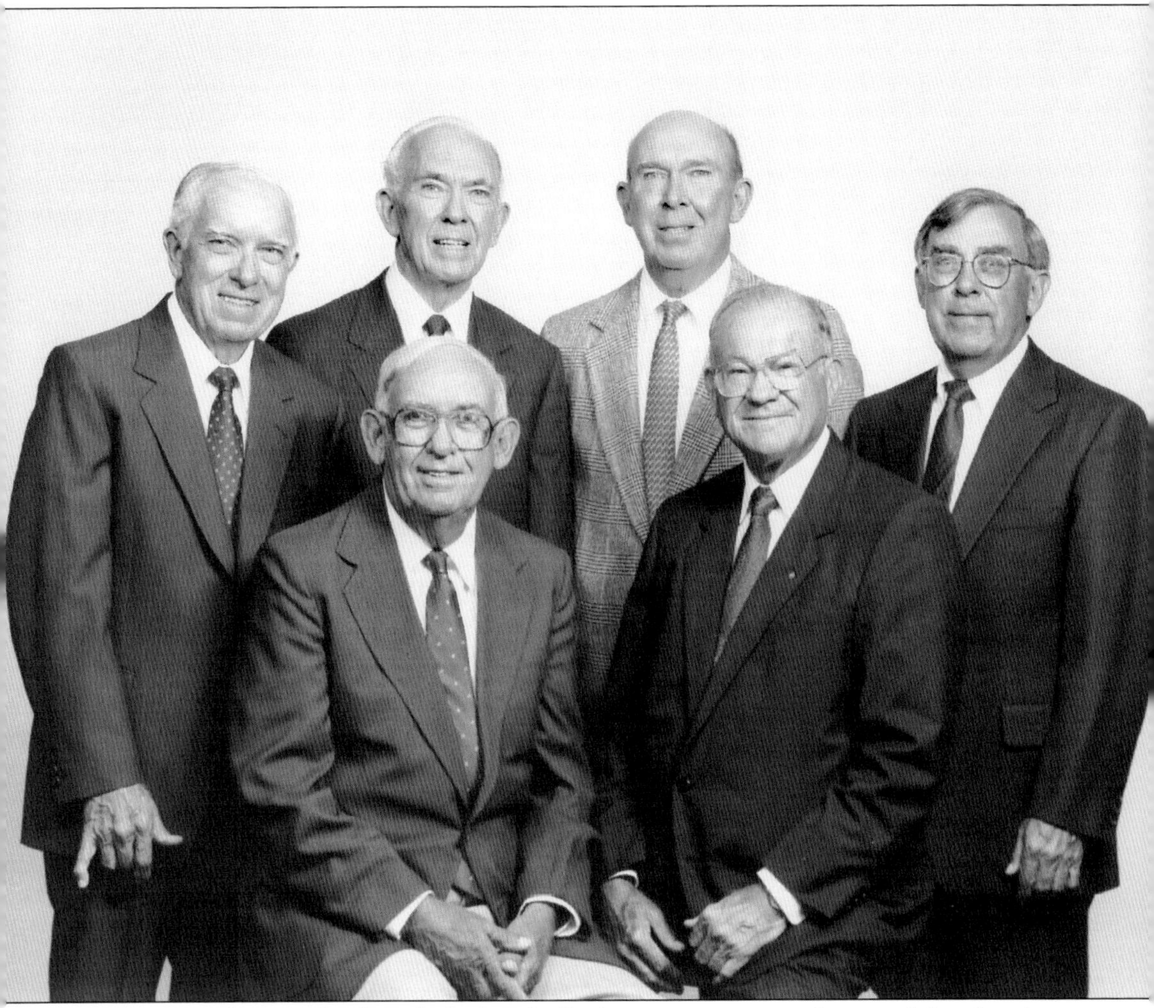

The Kernodle name has been linked to the Burlington community for several decades. At one time, there were five brothers and a cousin who practiced medicine in Burlington. In 1949, two of the brothers, Harold Sr., Charlie, and their cousin John Robert, formed the Kernodle Clinic. Later G. Wallace Kernodle, Dwight Kernodle, and Donald Kernodle finished their medical education and practiced in Burlington as well. The Kernodle doctors are shown in this group photograph. Seated is Dr. Harold Kernodle Sr. (left) and Dr. John Robert Kernodle. Standing from left to right are Dr. Charlie Kernodle, Dr. G. Wallace Kernodle, Dr. Donald Kernodle, and Dr. Dwight Kernodle. The Kernodle Clinic today has 75,000 square feet of space adjacent to the Alamance Regional Medical Center, with other locations in east Burlington, Elon, and Mebane. (Photograph by Westbrook Studios; courtesy of Kernodle Clinic.)

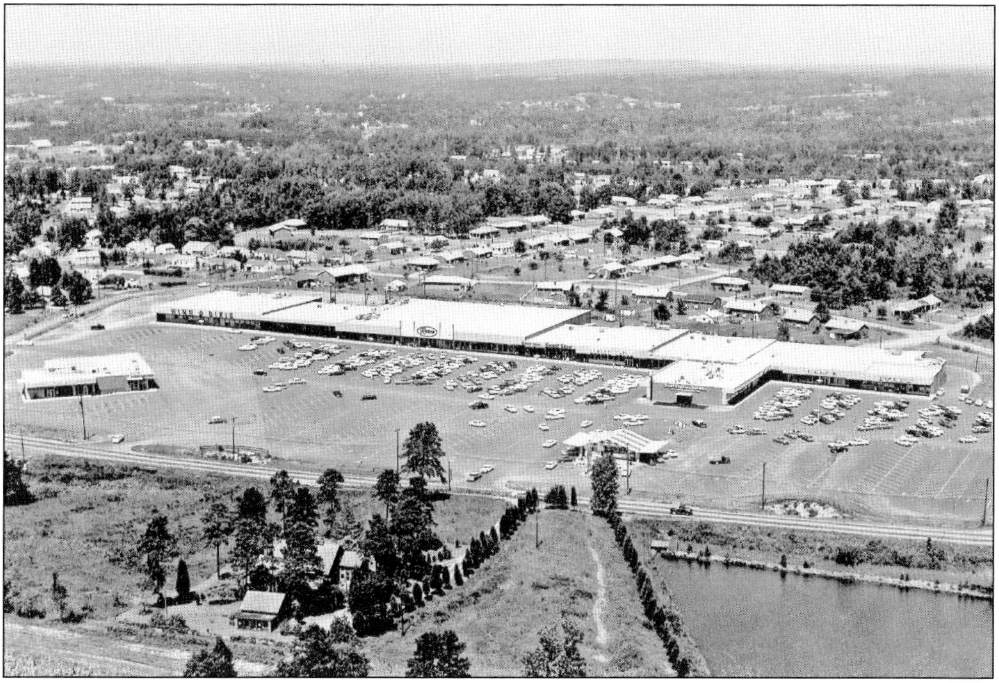

The Cum-Park Plaza was Alamance County's first shopping center. In 1963, Hugh M. Cummings and Carl Parks formed the plaza on North Church Street in east Burlington. One of the major tenants was Rose's 5 and 10 Store. For many years, Rose's had been downtown in a store opening on to three streets. Rose's was the first major business to leave downtown. (Courtesy of Alamance County Area Chamber of Commerce.)

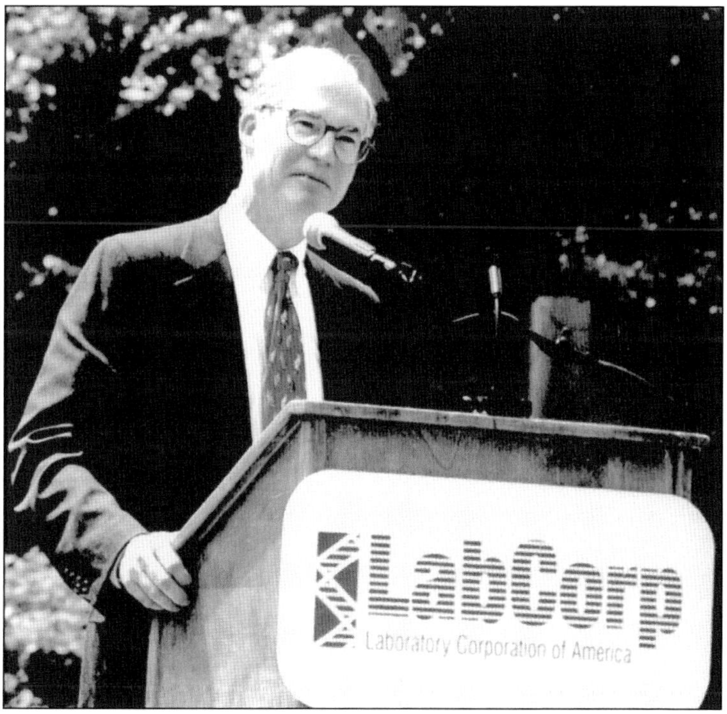

Dr. James Powell Jr., with brothers Thomas and John, formed a small medical testing laboratory in the building vacated by the Alamance General Hospital in 1969. The firm later became part of the Roche organization and finally a part of the Laboratory Corporation of America (LabCorp). Through Dr. James Powell's efforts, LabCorp established national headquarters in downtown Burlington and is now the major employer in the county. (Courtesy of Anne Powell.)

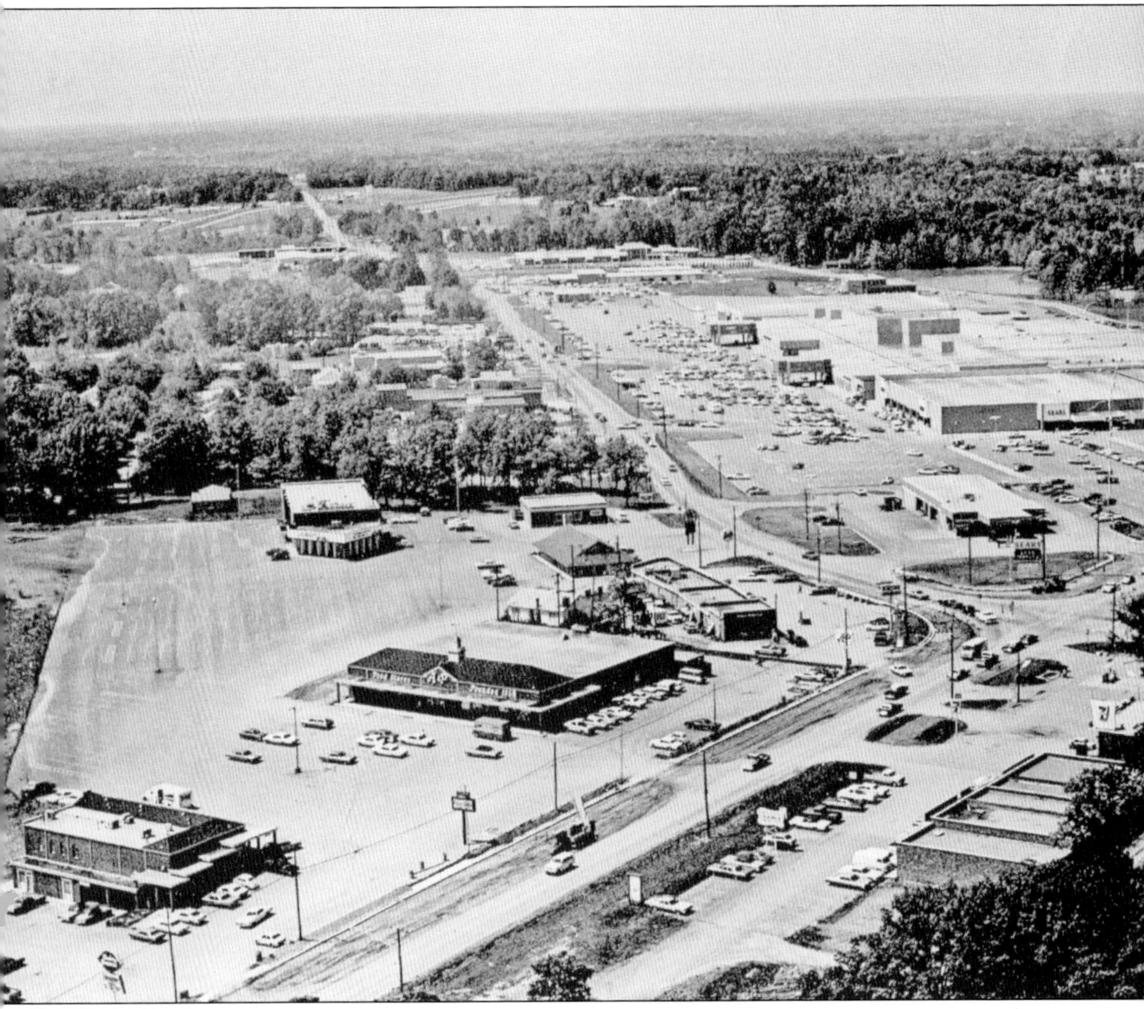

In 1969, one of the South's major shopping facilities opened on Huffman Mill Road in west Burlington. The Holly Hill Mall (at upper right) attracted four major anchors—the Belk-Beck Company; the Sears, Roebuck, and Company; the F. W. Woolworth Company; and the J. C. Penney Company. All four moved out of downtown Burlington, leaving a huge void in the downtown shopping community. This marked a significant change for the downtown community. The new mall acted as a magnet to new businesses along Huffman Mill Road. It quickly became a major business corridor, linking Burlington traffic to U.S. Interstate 85, a short distance south. The mall's big lineup of stores attracted shoppers from throughout the Piedmont region as well as from southern Virginia. Holly Hill went through ownership changes, and its name was changed first to the Colonial Mall and then to the Burlington Mall. In 2007, a new major shopping area, Alamance Crossing, opened south of the mall, and Belk and J. C. Penney moved to the new location, as did other smaller stores.

Seven

BURLINGTON'S STREETS, EVENTS, AND PEOPLE

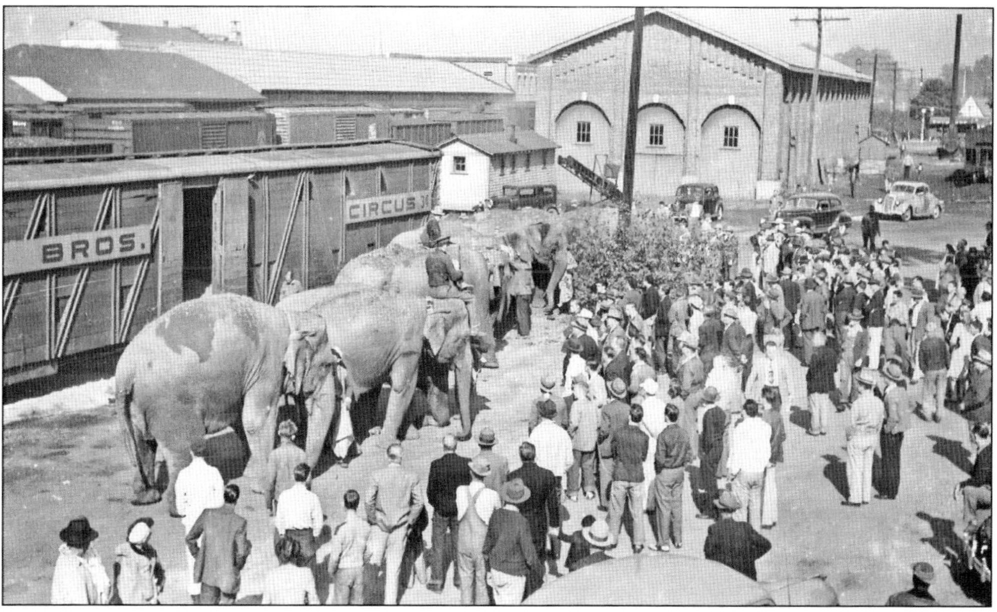

In this 1919 photograph, circus elephants were the big attraction in the railroad yard in Burlington. This was not a touring circus though. The elephants were a part of Burlington's own Heritage Brothers Circus. The local operation traveled the country and wintered in Burlington. The building in the background is the railroad engine house, built in 1856. In recent years, it became Burlington's passenger depot.

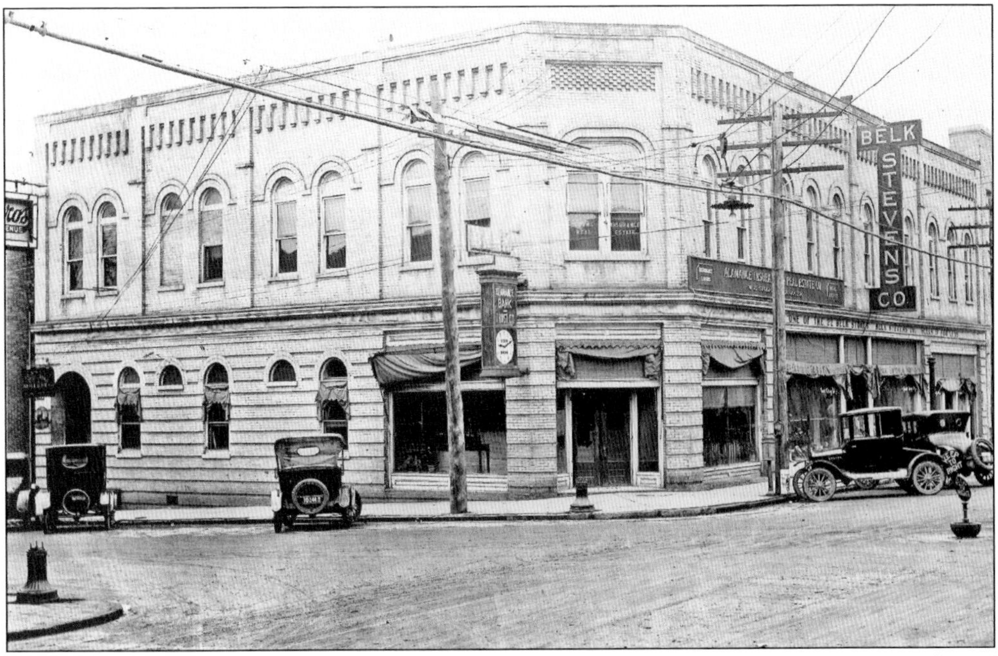

This building at Main and Davis Streets, pictured in the 1920s, has been home to a number of businesses over the years. In this photograph, a bank occupies the site, and around the corner is the Belk-Stevens Company, the forerunner of the Belk-Beck Company. The Belk-Beck Company later had a major store on this block with entrances on three streets. Raylass was the last occupant of the corner. (Courtesy of the Alamance County Area Chamber of Commerce.)

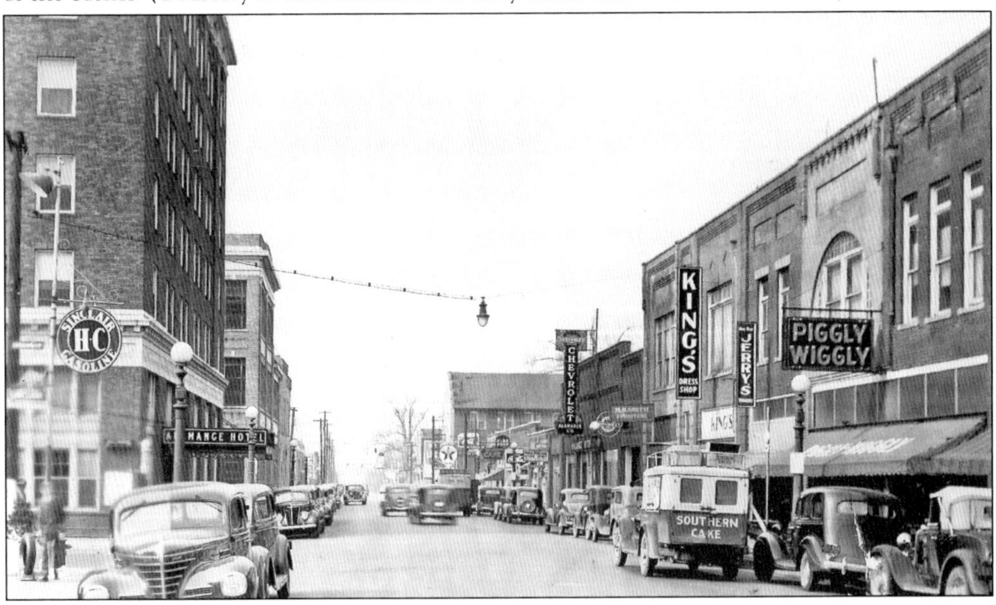

South Main Street at Maple Avenue in the 1930s was a busy business area. The Alamance Hotel is at left, and on the right is the Piggly Wiggly LLC, one of the early supermarkets in town. Down the street is Alamance Motors, the Chevrolet dealer in Burlington. In later years, all the buildings at right were demolished, and a bank occupied the entire site. (Courtesy of the Alamance County Area Chamber of Commerce.)

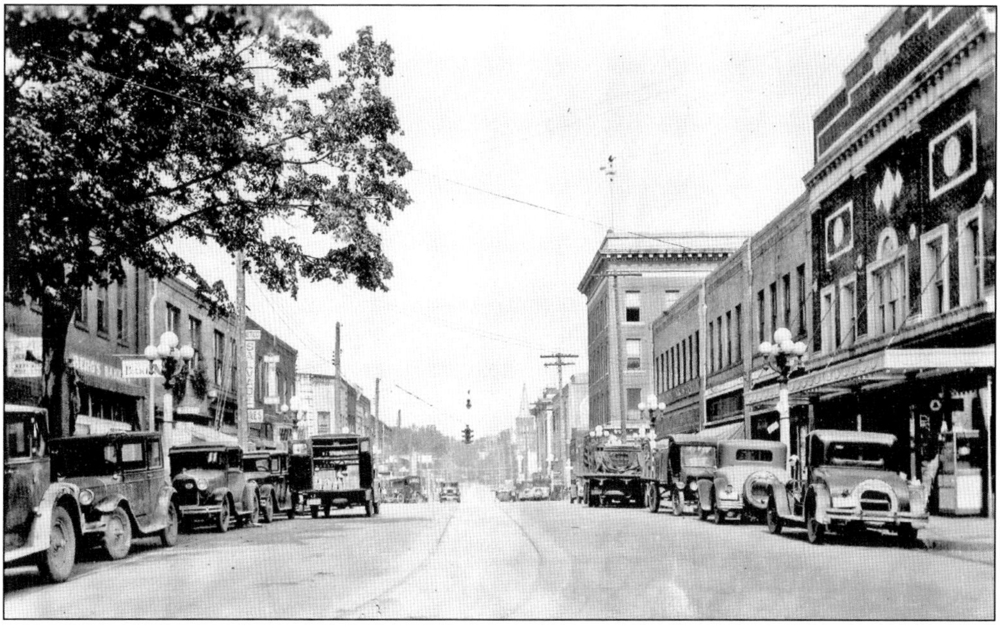

This photograph was made of the 100 block of East Front Street in 1934. The Paramount Theater is at far right, and the National Bank Building is at the corner of Main Street. Some of the first business buildings in the city were constructed along this street. The streetlights of clustered white globes were installed in 1921 and first lit at a huge downtown party.

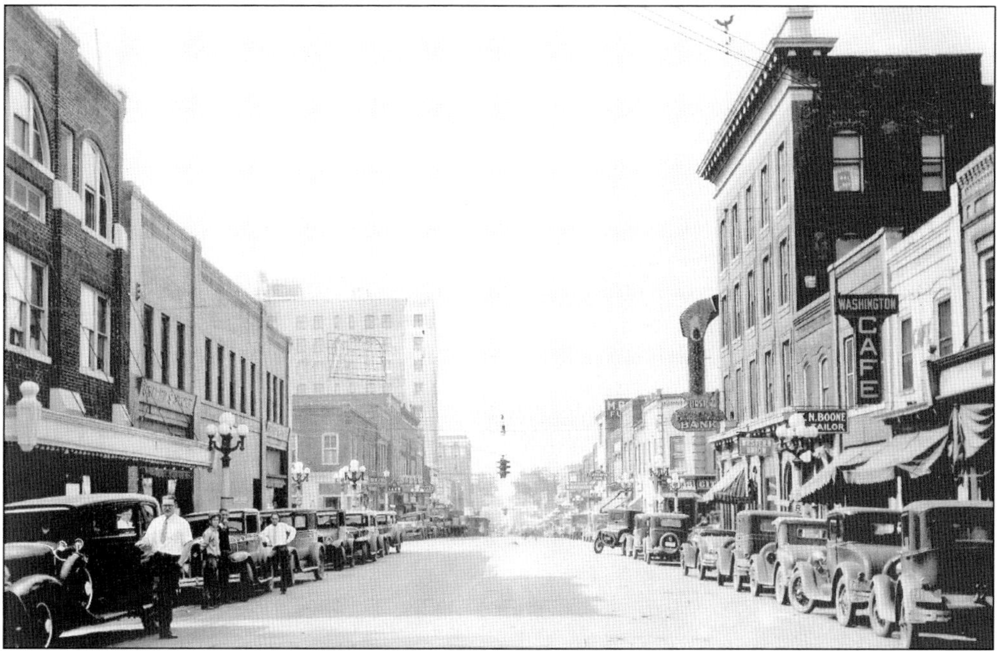

Downtown Burlington is seen on a summer afternoon in 1934. Main Street was filled with automobiles in front of businesses that are now memories. The Carolina Theater was at left, and the Washington Café is seen at right, along with T. N. Boone Tailors, Western Union, and the National Bank. All of this block at right and most of the one at left were demolished in the 1970s.

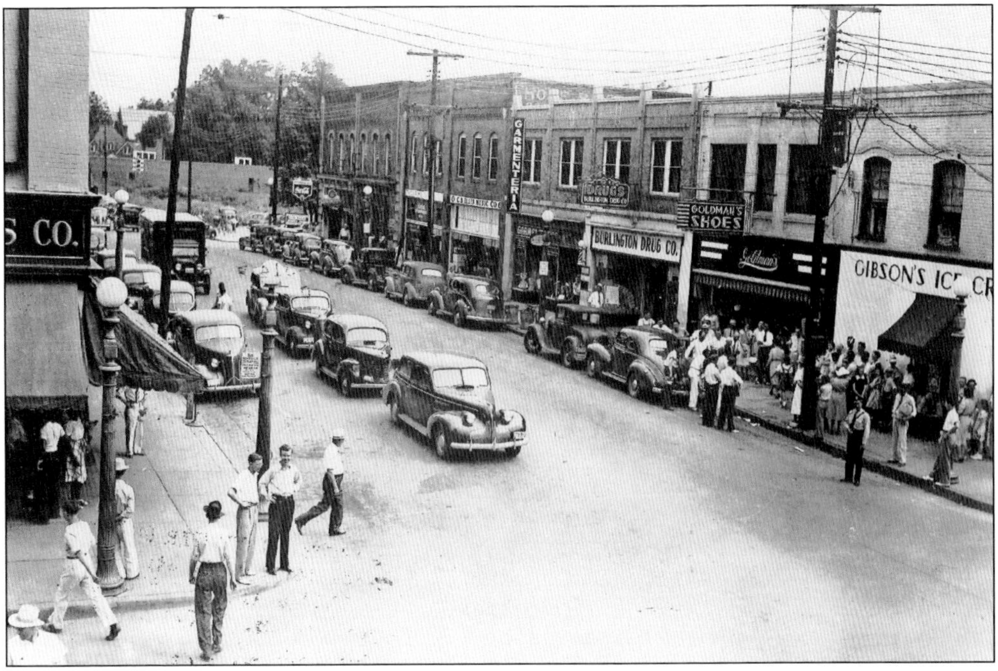

Front Street at Main Street was a busy intersection, especially on Saturdays. It was here that street preachers came every week for years to proclaim the gospel. There is a group listening to one of those preachers at right in front of Gibson's Ice Cream Shop. That building later would be the home of Biller's Jewelry Store for several decades.

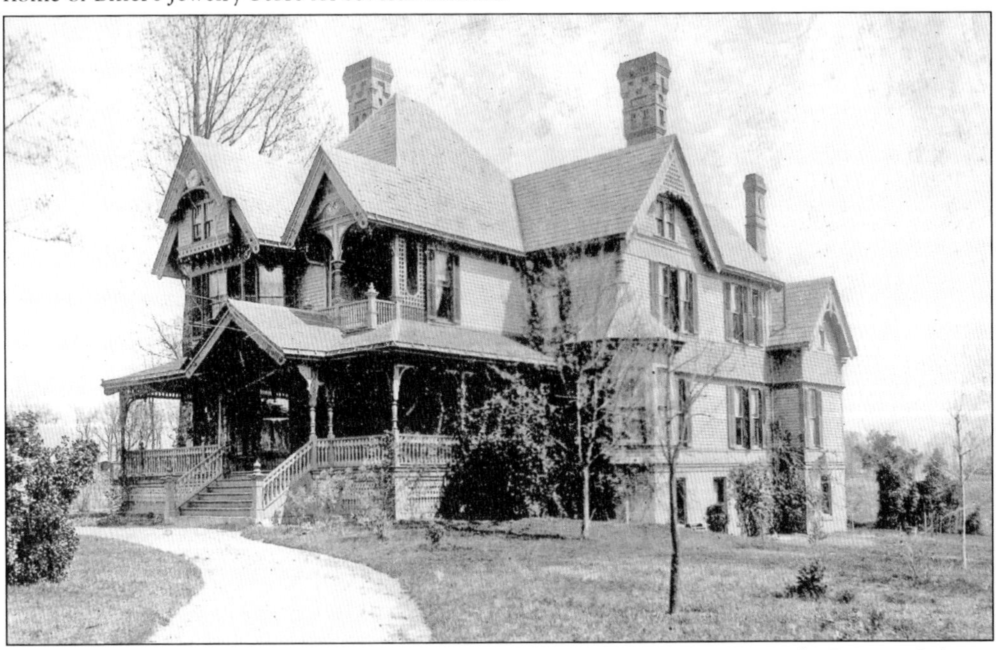

This beautiful home was built by John Q. Gant, the founder of Glen Raven Mills. Bonnie Oaks, as it was named, was in a block next to the downtown business area. East Front Street runs through the property today. The house was on land bound by Spring and East Davis Streets, Webb Avenue, and Lexington Avenue. (Courtesy of Edmund Gant.)

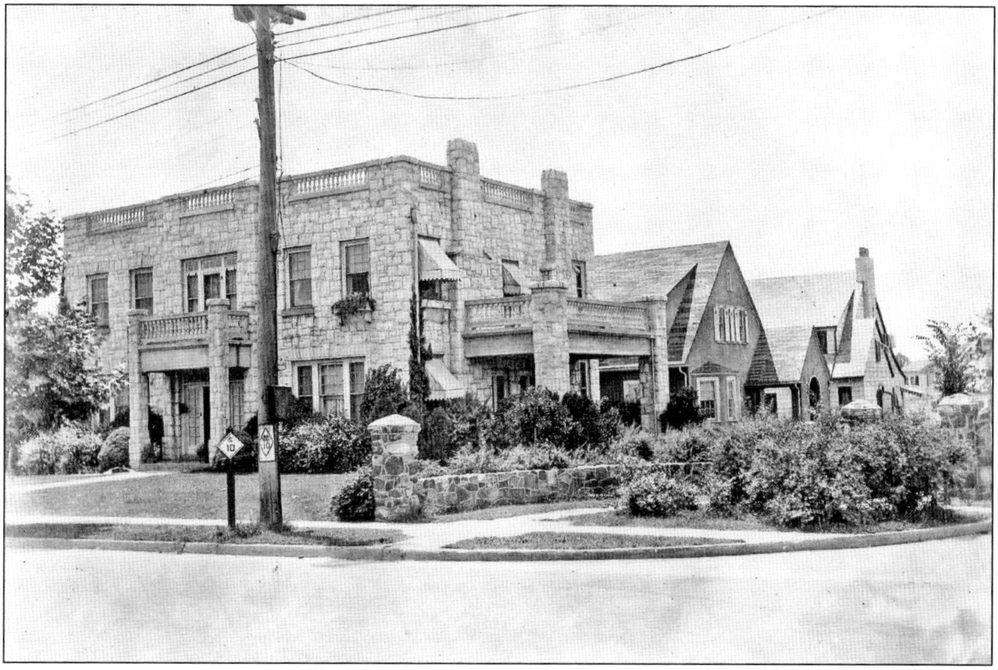

A Burlington realtor, Harold C. Pollard built this stone house in 1918 at West Davis Street and Fountain Place. A few years later, C. Freeman Neese, the owner of C. F. Neese Jewelers, purchased the house. Neese was the first child born in Burlington after the city's name was changed from Company Shops in 1887. (Courtesy of the Alamance County Area Chamber of Commerce.)

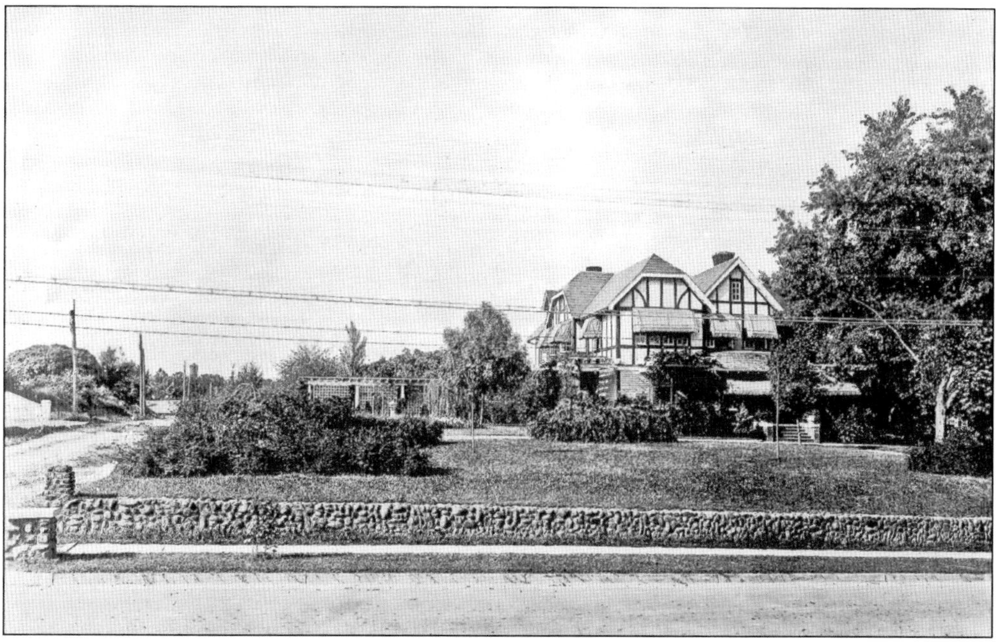

This house originally was a one-and-a-half story Victorian cottage, but its first owner, Walter Sharpe, revised the structure and made it into a much larger, Tudor Revival–style home. Realtor C. G. Somers purchased the home in the 1930s. The house sits at the corner of West Davis and Peele Streets. (Courtesy of Alamance County Area Chamber of Commerce.)

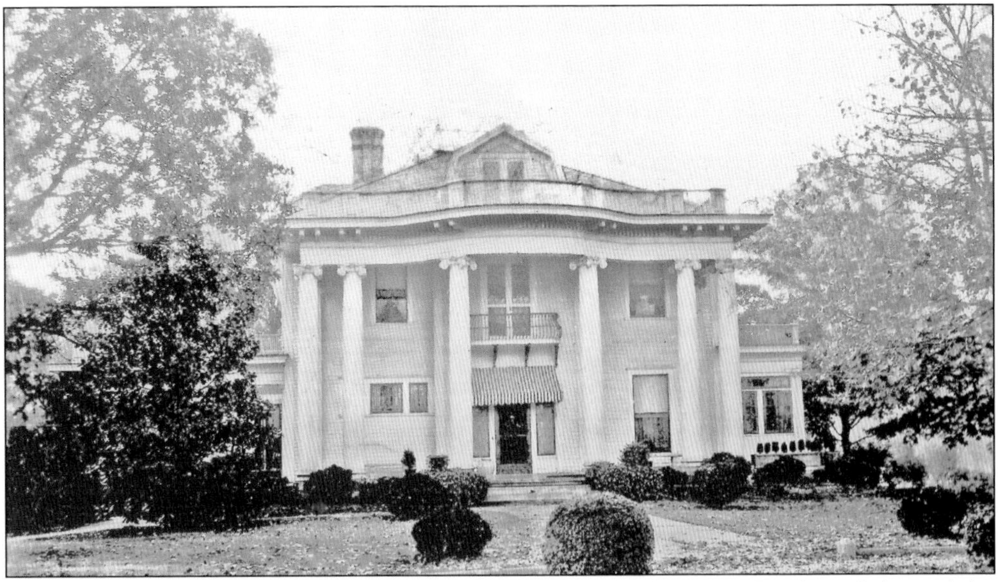

This house on West Davis Street was the home of F. L. Williamson's family and then of the W. H. May's family. In the early 1950s, this house was demolished to provide a new location for the First Presbyterian Church. Williamson was the grandson of textile pioneer E. M. Holt, and May was one of the principals in the May Hosiery Company. (Courtesy of the Alamance County Area Chamber of Commerce.)

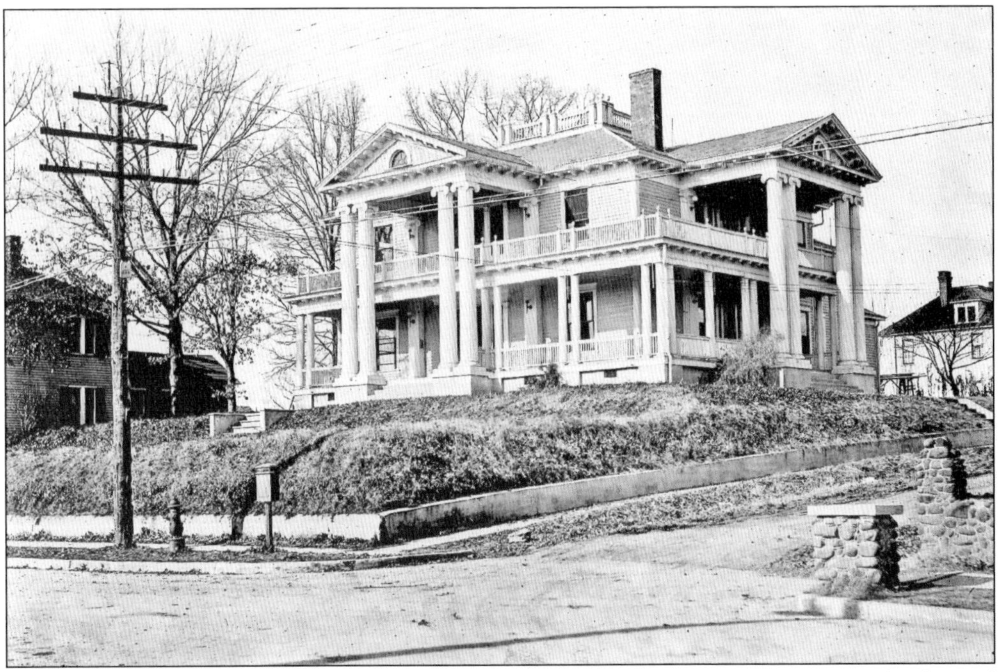

This house was built in the beginning of the 20th century for J. W. Murray, a civic leader and president of the Piedmont Bank and Trust Company. Murray died in 1915, and Dr. J. L. Kernodle, a medical doctor who was also active in civic affairs, later owned the house. The house sits at the corner of West Davis and Peele Streets. (Courtesy of the Alamance County Area Chamber of Commerce.)

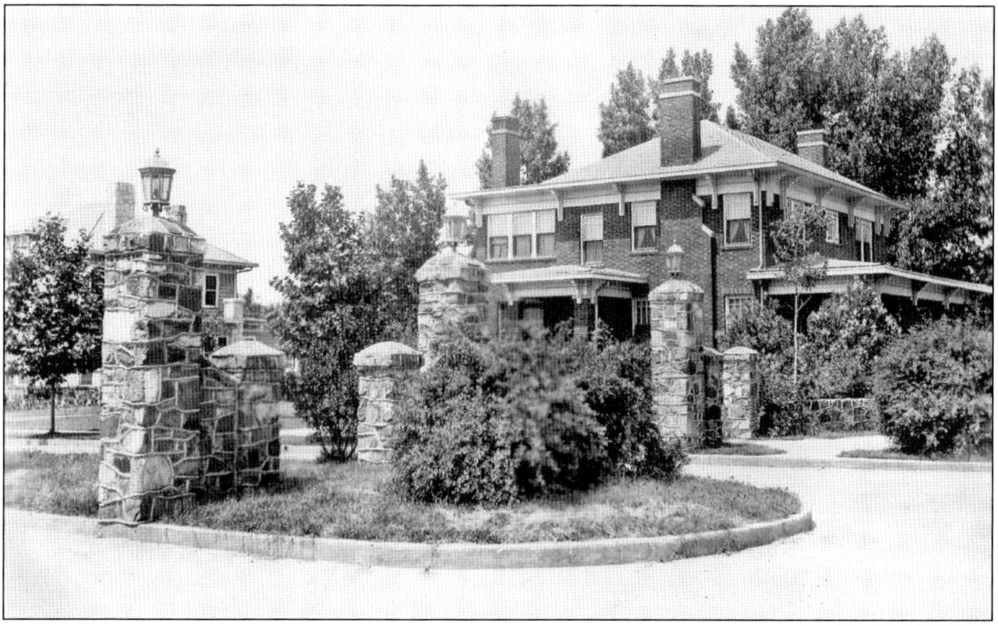

The first significant residential subdivision in Burlington was Fountain Place. Walter E. Sharpe purchased land in 1919 off West Davis Street and laid out a residential development plan. The street was divided, and halfway along its length, a large fountain was built in the middle of the street. Trees and lighting were provided, and this stone gate at Davis Street marked the entrance. (Courtesy Alamance Area County Chamber of Commerce.)

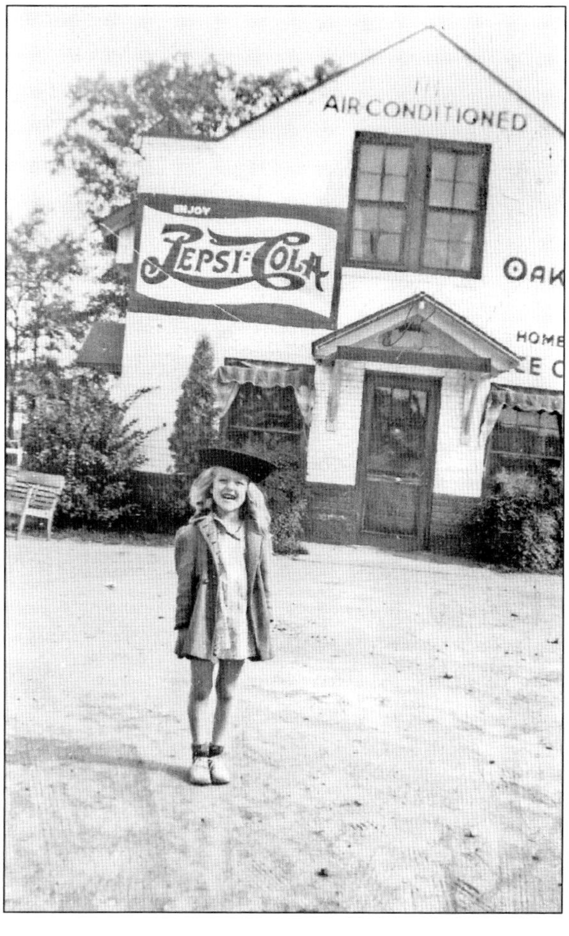

Beverly Morton poses in front of the old Oak Grove Café, which, in 1939, was far outside the city limits. The restaurant was at the intersection of South Church Street, Chapel Hill Road, and Alamance Road. The café was across the street from another famous spot, a restaurant known as Brown's Number Two. The Oak Grove Café, in more recent years, became La Fiesta, a Mexican restaurant. (Courtesy of Beverly Crnkovic.)

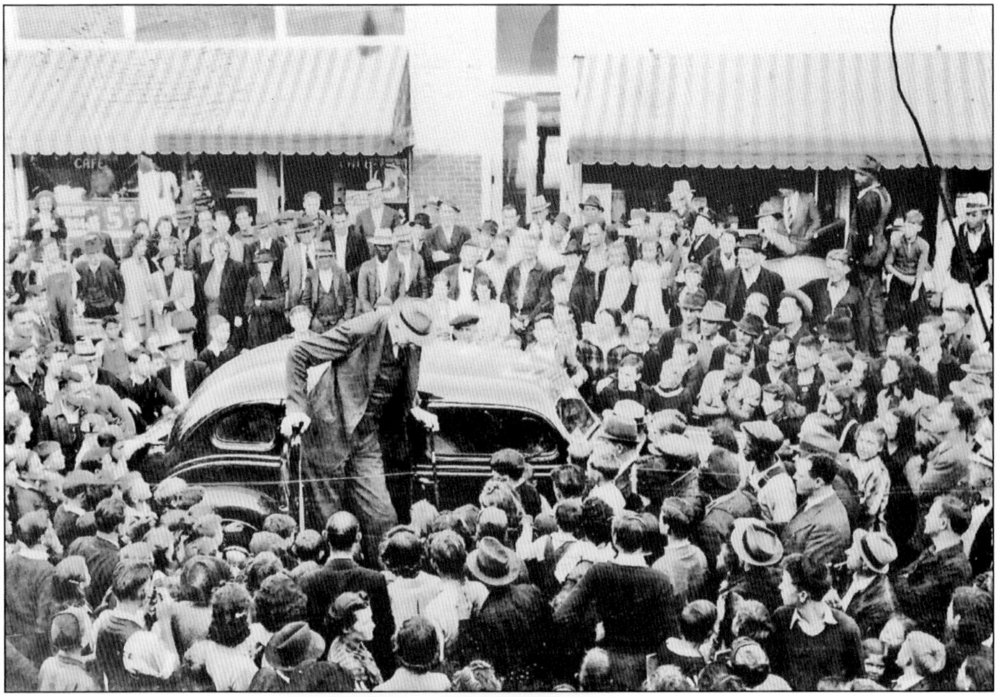

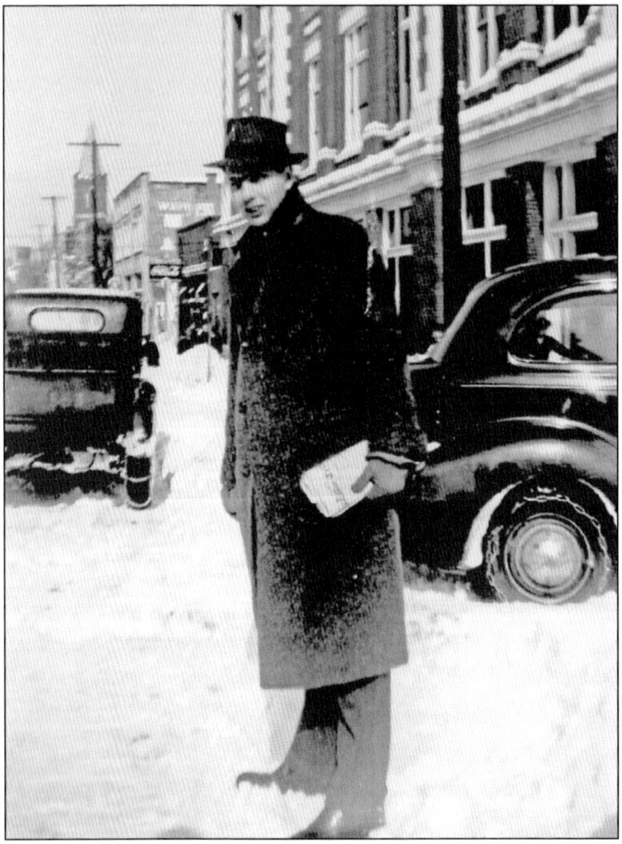

Robert Wadlow was 8-feet, 11-inches tall, which is still the record as the tallest man in the world. He came to Burlington and drew a huge crowd in front of Bell's Shoe Store on East Davis Street in Burlington. Wadlow was on a promotional tour for a shoe company and visited the local store as part of the tour. The photograph was dated 1939.

Paul Morrow makes his way to work in downtown Burlington in late January 1940. One of the area's major snowfalls hit during the last week of the month, with depths of 24-inches in most areas of the city. Also during that period, the temperature dropped to what may be its lowest level recorded in Burlington. The temperature was below zero several nights and minus-12 on the coldest night.

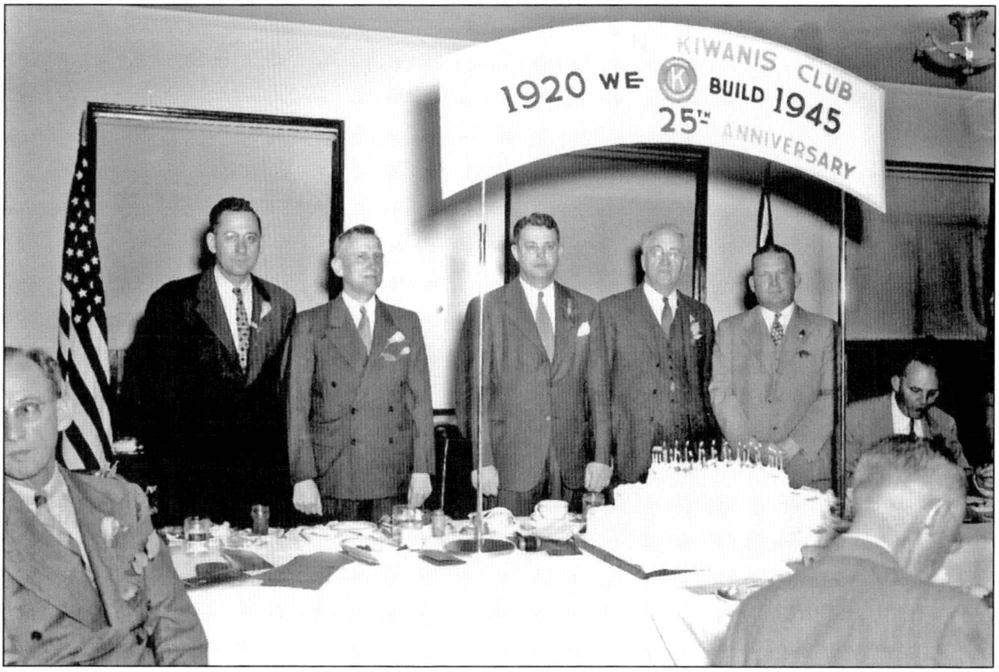

The Burlington Kiwanis Club celebrated its 25th anniversary in 1945 with a banquet at the Alamance Hotel. The president of the club at the time was W. Cliff Elder, a Burlington hosiery executive and civic leader in the community. He is in the middle of this group of Kiwanians taking part in the anniversary program.

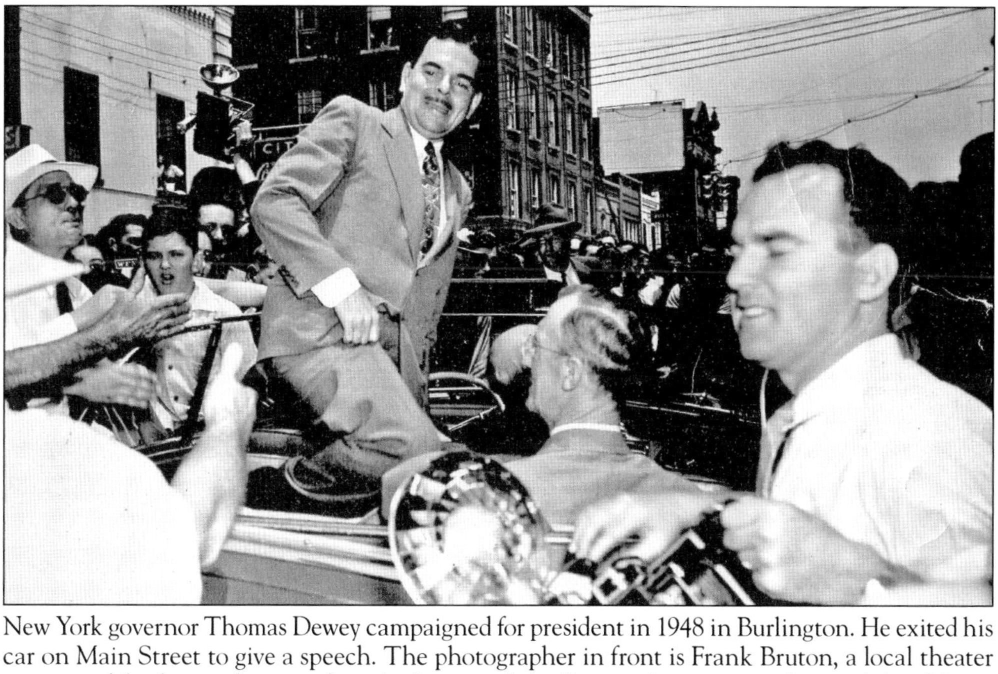

New York governor Thomas Dewey campaigned for president in 1948 in Burlington. He exited his car on Main Street to give a speech. The photographer in front is Frank Bruton, a local theater owner and freelance photographer. A photograph by Bruton during a visit by candidate Henry Wallace was shown in *Life* magazine that year. The photograph showed Wallace being chased out of town and pelted with tomatoes. (Courtesy of Tommy Bruton.)

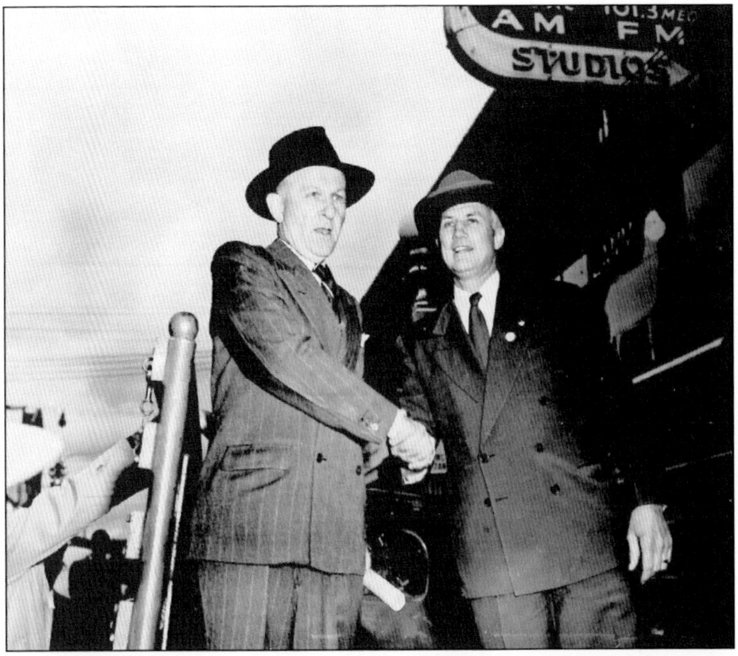

South Carolina governor Strom Thurmond (right) was another presidential candidate who visited Burlington in the 1948 campaign. He is shown in this photograph with J. E. Baker, a local hosiery executive, at left. Thurmond, running on the Dixiecrat ticket, campaigned in Burlington, as did Thomas E. Dewey and Henry Wallace. Harry Truman, the only candidate not to visit Burlington that year, won the race.

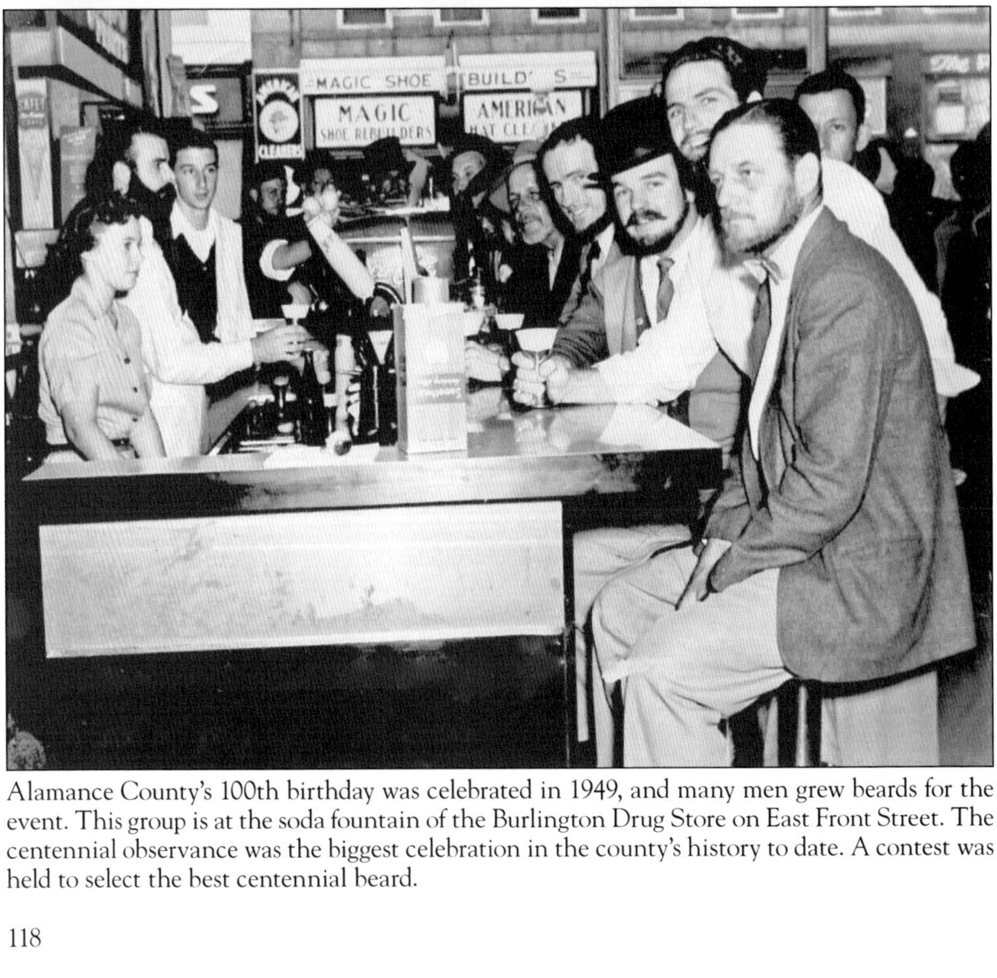

Alamance County's 100th birthday was celebrated in 1949, and many men grew beards for the event. This group is at the soda fountain of the Burlington Drug Store on East Front Street. The centennial observance was the biggest celebration in the county's history to date. A contest was held to select the best centennial beard.

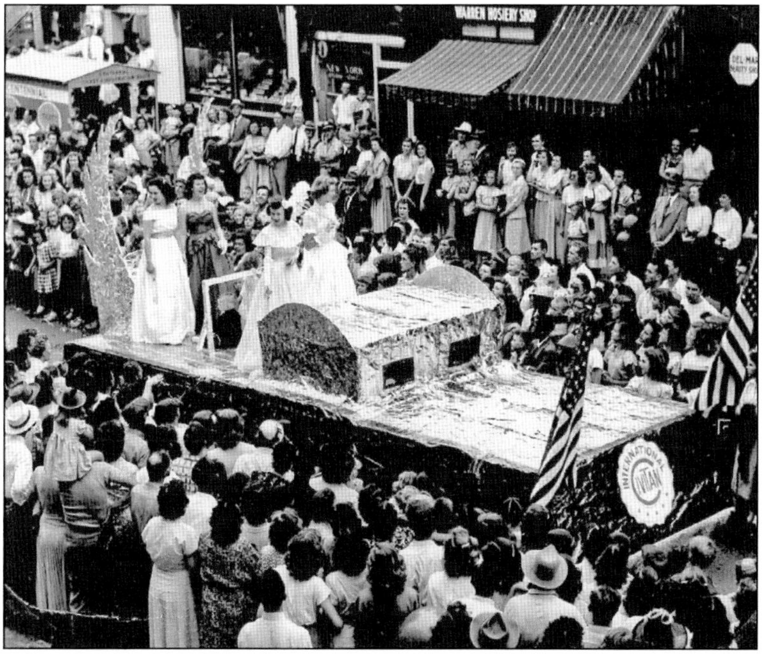

There were parades in Burlington, Graham, and Mebane during the weeklong centennial celebration in 1949. This parade is on Main Street near Front Street in downtown Burlington and shows the float sponsored by the Burlington Civitan Club. The crowd at this parade was said to be the largest group to see a parade in Burlington up to that time.

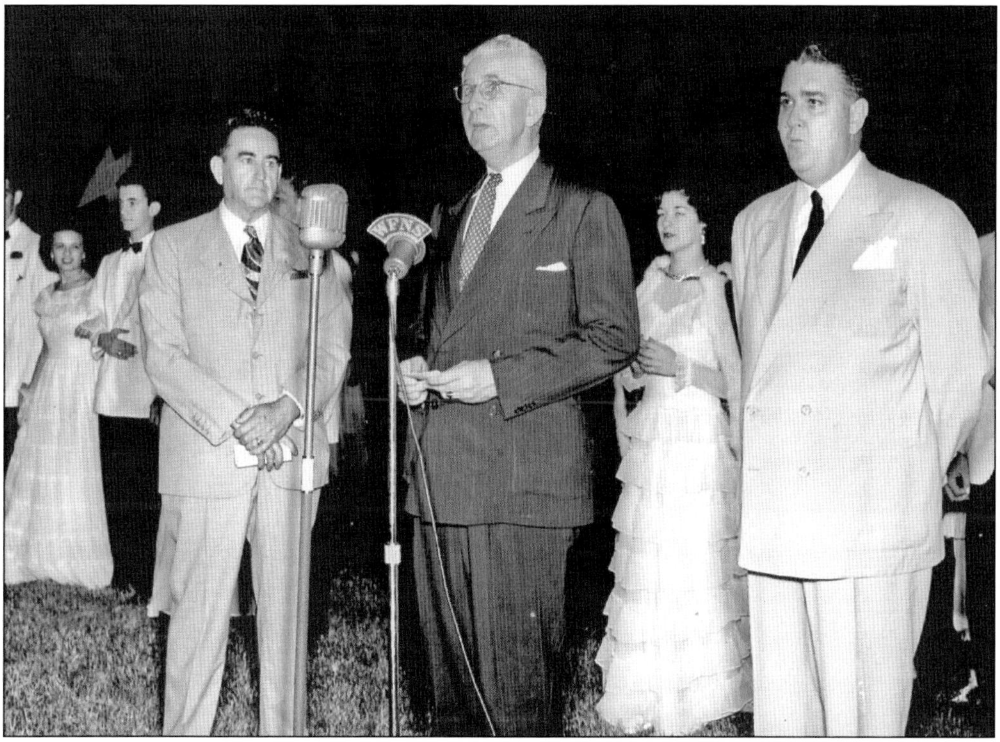

North Carolina congressman Carl Durham addressed the crowd at the Alamance County centennial pageant in May 1949. In the photograph, from left to right, are Jeanette Zimmermann; Ralph Holt Jr.; Gov. W. Kerr Scott of Alamance County, Durham; Carolyn Holt who was crowned pageant queen; and T. D. Cooper, Burlington attorney. The pageant was held at the new Memorial Stadium in Burlington.

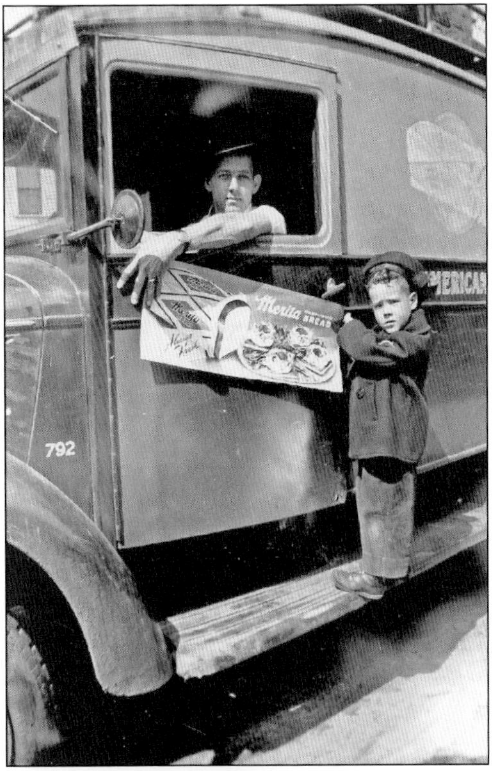

Young John Kinney helps his father, Melvin, display an advertising sign promoting Merita bread. John's father drove a bread truck for the Merita Bread Company, serving the Burlington area in the 1940s. The Merita Bread Company was one of the early major bakeries in the area. Earlier local bakeries served Burlington's needs, one of the most popular being Berg Bakery, which was on East Front Street for many years. (Courtesy of John Kinney.)

Local growers were always proud of their big vegetables, and the *Times-News* often ran photographs of the largest ones. Duncan Bryan (below, right), a local farmer and longtime grocer, proudly displays some of his oversized produce for Staley A. Cook, who was then editor of the newspaper. The *Times-News* was then located on Maple Avenue near Spring Street.

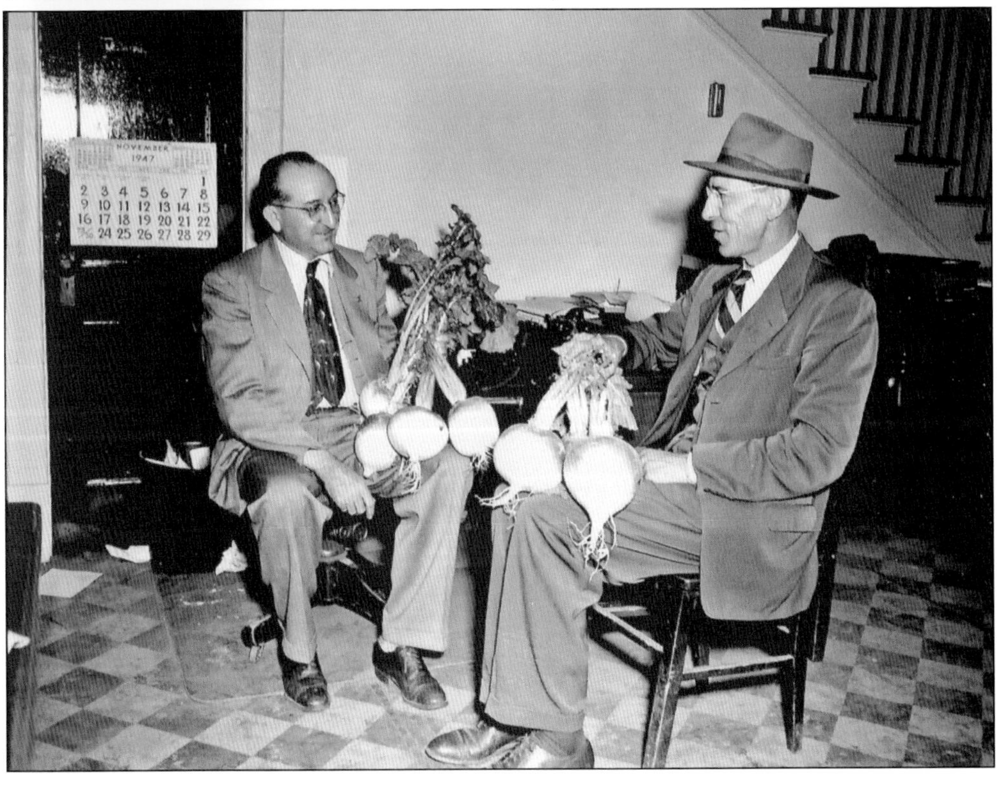

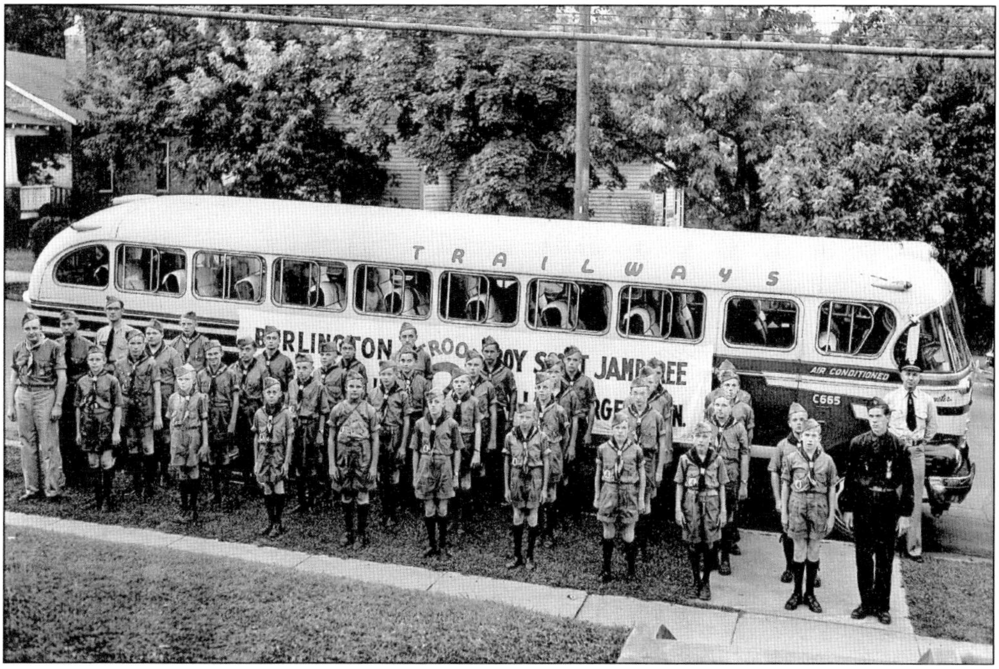

Area Boy Scouts were ready to leave for the national jamboree when this photograph was made beside the First Baptist Church in August 1950. The jamboree was held in Valley Forge, Pennsylvania. The scoutmaster leading this delegation was Allen Cammack Jr., standing at far left in the photograph. (Photograph by Westbrook Studios; courtesy of John Kinney.)

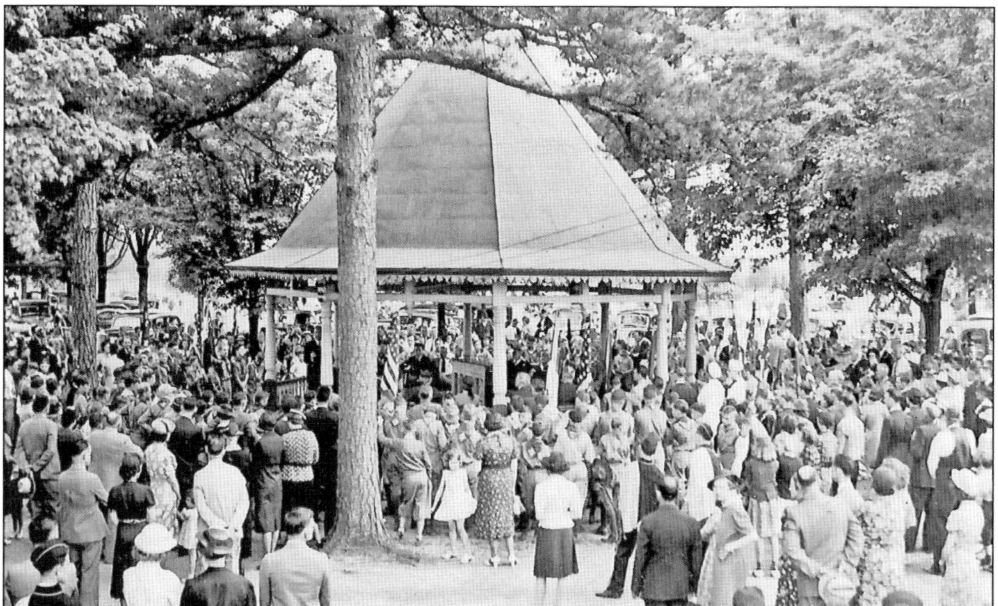

The gazebo in the Pine Hill Cemetery has been the scene of many local functions. It has been used for musical concerts, patriotic programs, speeches, and for Memorial Day events. The Boy Scouts used it for many years for a program on Mother's Day. The gazebo is located in the cemetery off Main Street. The Pine Hill Cemetery is a city-owned cemetery from the late 19th century.

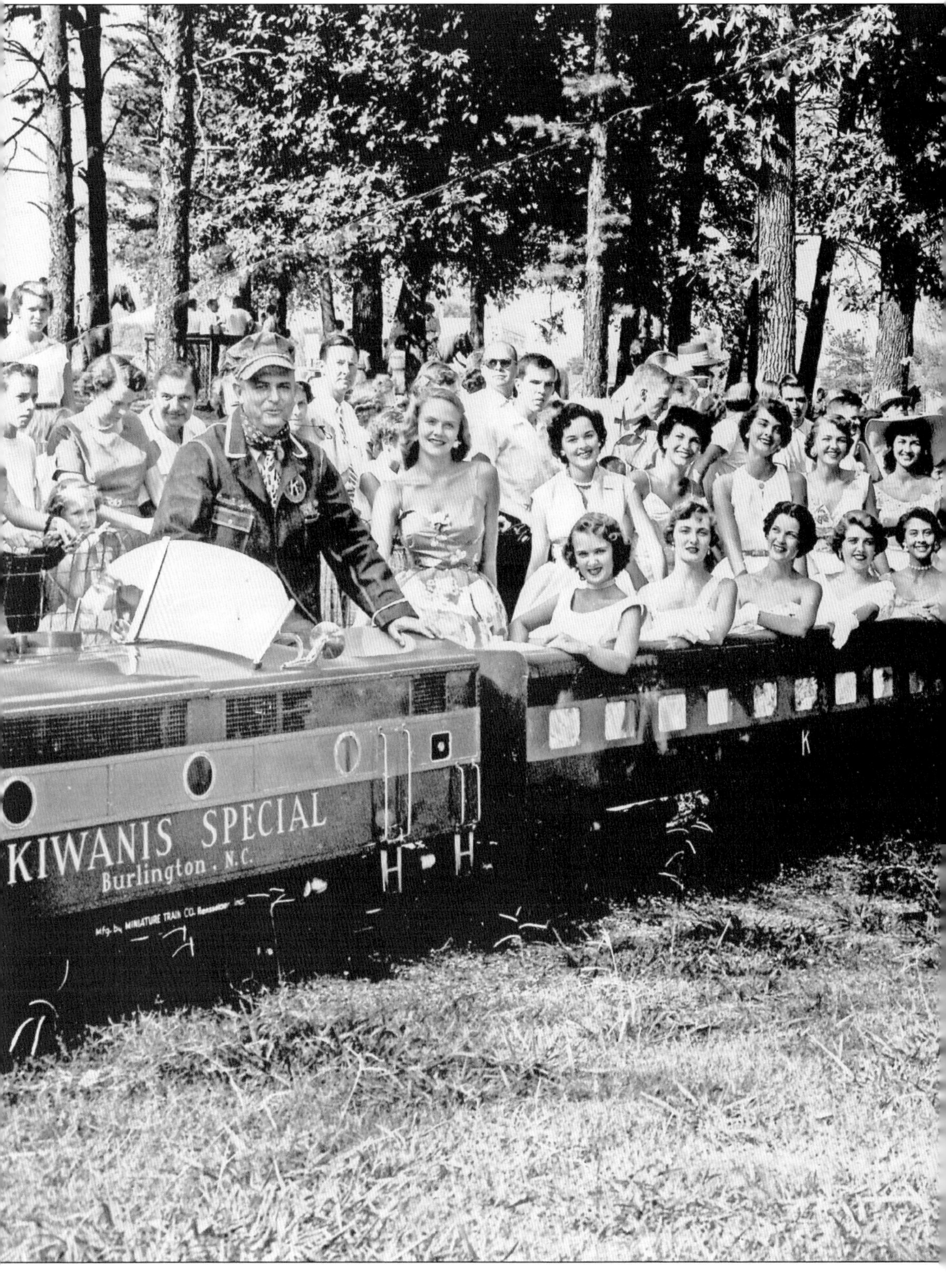
KIWANIS SPECIAL
Burlington . N.C.

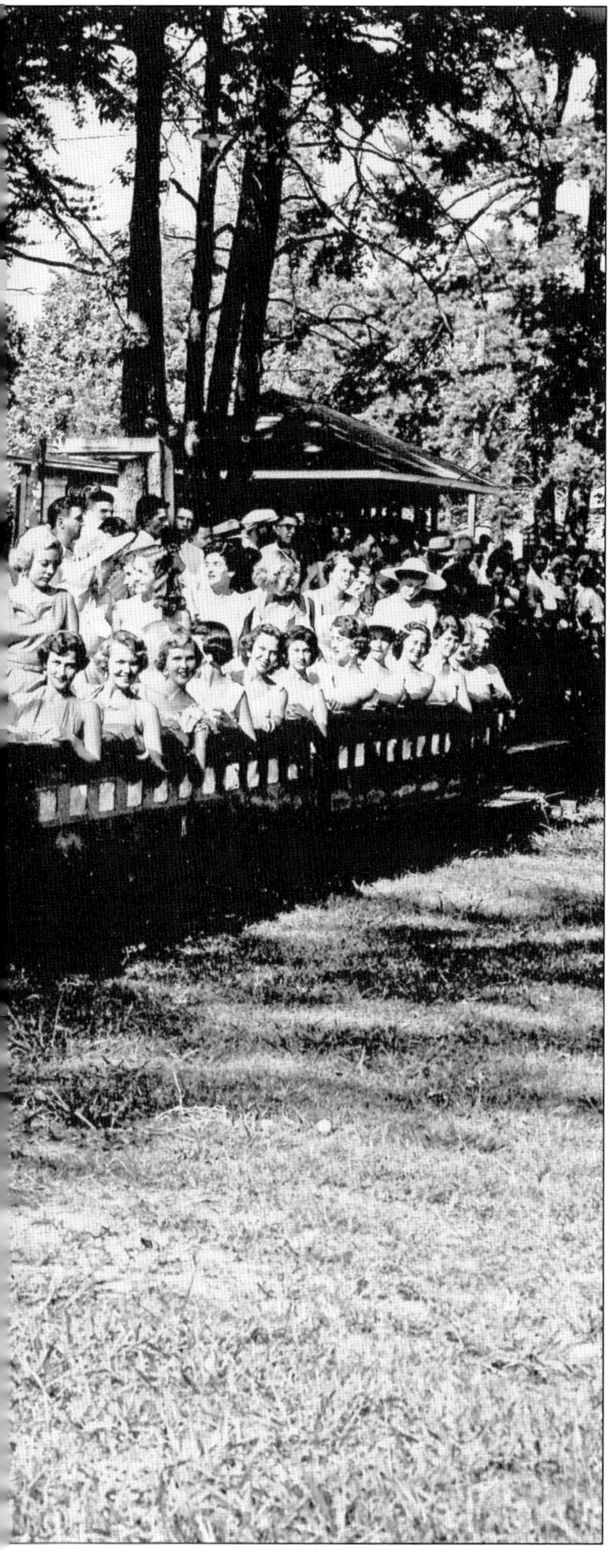

Until 1951, the Miss North Carolina Pageant had always been at a beach location. In 1951, though, the Burlington Jaycees made a successful bid and brought the pageant to Burlington. They staged the largest preliminary event in the history of the Miss America Pageant. The Jaycees brought the program back to Burlington in 1954 and 1957. Each year, the contestants rode the Kiwanis Special, the miniature train in City Park, and attracted hundreds of spectators. This is the 1954 group, led by Evelyn Ay, Miss America 1954. She is next to Kiwanian W. Cliff Elder who is the engineer. The pageants were held in the auditorium of Williams High School, the largest auditorium in the Burlington area at that time, and there was a full house every night of the events. (Photograph by Ed McCauley; courtesy of the *Times-News*.)

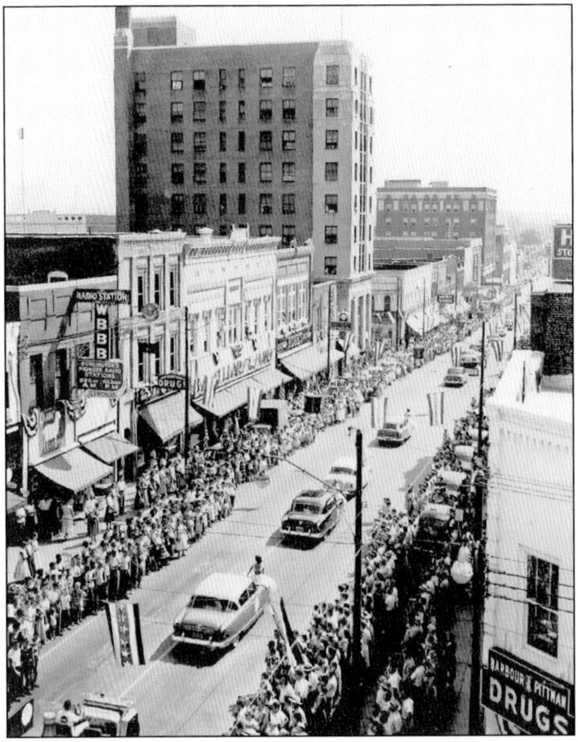

The Miss North Carolina Pageants in Burlington were extremely popular events. The contestants were headquartered at the Alamance Hotel, and crowds gathered there throughout the week to see the girls. Contestants paraded down Main Street in convertibles each of the three years. This photograph from 1951 shows the streets lined with a crowd estimated by some sources as high as 75,000 people.

Dr. B. B. McDade was a Burlington physician with a hobby of hunting big game around the world. For many years, his trophies were displayed in the McDade Wildlife Museum in Burlington's City Park. It was a major attraction, but after a number of years, the displays were moved to a museum in Greensboro and to other locations in North Carolina. (Courtesy of the Alamance Area Chamber of Commerce.)

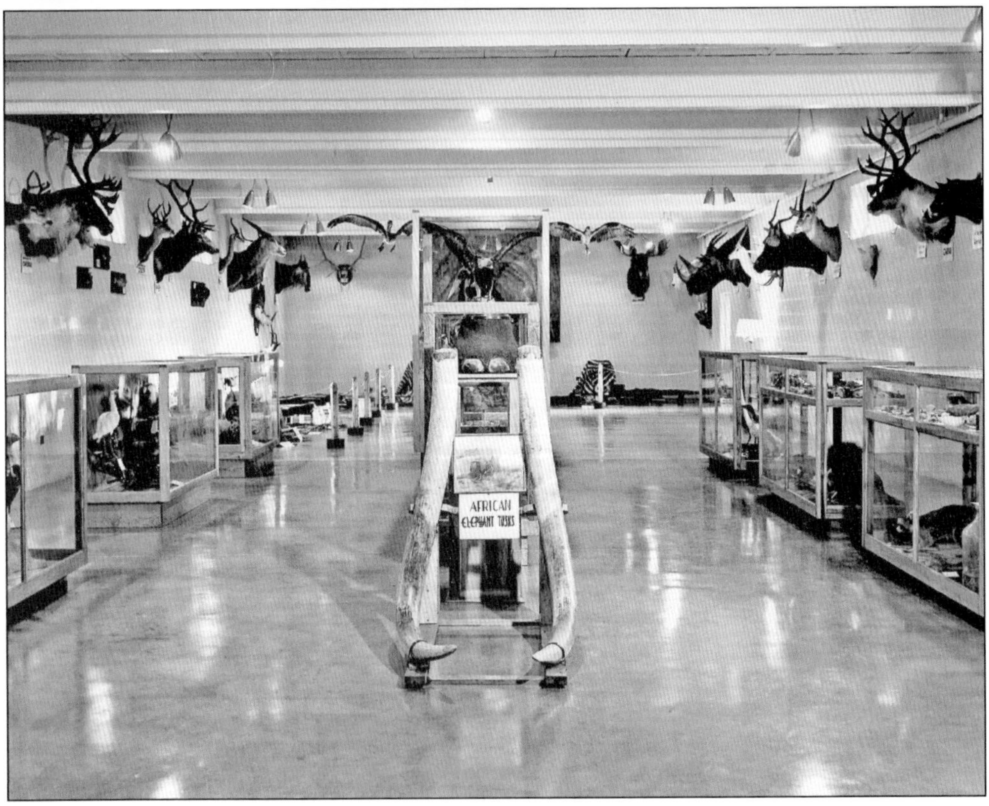

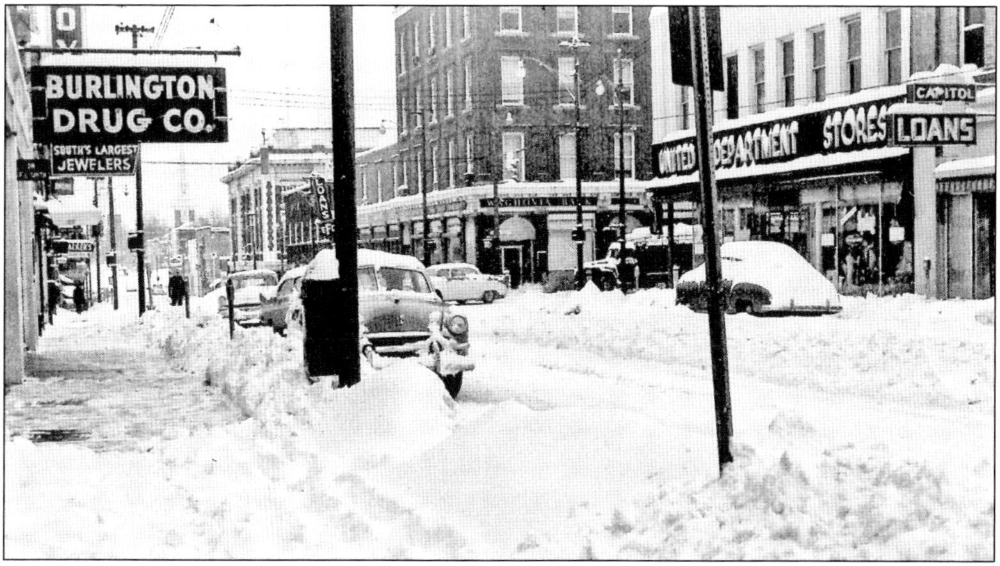

In March 1960, snow fell on the first three Wednesdays of the month. At one time, there were 18 inches on the ground, and spring seemed a distant dream. This is East Front Street following one of the storms. Police officer Jack Bell is barely visible in the background. He had little traffic to direct, as almost everything in the area came to a halt. (Courtesy of Jack Bell.)

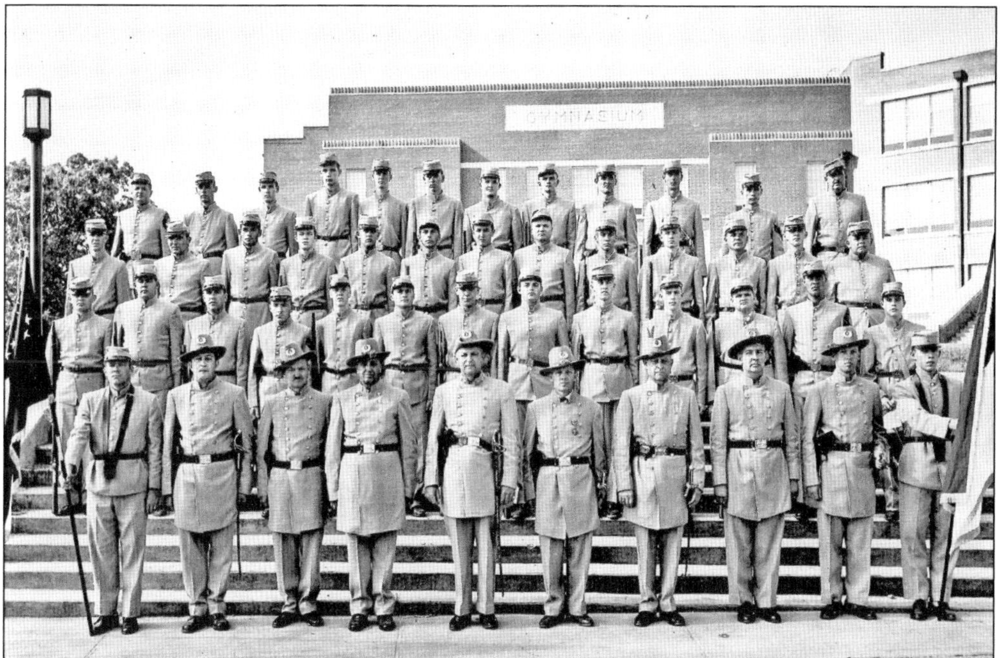

In the 1960s, there were many events marking the centennial of the Civil War. These men were members of a special team that reenacted Civil War battles. It was called the North Carolina Sixth Regiment Volunteers and was named for a unit that was formed in the area during the war 100 years earlier. They participated in many reenactments throughout the South. (Photograph courtesy of Ben Lowe.)

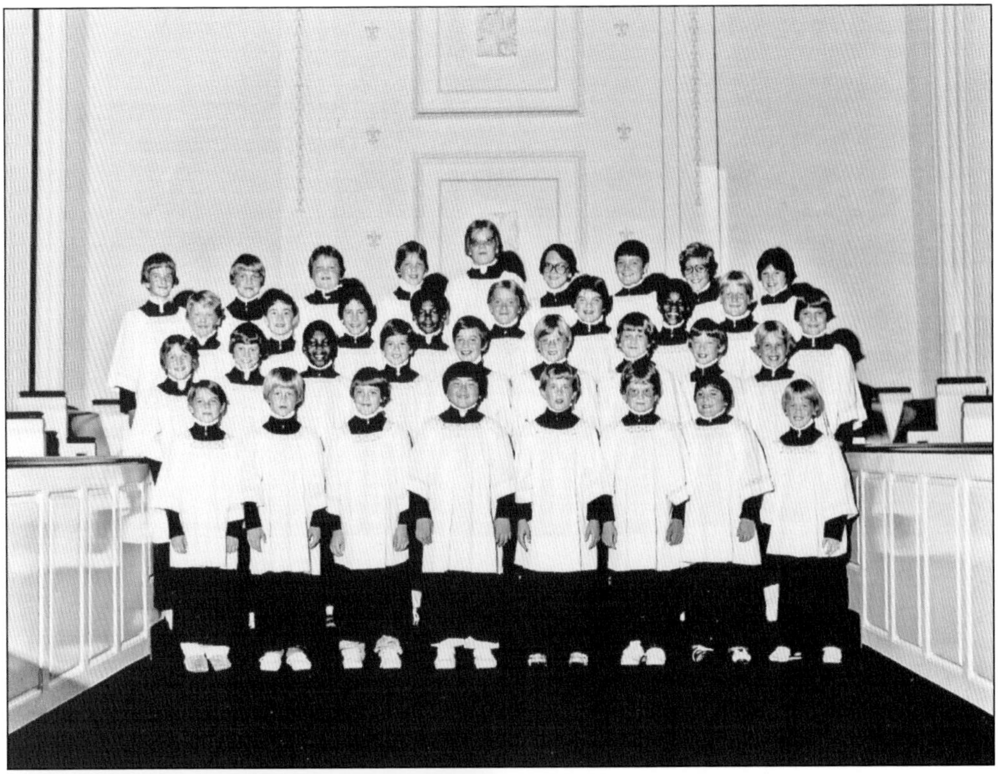

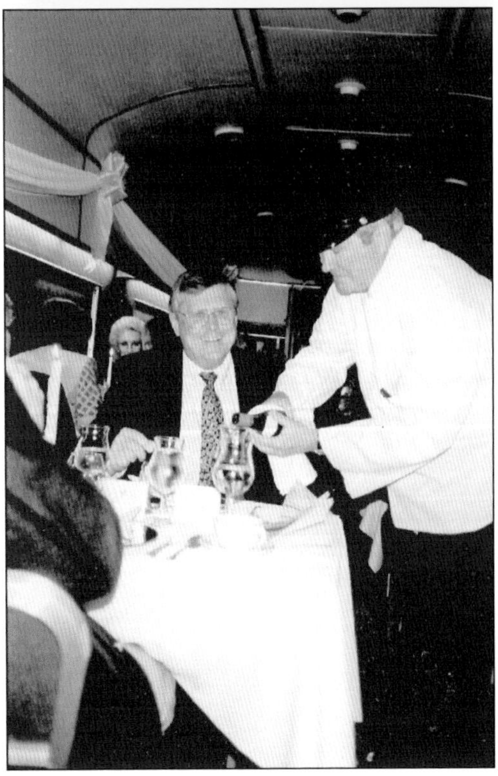

The Burlington Boys Choir was formed in 1959 by city school teacher Eva Wiseman with sponsorship by the Burlington Rotary Club. Since then, the choir has performed at the White House four times, made seven tours of Europe, and appeared at other concerts across the state and nation. This is the group in 1979. (Courtesy of Barry and Barbara Carroll.)

Burlington marked the 100th anniversary of its charter in 1993. A number of events were held over the period of a week, and many had a railroad theme, owing to the origin of the city as a railroad center. William Hawks, a hosiery executive, served as a waiter for James Copland, Copland Fabrics's president, at a dinner held in a railroad dining car brought to Burlington for the celebration.

In 1986, Rachel Oliver of Burlington was chosen as Miss Black America. Oliver later became a recording artist and developed a special scholarship and talent development program for teenage African American girls. A year later, Rachel's mother, Donna Oliver, achieved another national honor for the family—National Teacher of the Year. (Courtesy of Rachel Oliver-Cobbin.)

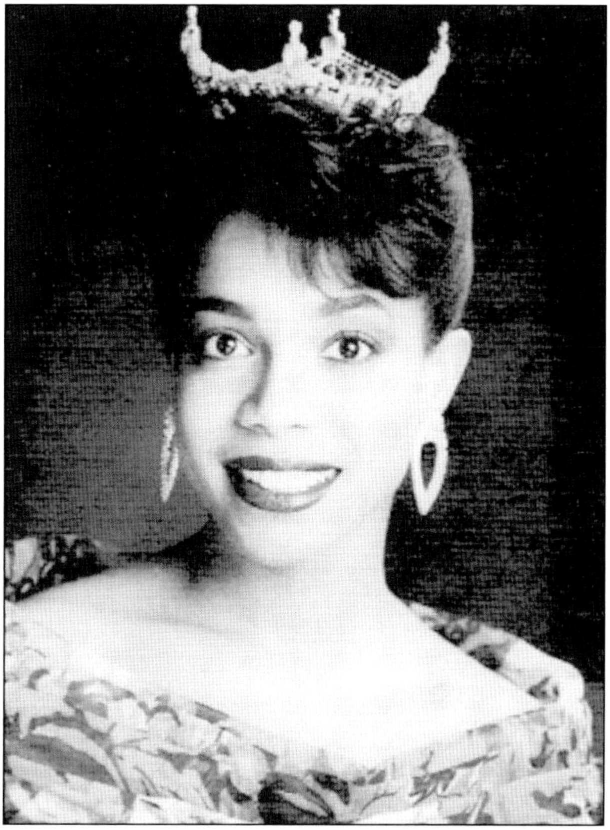

In April 1987, U.S. president Ronald Reagan recognized Donna Oliver, a teacher at Cummings High School in Burlington, as the National Teacher of the Year. Oliver is at center in this photograph in the Oval Office. From left to right are Donna's daughter, Rachel, who a year earlier had been named Miss Black America, President Reagan, Donna, her husband, James, and her sister Annette Woods.

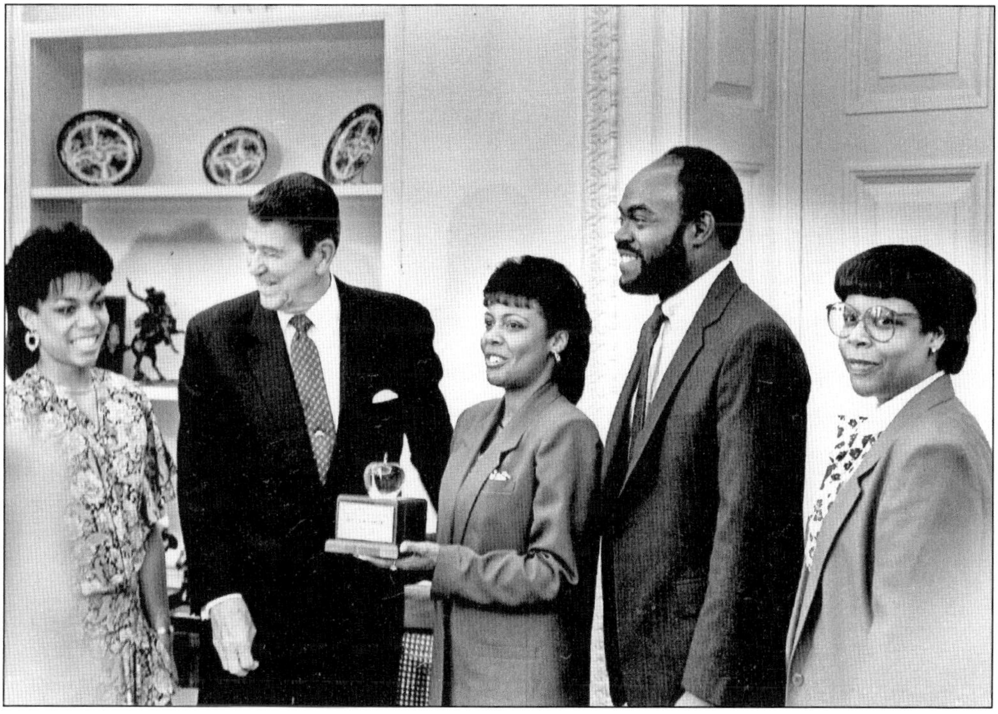